ADULT LEARNING AND DEVELOPMENT

Multicultural Stories

Edited by
Lisa Baumgartner
and
Sharan B. Merriam

KRIEGER PUBLISHING COMPANY
MALABAR, FLORIDA

Original Edition 2000

Printed and Published by
KRIEGER PUBLISHING COMPANY
KRIEGER DRIVE
MALABAR, FLORIDA 32950

Copyright © 2000 by Krieger Publishing Company

Library of Congress Cataloging-In-Publication Data

Adult learning and development : multicultural stories / edited by
 Lisa Baumgartner and Sharan B. Merriam.
   p.   cm.
  Includes bibliographical references (p.   ) and index.
  ISBN 1-57524-104-8 (hardcover : alk. paper).—ISBN 1-57524-097-1
 (pbk. : alk. paper)
   1. Adulthood—Psychological aspects. 2. Learning, Psychology of.
 3. Maturation (Psychology) 4. Pluralism (Social sciences)
 I. Baumgartner, Lisa, 1964–   . II. Merriam Sharan B.
 BF724.5.A34 2000
305.24—dc21   99-21494
                                                        CIP

10 9 8 7 6 5 4 3

Contents

Preface

From Confucius's six stages of life, to the Talmud's version of the life cycle, to Shakespeare's "Seven Ages of Man," poets, philosophers, and spiritual leaders have long been observers of how people change as they age. It has only been since the mid-twentieth century, however, that such changes have been studied scientifically as part of the field of lifespan or developmental psychology. At first, childhood, adolescence, and old age received more scrutiny than adulthood; there are, after all, more dramatic physical changes that are easily observable at these ages. However, an increase in life expectancy to where now the longest segment of the lifespan is adulthood, combined with more sophisticated research tools, are two factors contributing to *adulthood* being studied and documented. Indeed, this longest period of the life cycle has itself been divided into the segments of young, middle, and older adulthood; in some models these segments are further subdivided as for example, young-old, old-old, and very-old.

Until recently, the study of adulthood has been from a traditionally psychological perspective wherein the individual is the focus; that is, how do individuals grow and change over time and how are these changes manifested in their behavior? Are there commonalities in development across individuals? To what extent is development genetically predetermined versus a function of individual choice? Today scholars and researchers are recognizing that we can learn more about development by considering how the individualized self is also collectively defined by the society in which he or she lives. Each society has defined norms of behavior based on ethnicity, age, sexual orientation, the color of our skin, physical attributes and able-bodiedness, and whether we are male or female, rich or poor. The question is not only how maturation and personality structure development; of equal importance is how sociocultural factors *shape* the life course. Neugarten (1976) was one of the first lifespan psychologists to recognize the importance of this social dimension. "Every society," she writes, "is age-graded, and every society has a system of social expectations regarding age-appropriate behavior. The individual passes through a socially regulated cycle from birth to death as inexorably as he [*sic*] passes through the biological cycle: a succession of socially delineated age-statuses, each with its recognized rights, duties and obligations" (p. 16). More recently, Tennant and Pogson (1995) see adult development as an interaction between "the organism, with its constitutionally endowed equipment; and the social environment, with its historically given social and cultural formations. Development thus proceeds through a constant interaction between the person and the environment. [And] because development is contested, and because different versions of development serve the interests of different groups, it is as much a political as it is a psychological construct" (pp. 198–199).

Important to note about this perspective is that it is usually a combination of a number of these sociocultural factors, rather than a single factor, that impact development. For example, in the memoirs of the Delany sisters (1993)—two African American centenarians—it becomes clear that socioeconomic class and education as well as race and gender defined who they were. Though black and female, these upper class women were able to attend not only college but graduate school and, remarkably, establish careers as a teacher/supervisor and dentist at a period in our history when most whites never made it to college. Likewise, Wilson (1996) documents her identity development as a lesbian Native American. Treating "sexual and racial identity as independent developmental pathways" she feels, misses much of the picture. "While this simplifying division may make it easier to generate theory, it may also make it less likely that the resulting theory will describe people's real-life developmental experiences" (p. 303).

Of the six conditions that Bee (1996) identifies that impact development, only two are psychological—intelligence and personality. The other four are sociocultural—gender, race and ethnicity, social class, and education. All of these conditions affect development in varying ways. One's race or ethnicity, for example, is accompanied by a culture of shared values, beliefs, and meanings that determine age-appropriate social roles and behaviors. Hispanic, African American and Asian American elderly are more likely to live with family and less likely to be institutionalized than Anglos, for example. "Such differences reflect . . . the strong emphasis on family interaction and family solidarity in each of these ethnic groups" (Bee, 1996, p. 38). Other lifespan and lifestyle differences connected to race and ethnicity listed by Bee are (1) White women and men have a longer life expectancy than nonwhites; (2) Blacks and Hispanics of all ages are of a lower socioeconomic status on average, than whites; (3) Family experiences (rate and age of marriage, female-headed households, births to single women, etc.) "are, on average, quite different in black than in white families" (p. 39); (4) Blacks and Hispanics have lower levels of education than whites, while Asian Americans have the highest levels; (5) Blacks are less satisfied with life than whites, although whites have a higher rate of suicide.

In summary, the study of development in adulthood is changing from a purely psychological perspective to a framework that acknowledges the role of both psychological and sociocultural factors. Further, that American society is becoming more ethnically and culturally diverse is common knowledge. The voices of previously marginalized groups are now being heard in popular culture, the media, education, business, the arts and literature.

One of the more powerful mediums for understanding the experiences of others is through literature. Great literature is timeless because of its ability to speak to the human condition; readers are able to see, feel, and hear what the protagonist experiences. Shakespeare's King Lear, Ibsen's Nora, Ellison's invisible man, are as real as the family patriarch dividing up the property, the middle-aged wife and mother who seeks her own identity, the black man who has to negotiate a racist society. Insights about people, about life's dilemmas, about growth and development in adulthood can be more easily gleaned from in-depth encounters with three-dimensional adults than from textbooks, fact sheets, and research reports.

Adult Development and Learning: Multicultural Stories is designed to bring about just such an encounter. The book is a collection of stories and poems about growth and development in adulthood. The protagonists, however, are other than white, middle-class men. Selections were purposely chosen to reflect the diversity of American culture and the sociocultural factors of race and ethnicity, gender, class, sexual orientation, able-bodiedness and so on that impact development in adulthood. The intended audience for *Adult Development and Learning: Multicultural Stories* includes students in various disciplines interested in multicultural and diversity issues. Courses in adult education, gerontology, social work, adult development and aging, learning, women's studies, ethnic studies and so on, may refer to works in this book to illustrate various discipline-based concepts and theories from a multicultural perspective. Finally, practitioners in any of these fields who are interested in gaining a greater understanding of the multicultural context of their practice will find reading these selections to be an enlightening and enjoyable learning experience.

Overview of Contents

A number of decisions had to be made with respect to the selections included in this book. First, we wanted a representative sample of literature from various ethnic groups living in America. To that end we have stories about African Americans, Hispanics or Latinos/Latinas (we are using these terms interchangeably), Native Americans, and Asian Americans. Other factors that often intersect with racial and ethnic identity and which are represented in some of the stories are religion, socioeconomic class, gender, sexual orientation, and physical able-bodiedness. Since the theme of the book is adult development, we also wanted an age spread among our protagonists spanning young adulthood, middle, and older adulthood. Although most of our selections are by authors from the particular racial or ethnic group of the protagonist, we also had Native American readers review the Native American stories, African American readers the African American stories, and so on, to ensure that the stories would be seen as representative of that group's culture. Other readers representing adults with disabilities, a homosexual orientation, or some combination of conditions also assisted us in screening the selections. Through this process, we feel we have been able to compile a selection of readings that do in fact touch upon many, if not most of the diverse sociocultural factors that shape development in adulthood.

The selections are organized into six different themes or arenas of adult life where development takes place. The themes are Identity, The Importance of Work, Intimacy, The Family Life Cycle, Physical Development, Health and Aging, and Learning in Adulthood. Readers will note that nearly all of the stories could have been placed under several different themes. One's identity is often associated with one's work, for example, and certainly issues of love and friendship can play out in the family. Finally, development in adulthood, whether it be in terms of an empowered sense of self, a greater capacity to love or to work, making age-appropriate physical demands on one's body, and so on, all involve *learning*. Although featured in the section, "Learning in Adulthood," learning is implicit in all the other selections.

The first section, "Identity," contains stories that demonstrate how culture, race, gender, ethnicity, and sexual orientation intersect in identity formation. In *A Sistah Outsider,* an undergraduate grapples with her dual identity as an African American lesbian. Also a young adult, Jaimi Carter copes with her multiracial identity and a relationship with a father who tells her he doesn't love her in *Are You Writing A Book?* Perri Klass's *Flip-Flops* shows how cultural beliefs and socialization prevent a woman from truly believing she is a medical doctor. The main character in *You're Short, Besides* recognizes the physical, cultural, and mental challenges she faces as a result of a disability caused by her childhood bout with polio. She wonders how her handicap has affected her identity. Cultural identity is the theme of *A Dictionary of Japanese-American Terms* where the protagonist journeys to Japan to find her cultural heritage. Ben Inaba, the protagonist in *Three Steps a Minute,* describes how race and historical time can influence one's life. In *How I Got to be Jewish,* author Erica Jong shows how ethnicity and class impact identity formation while Alexis De Veaux poignantly demonstrates how colorism affects identity within the African American community in *Dear Aunt Nanadine.*

Work is a central, defining characteristic of who we are as adults. But like other aspects of our lives, historical time as well as race, class, gender, and so on, intersect in shaping a particular individual's work life. The second section on "The Importance of Work" contains three selections, two stories and a poem, each of which demonstrates how various factors affect an adult's work. Dale Brown's *Learning to Work* shows how a learning disability can affect job performance. When the problem is diagnosed, the protagonist learns compensatory strategies and becomes a productive employee. In *Sweetheart,* Bev obtains her diesel mechanic job through a court order. Though she has a positive outlook, she has to deal with sexism and harassment on a daily basis. The last selection is a poem entitled *Piece Work* which captures the sex, ethnicity, and class-segregation of the workplace.

Love knows no bounds and in the section "Intimacy" we see how culture, class, education, and sexual orientation impact relationships. In Ella Leffland's *The Linden Tree,* George and Guilio, a gay, interracial couple, have lived together for fifty years. Guilio's heart ailment causes George to reflect on their life together. The love of an African American church community for one of its members afflicted with AIDS is the subject of *Church.* In *Is This the Reward of a Catholic Girlhood?* the young protagonist recognizes her passion for women, while the main character in *Between* is emotionally attracted to both her boyfriend and a gay, male friend. The relationship of Japanese American high school sweethearts is affected by class and differing educational aspirations in R. A. Sasaki's *First Love.*

The fourth section, "The Family Life Cycle," looks at how culture affects events in the family. In *The Management of Grief,* an Indian-Canadian woman regrets that her upbringing did not allow her to verbally express affection for her husband who has perished in a plane crash along with her sons. In *This Place,* David's medicine-man grandfather helps David grapple with his life and impending death while imparting the values of Mohawk culture. Culture, in the form of family stories are passed down to Jose, by his grandmother, Lola Silang in *The Storyteller.* Marriage, a facet of the family life cycle, is also influenced by culture. Marie Hara's *1895 The Honeymoon Hotel,* allows us to witness the beginning of two arranged marriages as Chika and Sono emigrate to Hawaii to meet their husbands. The courtship ritual can also be a family affair as in *Groom Service* where mothers arrange a courtship ritual between two young Native Americans, Marie and Bernard.

The fifth section, "Physical Development, Health and Aging," includes pieces that span young, midlife, and retirement stages of adulthood as well as conditions of gender, race and ethnicity, and physical disability. In *What I Know from Noses,* a young Jewish woman reconsiders her earlier-life decision to have cosmetic surgery in light of her now feminist consciousness. Also a young adult, Finch in *Finch the Spastic Speaks,* allows the reader to get inside the mind of someone with his physical disability. It is a poignant portrayal of the agony of dealing with the disability while at the same time, trying to be a "normal" young adult grappling with the issues typical of this stage of life. The menopausal, middle-aged woman of *Combustion* presents a positive spin on dealing with the "change of life." Finally, in *Hector Quesadilla* we see a man past his prime who escapes his aging body through memories and fantasies of younger years as a star baseball player.

The final section of the book focuses on "Learning in Adulthood." Here we have included three selections which illustrate how learning can be both additive and can contribute to developmental change. What we learn is also deeply embedded within the cultural context of our lives. *La Tortillera* for example, is more than learning to make tortillas—it is learning one's cultural heritage. *Talking to the Dead* is about learning traditional Hawaiian death rituals. In *Mountain Biking and the Pleasures of Balance,* the protagonist not only learns a skill but also becomes empowered as she develops a stronger sense of self.

In summary, we have tried to bring together a selection of stories that illustrate both the similarities and differences in our lives. The stories show the sameness of human experience in that everyone forms an identity, for example, and they also demonstrate how sociocultural factors such as race, gender, ethnicity, and class cause people to experience life events in unique ways. Most important, these tales help us appreciate adult learning and development in adulthood.

Acknowledgments

We would like to thank all those who contributed to our efforts in putting this volume together. Numerous colleagues suggested readings, reviewed our selections, and provided support during the process. We would also like to thank Mary Roberts, Elaine Rudd, and Marie Bowles at Krieger Publishing Company for their support in this project.

About the Editors

Lisa Baumgartner is a doctoral student in adult education at the University of Georgia. She received her B.A. (1986) in psychology from Augsburg College and her M.A. (1989) in counseling psychology from Ball State University. She taught English in Japan and is interested in the influence of culture on adult learning and development.

Sharan B. Merriam is a professor of adult and continuing education at the University of Georgia. Her research and writing interests include adult learning and development, adult education, and qualitative research. She is the author of numerous publications including *Themes of Adulthood Through Literature* (1983), *A Guide to Research for Educators and Trainers of Adults* (with E. L. Simpson, 1995, second edition), *The Profession and Practice of Adult Education* (with R. G. Brockett, 1997), *Qualitative Research and Case Study Applications in Education* (1998, second edition), and most recently, *Learning in Adulthood* (with R. S. Caffarella, 1999, second edition).

About the Authors

Mona Elaine Adilman graduated from McGill University in Montreal, Quebec, Canada. Her books include *Beat of Wings* (1972), *Piece Work* (1980), and *Cult of Concrete* (1977). She edited *Spirits of the Age: Poets of Conscience* (1989).

James Laus Baluyut emigrated to the United States from the Philippines in 1989. He was at the University of Michigan's Residential College studying comparative literature and creative writing when "The Storyteller" was published in *Into the Fire: Asian American Prose* edited by S. Watanabe and C. Bruchac (1996).

Beth Brant is a Bay of Quinte Mohawk from Tyedinaga Mohawk Territory, Ontario, Canada, and has spent much of her life in Michigan. Her works include *Mohawk Trail* (1990), *Food and Spirits* and "Her Name is Helen" in J. Barrington's *An Intimate Wilderness: Lesbian Writers on Sexuality* (1991). Awards include a literary fellowship from the National Endowment of the Arts and grants from the Michigan Council for the Arts and the Ontario Arts Council.

Dale Brown is a government administrator and educational program director. She founded the Association for Learning Disabled Adults (ADLA) and the National Network for Learning Disabled Adults (NNLDA). Recent writings include *Working Effectively with People Who Have Learning Disabilities and Attention Deficit Hyperactivity Disorder* (1995) and *I Know I Can Climb the Mountain* (1995).

T. Coraghessan Boyle is a native of Peekskill, New York. His first novel, *Water Music* was published in 1982. Other works include *Budding Prospects: A Pastoral* (1984) and *Greasy Lake and Other Stories*

(1985). His short stories have been published in *Esquire, Atlantic Monthly,* and *Harper's.*

Jaimi Carter is a graduate of Macalaster College in St. Paul, Minnesota. She grew up in Southern California.

Sucheng Chan was born in Shanghai, China, and emigrated to the United States. Her books include *Asian Americans: An Interpretive History* (1991), *Asian Californians* (1991), and *Quiet Odyssey: A Pioneer Korean Woman in America* (1990). She received the Association· for Asian American Studies Outstanding Book Award for *Quiet Odyssey* in 1991.

Margaret Cruikshank was born in Duluth, Minnesota. She is a member of the National Women's Studies Association. Awards include selection as an affiliate scholar at the University of California—Berkeley, 1996–1997. She is the editor of *The Gay and Lesbian Liberation Movement* (1992) and *Fierce with Reality* (1995).

Alexis De Veaux has served as an editor-at-large for *Essence* magazine. She is a member of the Organization of Women Writers of Africa, Inc., (OWWA). Recent writings include "Twilight" in *Arc of Love: An Anthology of Lesbian Love Poems* edited by Clare Coss (1996) and a short story titled "Bird of Paradise" in *Does Your Mama Know?* edited by Lisa Moore (1997).

Michael Dorris was a recipient of the Indian Achievement Award in 1985. He was a member of the Native American Rights Fund and founded and served as chairman of the Department of Native American Studies at Dartmouth College from 1972–1985. His creative works include *Sees Behind Trees* (1996), *Morning Girl* (1992), and *Rooms in the House of Stone* (1993).

Elizabeth Graver is a native Californian. She won the Drue Heinz Literature Prize for *Have You Seen Me?* (1991). Her articles and stories have appeared in periodicals such as *Southern Review, Story,* and, *Prism International.*

Marie M. Hara is a writer, editor, and teacher who lives in Hawaii. Her book *Bananaheart and Other Stories* was published in 1994.

Susan Carol Hauser lives in Minnesota and received the 1989 Minnesota Book Award for *Meant to Be Read.* Other books include *Girl to Woman* and *Which Way to Look.*

Anndee Hochman is a freelance writer whose work has appeared in *Ms.* and *Philadelphia Magazine*. Her articles include "Tales Out of School" (*Ms*, July, 1997) and "Confessions of a Feminist Bartender" (*Philadelphia Magazine,* March 1994). She has also written a book titled *Everyday Acts and Small Subversions: Women Reinventing Family, Community, and Home* (1994).

G. Winston James's work has appeared in *Waves: An Anthology of New Gay Fiction* (1994), *The Road Before Us* (1991) and *Words of Fire* (1996).

Erica Jong is the author of numerous novels and collections of poetry. Recent publications include *The Devil at Large* (1993), *Fear of Fifty: A Midlife Memoir* (1994) and *Inventing Memory* (1997).

Perri Klass was born in Tunapuna, Trinidad, East Indies. She is a pediatrician and writer. She is an American Academy of Pediatrics Fellow. She won four O. Henry Awards for short stories. Her writings include a collection of short stories *I Am Having an Adventure* (1986) and *Baby Doctor* (1992) in addition to numerous articles to medical magazines.

Ella Leffland has lived and worked in northern California. Her books include *Mrs. Munck* (1970), *Love Out of Season* (1974), *Rumors of Peace* (1979) and *Last Courtesies and Other Stories* (1980).

Molly Martin is an electrician and also an editor of *Tradeswoman* Magazine. She founded *Tradeswoman, Inc.* which is a national organization for women in the trades.

Patricia Preciado Martin is a native of Arizona. She is active in the Chicano community in Tucson. Her creative works include *Songs My Mother Sang to Me: An Oral History of Mexican American Women* (1992), *Images and Conversations: Mexican Americans Recall a Southwestern Past* (1983) and *Days of Plenty, Days of Want* (1988).

Bharati Mukherjee was born in Calcutta, India, and emigrated to the United States to pursue studies in English at the University of Iowa. Her writing reflects her cross-cultural experiences. In 1988, she was awarded the National Book Critics Circle Award for best fiction for *The Middleman and Other Stories*. Recent works include *Regionalism in Indian Perspective* (1992) and *Leave It to Me* (1997).

Shamara Shantu Riley received her bachelor's degree from the University of Illinois at Urbana-Champaign. She was a founding member and president of Black/Out, a campus organization for black lesbians, gays, and bisexuals.

R. A. Sasaki grew up in the Richmond district of San Francisco, California, and is the author of several short stories which have appeared in numerous anthologies including *Growing Up Asian-American* (1993), *Making Waves* (1989) and *Growing Up Female* (1993). She was the recipient of the American Japanese National Literary Award in 1983.

Ruth Shigezawa grew up in Southern California. She is a fourth generation Japanese American and has written about the experiences of first generation Japanese Americans. She is the author of *Celeste* (1993) and *A Photo Marriage* (1984). She is a recipient of the American Japanese National Literary Award.

Marti Stephen is a native of Colorado has served as a mountain-bike editor for *Velo News* which is a magazine for competitive cyclers.

Gordon Weaver grew up in Illinois. His books include *A World Quite Round* (1986), *The Eight Corners of the World* (1988), and *Men Who Would be Good* (1991). He has also served as the general editor for the *Twayne Series of Short Fiction Studies*. Awards received for his writings include two National Endowment for the Arts Fellowships, the Pushcart Prize, and the O. Henry First Prize.

Sylvia A. Watanabe was born in Hawaii. She co-edited *Into the Fire: Asian American Prose* and *Home to Stay: Asian American Women's Fiction* (1990) with Carol Bruchac. Other works include *Talking to the Dead* (1994), and *Talking to the Dead and Other Stories* (1993, 1994).

PART I
IDENTITY

IDENTITY

"Who am I?" This question, prominent in adolescence and early adulthood, is revisited throughout adult life. We define ourselves through our work, relationships with others ("I'm Sarah's mom" or "I'm Tim's partner"), learning strengths and weaknesses ("I'm not a math person, word person, mechanically inclined"), and physical attributes. Continual identity revision occurs as new meaning is made of past and present experiences.

Paradoxically, a person's identity changes and yet remains fundamentally the same. Personality traits such as extraversion, agreeableness, openness and neuroticism remain stable (Costa & McCrae, 1984). Bee (1996) explains this irony by saying that there are two layers to our personality. One layer is genetically hardwired and includes the factors listed above. Bee notes that the second layer contains individual "motivations, desires, strategies for achieving goals, defense mechanisms and coping styles. . . . Naturally, these two levels are linked to one another in each of us: our enduring traits flavor our experiences, affecting our choices and motives" (Bee, 1996, p. 311).

Identity is not produced in a vacuum. Erikson (1968) states that identity occurs both "within the core of the individual and yet also in the core of . . . communal culture" (p. 22). Individuals are influenced by experiences in the world and continuously redefine themselves as a result of those experiences. If the dominant culture does not validate individuals' identities, they face additional identity development challenges.

The environment prompts us to refine who we are. This lifelong project of identity formation occurs through the processes of assimilation and accommodation (Whitbourne & Weinstock, 1986). Whitbourne and Weinstock define assimilation as "The process through which the adult imposes his or her existing framework of self-knowledge of identity onto experiences. This process makes the

environment a place that can be understood in terms that are familiar to the individual's existing identity structure" (p. 179). The
person approaches each situation with what she knows about herself and values in the world. For example, if a person values helping people and being seen as a helpful person, she may see every
social interaction as an opportunity to help and may view her in-
teractions with co-workers in terms of how helpful they think she
is. However, if she discovers that her co-workers consider her nosy
and don't want her help, she may engage in the process of accommodation, defined by Whitbourne and Weinstock as "incorporating
new information gained from . . . experiences" (p. 179). She takes
in the new information and decides to refrain from offering advice
to co-workers unless she's directly asked.

Audre Lorde defines the "mythical norm" in U.S. culture as,
"white, thin, male, young, heterosexual, Christian, and financially
secure" (Lorde, 1984/1995, p. 285). Society rewards these attributes
and if individuals do not fit this profile, they are considered aberrant
and may struggle with aspects of their identity. In fact, one must
cope with multiple identities (and multiple oppressions) as a result.
There are a multitude of identity concerns for those who don't fit the
"mythical norm." Older adolescents and young adults sometimes find
difficulty reconciling ethnic identity with national identity (Phinney,
1993). How can they be both Mexican and American? Some come to
terms with this ambiguity by recognizing the value of being both
(Phinney, 1993).

Others choose to focus primarily on one aspect of their identity. A
qualitative study by Shorter-Gooden and Washington (1996) ex-
plored the challenges young, black women have in forming an identity and found that of the seven identity domains discussed, racial
identity was the most salient. This was followed by gender identity.
The authors state that:

> Race, more than any other area, was a source of self-definition for
> these women. These women varied in their experience of racial iden-
> tity . . . in how actively they struggled with issues of racial identity,
> and in the context of their racial identity beliefs and attitudes. Despite
> these variations, in general the women seemed to have positive atti-
> tudes about being Black. This suggests that while the societal context
> of racism may contribute to the salience of racial identity, it does not
> automatically mean that the resultant identity will mirror society
> views and thus be negative. (p. 471)

It was also noted that African American women mentioned devel-
oping a sense of strength as a result of "struggling with two ascribed

identities—race and gender—that are devalued; or alternatively, the more racism and sexism an African American woman perceives, the more likely she is to have an identity that includes a sense of strength" (p. 473).

This growing sense of strength evidences itself in a story included in this volume by Shamara Shantu Riley. In *A Sistah Outsider* the protagonist is African American, female, and gay. Through selected diary entries spanning her undergraduate years, Shamara reveals her awakening black consciousness and her emerging identity as a feminist and lesbian. She recognizes the developmental aspects of identity (and the dominant culture's insistence on heterosexuality) when she says, "What I've learned most from my college experiences, is that constructing one's decolonized identity is not a one-step, but rather a continuous process. The next step in my process of undoing internalized homophobia is to come out to my family in order to remove myself from the half-truths I've told in order to be accepted and keep the peace."

People with different ethnic heritages often struggle with their identity. One writer of African American and Japanese descent believes that people of mixed racial identity handle the subject in one of several ways: They see it as "inherently problematic" (Thorton, 1996, p. 108), or an issue of assimilation during the identity process where race plays only a small part in identity formation. Or, some literature suggests people go through stages while coping with their multiracial identity, finally reaching the stage of acceptance and appreciation for the strengths their identity gives them (Thorton, 1996).

In *Are You Writing A Book?* Jaimi Carter grapples with her ethnic identity and her relationship with her father. She does not know her father's heritage. She searches for clues and writes her father's side of the family but receives no response. She concludes:

> And at twenty-two, I conclude that I will, I must, define myself out of a half-past, and a present. I am not a "what," I am a "who." I am Jaimi, who has a mother who happens to be white; who has . . . an un-dad who happens to be black, or at least part black . . . I am a body of experiences and though not restricted to (yet not excluding) the 'what' that people seem to have such difficulty defining . . . such a need to define.

The largest group affected by the dominant culture's values is women. Although more women are assuming positions of power in the government and the workforce, many still have difficulty believing they belong in those environments. Additionally, women sometimes question their abilities to do a job (Stiver, 1991). Such is the case with the protagonist in *Flip-Flops*. A medical doctor, she runs to the scene of a motorcycle-truck accident. Although she recognizes her professional position, she also realizes her credibility is undercut because she is a woman and she's wearing flip-flops. She notes, "There are time-honored styles of male authority in the hospital . . . But women have to earn their authority." She has been socialized not to assert her power and also has difficulty accepting her identity as a doctor. She says of a previous emergency room situation, "I heard the nurse say, 'You know, it's at moments like these that I'm really glad that I'm the nurse and you're the doctor.' So I looked over my shoulder to see what doctor she was talking to—but there was no one else there. She was talking to me."

Cultural beliefs regarding physical handicaps have an impact on Sucheng Chan, a physically challenged, Asian American woman whose leg is deformed as a result of polio. Because the Chinese believe physical deformity is equated with being "morally flawed" and the "fate of one [family] member can be caused by the behavior of another," Chan's father believes that her handicap is retribution for his behavior. Although Chan's American friends don't equate her physical disability with the "state of [her] soul," instead of asking about her leg, as her Chinese friends would, Americans either ignore her disability or become "jovially patronizing." She recognizes the physical, cultural, and mental challenges she faces because of her physical disability and wonders if her handicap has made her a different person.

R. A. Sasaki's ethnic identity development unfolds in *A Dictionary of Japanese-American Terms*. In grade school she wasn't certain how she could be both American and Japanese. Sasaki travels to Japan to discover her heritage. She says, "going to Japan was like . . . breaking through the fog and seeing, for the first time, in full light, where I had come from. . . . Until I went to Japan, I was a person without a past; I looked into a mirror and saw no reflection."

Historical time also shapes our identity. For example, World War II impacted children's and young adults' identity development differently. We see the influence of race and historical time on Ben Inaba, the protagonist in *Three Steps a Minute,* as he reviews his life. An immigrant, he studied to be a CPA but no one hired him so he picked crops for a living and currently lives in a run-down hotel. Satisfied with his life, he wants no sympathy.

In *How I Got to Be Jewish,* we see the increasing importance of ethnicity and its intersection with class in the main character's identity development. The author states, "The older we get, the more Jewish we become in my family. . . . When we're young and cute, we can hang out with goyim—but as the sun goes down, we revert to knishes and knaydlach." As a child, she realized class was, in part, determined by ethnicity and says, "My best friend Glenda Glascock . . . was considered classier than me . . . Glenda's name ended with *cock* and mine did not. I knew that names ending in *cock* were intrinsically classier. The dominant culture . . . required names that did not *sound* Jewish or foreign."

She maintains that Jews are concerned about their identity because their "survival depends on it" because "A Jew is a person who can convert to Christianity from now to Doomsday, and still be killed by Hitler if his mother was Jewish." Writing, the author believes, helps Jews (and women) "reinvent [themselves]."

Finally, in *Dear Aunt Nanadine* Alexis De Veaux examines the influence of colorism within the African American community on the main character's identity. Her Aunt's admonition to not wear a red dress because it would cause people to notice her dark skin color, made the author aware of how her color affected her. The sixties taught the author to "learn to love the dark me . . . I could not get dark enough." She writes to Aunt Nanadine, "Remember that it is the impulse to love that comes between the silence between aunt and niece. Comes in the letter saying I love you. Comes, as I write, struggling to internalize beauty, because *color is still a critical issue between our people*" [italics in the original].

In summary, identity is a multifaceted, simultaneously changing and stable construct. Those outside the "mythical norm" may struggle with various aspects of their identity and use different methods to come to terms with their identities. Our sense of self is influenced by, among other factors, culture, history, sexism, and racism. Ultimately, however, we are responsible for making sense of ourselves to ourselves.

A Sistah Outsider

Shamara Shantu Riley

On and off since the fourth grade, I have recorded my thoughts and daily experiences in a diary or journal. I think my grandmother bought me my first lock-and-key diary at age eight partly to encourage writing skills. At first, my diary only revealed my youthful social activities. But as I grew older and more politically conscious, social issues became infused in my journals.

The inspiration for the title of my selected journal excerpts is from Audre Lorde's Sister Outsider *because the term typifies much of my life. Because of my multifaceted identity as a Black lesbian, I have often simultaneously felt like a "sistah" and yet still an "outsider" in the Black, lesbian, and womanist communities. In this contradictory space of sistah-outsiderhood, I am often expected to negate some component of my identity in the name of "unity" or in order to pass someone's litmus test of acceptance. In order to deal with these conflicts in my life, writing has increasingly become a hobby of mine. Writing gives me some sort of voice to articulate my thoughts about my identity in a world where people constantly try to deny me the right to have my own identity. Writing in my journal is also cathartic because it enables me to survive, to heal many of the wounds that have existed in my life.*

As my journal excerpts reflect, much of my undergraduate social life was spent trying to fit into some crowd to the detriment of my identity. Nevertheless, college, especially my later years, served as the catalyst of my increased consciousness and understanding about my relation to others in the world.

As I reflect on my journal writings throughout my undergraduate years, I think about how much I've grown in my consciousness about

the isms affecting not only my life but the lives of others as well. I also
think about those who've helped me with this ongoing process of
transformation—the women at the YWCA, the writings of various
womanists, and my queer friends.

First Year of College

After I graduated from high school, I decided to leave the sheltered,
middle-class sanctuary of St. Petersburg, Florida, for Chicago in or-
der to be more independent. Even though I had decided to major in
political science back in tenth grade, I still lacked a political con-
sciousness. In my first year at the University of Illinois at Chicago
(UIC), I was much more preoccupied with fitting in than about elim-
inating world oppression.

September 15, 1988

I am finally in college. Today was the first day of classes. College
seems so much better than high school. It seems much easier for me
to make new friends here in college than it ever was in high school.
I guess that's because I live on this floor with about fifty other fresh-
men who are also trying to fit in. I'm going to try to make a new life
for myself here in college. . . .

October 12, 1988

. . . I keep getting these feelings for other females. I kind of have a
crush on ____. Am I a lesbian simply because I find her attractive? I
still remember how I used to look at other girls in middle school, and I
was attracted to ____ in high school. Maybe it's just a phase I'm going
through. But are these feelings I keep experiencing even normal? . . .

October 18, 1988

Today I accidentally went to a lecture about homosexuality. I was
goofing around in the student union with nothing to do and encountered a large poster with this strange symbol that looked like two
stick people joined in hands. When I later asked what the symbol
meant, a woman told me that it was the symbol of womanhood and
two of those symbols meant lesbianism. The lecture was about this

white woman who was trying to gain custody of her disabled lesbian lover, but because lesbianism isn't recognized by law, the disabled woman's family got custody of her. The lecturer discussed how the case involved homophobia. I've never heard of this term before, but it's supposed to mean hatred of people who are gay. I feel sorry for her situation because it doesn't seem fair that she can't see her lover because of who she is. Why should it matter what people do in the privacy of their bedroom? I wonder why Julia and Sherrie looked at me funny when I told them how I had gone to the lecture? . . .

December 1, 1988

. . . My feelings for other women are getting stronger. I'm so confused about my sexual preference because I kind of like guys too. But I think I like women more because they're much easier to talk to and they're more serious about stuff. . . . People are starting to ask me why I'm not dating any guys, so I just make up stuff to change the subject. . . .

May 16, 1989

. . . Marcus asked me to go out with him and I said yes. Everyone else but me knew he liked me, and didn't even tell me. He's an OK-looking guy and isn't nearly as concerned about getting the panties as some of these other UIC guys. Maybe he'll help take my mind off the funny feelings I keep having. But I don't want to be intimate with him anytime soon. . . .

Sophomore Year

During my sophomore year, I started to have an inkling of race consciousness. I began attending more lectures on Black identity (which always connoted Black heterosexual male identity). I was even active in a campus group called the Black Student Retention Program (BSRP). However, I was still oblivious to a consciousness as a woman and queer. Sophomore year was a year where I continued to privately struggle with the social consequences of being a lesbian.

October 10, 1989

. . . Sherrie finally decided to sit down and talk to me after avoiding me for three days. Ever since I told her that I thought I might be gay, she has been squeamish. I'm not even sure if I am or not. When we talked, she said that she avoided me because when I told her that I liked someone female, she automatically assumed it was her. And to think that our friendship could have been ruined because she assumed wrong! But I hope that this news doesn't jeopardize our friendship. Sherrie's my best friend and she's like the older sister I never had. I don't know what I would do if she decides that she doesn't want to be my friend anymore because of this. Why should it even matter? I'm just like everyone else, except that I might be gay, that's all. I'm not even sure if it was right to tell her. . . .

October 22, 1989

. . . ____ asked me to go out on a date with her this afternoon, but I turned her down. How in the world did she find out about my sexual preference? I do kind of want to get to know her better, but I can't afford to let everyone know my business. I can't jeopardize my hard-built image by dating someone who also goes to UIC. If word gets around about this incident, I don't know what I'll do. . . .

December 13, 1989

. . . I think that I may be bisexual. In some ways, I kind of like guys, and in some ways, I kind of like girls. How does one determine what preference one has? Is it by whom you've dated, slept with, had a serious relationship with, or a combination? I don't know what my preference is. I wonder if anyone else feels the same way. . . .

February 4, 1990

. . . During halftime, the 1990 Homecoming Court all came out onto the court like we did during rehearsal. I was first runner-up. I was so happy that I called my family right after we got off the basketball court. I got a lot of votes for BSRP and Black Students for Communication. I finally feel accepted at UIC, but if people find out about my sexual preference, they won't want to hang with me anymore. . . .

February 8, 1990

. . . Sherrie told me that Brian asked about my sexuality. He asked her why I was never seen with any guys whom I am romantically involved with. Sherrie told me that she lied and told him that I had no boyfriend because I was busy with my studies. She also told me that Shawn was in the room and said that she also thought I was "strange." What do I do now that people are beginning to suspect about me? After all, I am dating—and she comes by my dorm room sometimes. . . .

March 10, 1990

. . . Tonight I was walking home from work and these Alphas harassed me in front of my dorm. . . . One of them said, "Hey, baby," but I just ignored him. They started making sexual comments about how they wanted to [have sex with] me and make me into a real woman. One of them said, "We don't like dykes around here. All you need is a good man and you'll come around." When I tried to move past them and enter my dorm, they blocked the door. I was so scared and felt so helpless because no one else was around. I didn't know what to do. Then they came away from the door and just started laughing at me. . . .

Junior Year

During my junior year, I transferred to the Urbana-Champaign campus of the University of Illinois. I publicly claimed that I had transferred because the Urbana-Champaign campus had a better political science program and more prestige. However, I now think that I transferred from the Chicago campus partly because of the rumors surrounding my sexuality. Because I pledged a predominantly white sorority, much of my junior year can be characterized as the year of the assimilation approach. Much of the year was spent trying to assimilate into mainstream society with drastic results. In the process, I ended up negating my identity as I sought to fit into my new school. Although I privately realized that I was a lesbian, I still dated men publicly because I saw myself as having an image to uphold as a Greek.

By March 1991, with a women's health conference as the catalyst, I began referring to myself as a womanist and reading womanist books. I had always believed that females should have equal rights to males; however, before the conference, I was part of the "I'm not a feminist, but . . ." group of young women. With this identification as a womanist, I began coming to terms with my Black womanhood as I sought information not only on the legacy of Black women, but on Black people in general.

Working at the Daily Illini (DI) *as a features writer and later as a columnist gradually enabled me to reclaim my own voice since I constantly had to defend my views on a conservative campus. In the end, these experiences made me more willing to speak up for myself and demand—not ask—to be heard.*

August 23, 1990

Today was the first day of classes. I'm glad I transferred from the Chicago campus because I didn't like its commuter-campus flavor. I like this campus much better. Unlike UIC, these surroundings make me feel as though I'm really in college. I will definitely be able to make a new life for myself here and put the past behind me. . . .

August 28, 1990

Today was the day all of the rushees were to pick up our bids at Illini Union. . . . I got a bid from Pi Beta Phi . . . Some Pi Phi seniors picked me up to take me to Sisterhood Night . . . I'm the only black person in my pledge class of forty-eight girls. We hung around the house and took pictures with the actives. I found out that there are 142 of us in all. My new sisters are really nice, although I do wish I weren't the only Black person. . . .

September 15, 1990

Ever since I pledged the Pi Phis, I've been gaining more friends although I now wish that I had decided to live in the dorms instead of an off-campus apartment. However, the Black kids on this campus look at me like I'm some traitor whenever I wear my Pi Phi attire around campus. The Black Greek Council members tease me even more than the independent ones do. They're just jealous because I didn't pledge any of their groups. Already, people have called me "Aunt Jemima" and "wannabee" behind my back. . . .

October 2, 1990

Today Rachel introduced me to this Black guy named Claude during lunch at the house. I guess she invited Claude to come over because she suspected that I wanted to get to know other Blacks in the

Greek system. Claude is the Phi Delts' VP and was our sorority's Ar-
rowman last year. We sat in the dining room and talked for a little
while, and then he suggested that we go for a walk. Claude said that
he wanted to take me out of the house so we could really discuss our
experiences in the Greek system. We walked along the Quad and discussed our experiences . . . At least I have someone who I can talk to
about being the only black in a white Greek group. . . .

October 11, 1990

. . . Tonight was our Halloween exchange with the Delta Sigs. I
knew I shouldn't have gone; I should have stayed home. . . . By midnight, I couldn't take it anymore and just left the party without saying good-bye to anyone. While I was walking along Armory Drive, Susan and Lesen saw me crying and wanted to know what was wrong.
I didn't tell them about how I felt so left out with all of those white
people because I didn't want to hurt their feelings. No one in my
sorority would understand. I tried to call Claude, but he wasn't
home; he must be at some party. I just feel so left out right now; I definitely don't belong in this sorority. . . .

November 1, 1990

. . . Tonight I went to Impromptu at Cochrane's with Claude. I had
a really great time. Claude is a really nice guy. We sat in my apartment and talked for a couple of hours. . . . While I was looking at
Claude, _____ flashed across my mind. I'm just not that interested
in having an intimate relationship with a man. . . .

November 7, 1990

. . . Tonight I depledged from Pi Phis. . . . I can no longer attempt
to be something that I'm not. Who will be my close buddies now? Now
that I'm out of the group, my sisters and I will not be as close, if they
speak to me at all. And most of the black people on campus seem to
hate my guts. . . . At least I can still hang with Claude; he's understanding about my decision. . . .

March 21, 1991

Today was the state conference on women's health at Jumer's.
Since it was free, I simply went by myself to get more information

about health issues. But I learned a lot today. . . . There was also a workshop on racism in the health-care system and virtually every woman of color in the room had an experience. I also told about my experiences with racism in the health-care profession when I went to the doctor at UIC that one time. . . . The conference really inspired me to learn more about women and their contributions to America. . . .

April 14, 1991

. . . Tonight was the Betty Friedan lecture in Illini Union. Just as I expected, she was very exclusionary in her speech. . . . She talked about how "our" mothers lived in the suburbs and were housewives before the 1960s women's movement began. . . . If this isn't a typical case of racism and classism in the women's movement, then I don't know what is. At least half of the women of color in the room left by the time she finished because she totally made us feel invisible. . . . I think I'm going to write a staffer's comment in the DI about how she basically implied that we made no contributions to the women's movement and how the women's movement must be more inclusive if it is ever to accomplish its goals. . . .

April 28, 1991

Today I found out that I will be one of the *DI's* columnists next year. Now I will finally be able to speak after people have ignored what I have had to say for so long. Now they will have to listen to what I have to say. . . .

Senior Year

By far in my twenty-one years of living, my senior year in college has been the most challenging and positive. During my senior year, I started to believe that I had value, I had worth. With this increase in self-esteem began my process of coming to terms with my multifaceted identity. I began seeing the interlocking nature of oppression as I started to analyze my internalized racism, sexism, and homophobia.

I also began to realize that I was not simply a passive victim of oppression, but that I could actually help make change and empower myself in the process. I became involved with a campus multicultural women's organization called Women Working for Progress (WWP), I also participated in one of WWP's support groups for Black women, the Womanist Circle.

By reading more about Black women through the Womanist Circle, I also learned more about my life as a Black lesbian. With increased political consciousness, I also realized that lesbianism is more than a bedroom issue and the people usually don't have a problem with queerness when it is kept so privately, but when it is just as out in the open as heterosexuality. A lecture by Kwame Ture served as the catalyst for my coming out on campus while the Second Annual Graduate Conference in Lesbian, Gay and Bisexual Studies, better known as the Queer Conference, served as a catalyst of my learning more about queer history and identity.

September 8, 1991

Today I did an article at work on my experiences as a Black lesbian, but later decided not to print it in the DI. So I have to do another one tomorrow. I decided not to have it printed because deep down I still don't have enough courage to come out to seventeen thousand people. I still don't want everyone to know my personal business and I'm afraid of how people will react to me when they read it. . . .

October 17, 1991

Today was the breakfast for Angela Davis to end her visit at the U of I. . . . I am totally in awe of this sister. She commands such a presence. I wish I had that effect on people when I speak. After breakfast, we all sat around and expounded on some of the issues that were touched upon in her lecture yesterday evening. I asked her about how we can deal with many Black women's misconceptions of womanism. . . . After she left to catch her plane, a bunch of us sat around and discussed political issues. While we were on the subject of homophobia, I managed to get enough courage to publicly state I was a lesbian for the first time—and to women who I didn't even know! . . .

October 30, 1991

. . . I've been catching a lot of flak for my article about how there can't be a Supreme Being. One woman wrote me and expressed anger that I would call God "It" instead of "He". . . . I just don't believe God exists. If there is such a thing, then the world wouldn't be in such a bad shape. And if this God is supposedly so good and kind, then how come It allowed slavery to happen? Why are people starving every day? . . .

November 7, 1991

. . . Tonight was the first time I entered Chester Street Bar, although it was so-called straight night. Will I be able to meet other sisters here? C Street is about the only place in the country where I'll have an inkling of a chance of meeting other women, so I hope. . . . I didn't dance with any women because I still haven't told Tahtia, Larry, and Meridee about my real sexual preference. I don't want to lose their friendship. . . .

November 27, 1991

. . . I also lied about my sexuality to Larry when he told me about the rumors floating around after I wrote the article about homophobia in the black community. I told the women at the Y because they looked like they would accept me anyway, but I don't know how Larry would react to it. Sabrina also told me that people have asked her about my sexuality. I purposely wrote the article to make my sexuality ambiguous because I can't deal with rejection right now. . . .

December 21, 1991

Tonight was the first time that I went to C Street on a gay night. . . . I wanted to ask some of the women there to dance, but I was nervous. I've never danced with another woman in public since my past girlfriends were even more closeted than I. While I was there, the question of whether I was nervous to ask other women to dance because of my shyness, fear, or both flashed across my mind. I think it might be a combination of both factors. . . .

December 28, 1991

. . . Today Grandma, Wes, and I were talking at the kitchen table and Grandma mentioned how her Bible study class had an interesting discussion yesterday. When I asked her what the topic had been, she said homosexuality and I immediately froze. While we had different views on the issue, I still tried to portray myself as a hetero who was just expressing a progressive opinion. I kind of wanted to come out to her since we were on the subject, but the "don't mess things up" message constantly came into my head. They've got to suspect by now. . . . I just wish they would just come out and ask me if I'm a lesbian so it would be easier to tell them. . . .

February 7, 1992

. . . Tonight I asked another woman to dance when I went to C Street. . . . I have finally overcome some of my shyness and fear of other people knowing my identity. . . .

February 8, 1992

. . . Tonight while I was at C Street, this guy named John asked me to dance. Because I had nothing better to do, I said OK. While we were dancing, this Black woman passed by and gave him a dirty look. He asked me if I knew her, and I said no. . . . Then he made some comment which I didn't hear because of the loud music. Then he said, "That was just a joke. But I know that you can't be a lesbian." When I told him that I was, he was astonished. "But you don't look like a lesbian, you look good," he said to me. I asked him if he thought that just because I was a lesbian, I had to be ugly too, but he had no response. It's funny how people have all of these stereotypes about lesbians. . . .

February 11, 1992

. . . Tonight was the Kwame Ture speech on Black liberation. Although he made some good points, some of his claims were very flawed. . . . Kwame claimed that because heterosexism was nonexistent in the Black community, homophobia was not an issue that needed to be addressed in the movement. He claimed that homosexuality was "tolerated" in the Black community and there were no incidents of gay-bashing. . . . I was one of the first people to get to the mike and challenge him on his views. When it was my turn, I outed myself in front of all of those people by questioning how he could claim to be for the liberation of all Black people and not even acknowledge heterosexism in the Black community. . . . He challenged me to name one gay-bashing incident in the Black community. When I proceeded to tell him about my experience at UIC, he tried to cut me off. . . . As we went back and forth, Dino tried to cut me off. But I wouldn't let him and basically told him to move aside because I had something to say . . . Now every Black person on campus will know about my sexual orientation, but oh well. I felt like a burden was lifted off my shoulders when I outed myself tonight. . . . My challenge obviously affected him, because he talked about the issue for a long time at the [African-American Cultural House] reception. At the reception, people looked at me funny, but I didn't care. . . . People probably think I'm crazy for daring to challenge the Black power man, but he is not exempt from holding misguided views. . . . I'm proud of myself for standing up to Kwame and Dino tonight. This is the first time I have stood up for myself.

February 23, 1992

. . . Tonight was the Black Women's Achievement Dinner. . . . Camille came up to me to tell me that she supported what I did at the Kwame Ture lecture. I've gotten a lot of support for standing up to him, but I've also gotten a lot of criticism. During dinner, Tahtia told me how she had to defend me several times against people who didn't like what I did. I have gotten flak for having been "disrespectful" to an elder like Ture. But when he dismisses the existence of me and other lesbians and gays in the community, am I just supposed to be silent? . . . The presentations at the dinner really inspired me and made me feel proud to be a Black woman. . . .

March 3, 1992

. . . This evening I read Suzanne Pharr's book in one sitting. . . . This book really has me thinking about how I've internalized negative imagery of myself, how I've been trying to achieve the good lesbian role so people will accept me. . . . We've been very lax at the YW about attacking the isms. . . . I'm going to approach Imani about doing that heterosexism workshop this semester. . . .

March 24, 1992

. . . Tonight Susana, Christy, and I facilitated the first part of the workshop series on heterosexism and homophobia. It went along OK,

although we were all very nervous at first. . . . We defined heterosexism and homophobia, and discussed the different ways it mani-
fests itself. . . . We also discussed internalized homophobia. . . . Although I know the language on how to move beyond internalized
homophobia, I just wish my personal life would catch up with my politics. Facilitating the workshop made me realize even more how
much I've internalized the oppressors' values and how I still have
stereotypes of what a lesbian looks like. Ever since I started dating
again, I seem to have back-slid. . . .

April 4, 1992

Today was the last day of the Queer Conference. . . . I guess the
conference was OK overall since I did learn about different people's
queer identities. I learned the most from the Black men who presented papers at the conference, and their papers really made me
start liking my identity. However, I am disappointed about the fact
that not one sister presented a paper at the conference. When I asked
some of the coordinators why this was the case, they told me that no
Black women sent in an abstract. . . . I'm definitely going to make
sure that I send in an abstract for next year's conference so there will
be no excuse for this blatant exclusion of our experiences. . . .

April 12, 1992

Today Steve and I were the guests at WBML's show on gays and
lesbians in the community. . . . I still didn't like the format of some of
the questions, and I told them so. The typical questions like when did
we realize that we were gay were on their list. . . . I hate when people try to address our experience without addressing the larger issues that affect that experience. Although the DJs were willing to
ask us about racism in our lives, they didn't want to get to the deep
issues of how heterosexism affects our lives. And they certainly
didn't want to get into the issue of heterosexism within the community because they probably would have to challenge themselves on
some of their assumptions. . . .

April 25, 1992

. . . Tonight was Tahtia's Q Sweet Ball in Illini Union. . . . After the
ball was over, these Omegas were trying to talk to _____ and me.

This one Omega from Nigeria tried to squeeze my phone number from me with these tired-ass pickup lines. . . . He asked me if I had a boyfriend, and my negative response was in such a way that he could tell that I was not the typical female he's encountered. "You've got a girlfriend?" he asked in amazement. I said yes. "Then you're, you're a lesbian? But you don't look like a lesbian," he said. I asked him what he thought a lesbian was supposed to look like, but he couldn't respond. For some reason, I get a pleasure out of messing up hetero men's world who try to stereotype us lesbians. . . . He then proceeded to ask me all of the stereotypical questions I get whenever I tell men about my sexuality. He asked me how lesbians make love, when I realized I was a lesbian, and all of that. When I asked him when he realized that he was heterosexual to show the absurdity of such a question, he was flabbergasted. He then pointed to _____ and asked if she was my girlfriend since we came together. Since _____ was giving me that don't-tell-him look, I lied and said no. I hate having to deny our relationship because _____ is fearful of what people will think of her. . . .

May 3, 1992

. . . Tonight was the Sistah Souljah speech in Krannert Center. Just as I expected, she was tripping hard. Many people left the auditorium, she was so outrageous in her male-identified views. . . . While she was supposedly discussing Black liberation, she made a statement that feminism was only for white women. . . . Then she stated that one of the keys to Black liberation was the family and emphasized the necessity of everyone being in hetero relationships. . . . I was so angry that I made sure I was the very first person at the microphone. I didn't even think about the consequences of my coming out to a packed auditorium of two thousand people who wanted to vent their frustrations over the Rodney King verdict on some scapegoat since she had fired everyone up. . . . I told her that as a lesbian and woman-identified woman, she was denying my reality and stated that she was in no way for Black liberation because of her comments. . . . She tried to bust me out and make me look stupid by claiming that what a person did in "his" own bedroom was "his" business and thus didn't need to be spread around. I wanted to tell her that people's problem with homosexuality is when it is out in the same level of visibility as heterosexuality, but she cut me off. . . . She also claimed that she was woman-identified also because she was a woman, which was downright ludicrous. . . . I left Krannert so mad! I am so hurt, I can't believe that my own people rejected me so much. . . . They booed me when I stated my case and cheered as she vented

her homophobic outrage at me for daring to challenge her views. . . .
Tonight makes me wonder whether I should even bother doing social
justice, whether we can have a true movement or just a spectacle. . . .

May 6, 1992

. . . Today _____ and I discussed various social issues. Because
she is so apolitical, she rarely wants to discuss such things. . . . It was
obvious that my challenge for her to analyze how she has internalized heterosexism and images that white is better irritated her. She
said that all I see is politics, that I always see things as a Black-and-
white issue. But everything is political . . . This is the first time I've
had a girlfriend who is overall much more closeted than me, and it's
hard to deal with. . . . When will she understand that holding my
hand, kissing me publicly is in itself a political act because of the way
society is structured? . . .

May 14, 1992

. . . I also found out that I got into the Ph.D. program in political
science at the U of I. I got a "minority fellowship." It's funny how with
all of the women in grad school, the financial aid is still referred to
as a "fellow"ship. And which minority group are they talking about?
. . . I have no idea what my Ph.D. thesis will be on, but at least I don't
have to decide right now. Maybe I'll just expand on my senior thesis
and go into more detail about statehood for D.C. But I kind of want
to do something about Black women and their political activism.
Who knows? . . .

May 15, 1992

. . . I went to the beauty shop today to get my hair done for graduation. While I was there, I saw Dauri, who was also there to get her
hair done for graduation. We talked for a while about our families
and I told her how I wanted to come out to my family. She told me
that all the coming-out books say to never come out to one's family
during a momentous occasion like graduation. She advised me to
wait until a regular time to tell them. But when will be the right time
to tell my family? Because my family lives so far away, whenever
they visit me or I visit them, it will be a momentous occasion. When
I told Rhonda about my thinking about telling my family, she told me

that they don't need to know anyway, but if I do tell them, I should wait until they ask me. I wonder what I should do? . . .

May 16, 1992

Today was the LAS graduation in Krannert Center. I have the distinction of being the first person in my generation in the family to graduate from college. . . . _____ also came to my graduation and sat right next to my family members. I'm sure they assumed _____ was just a good friend of mine. If they knew the nature of our relationship, I don't know how my family would react. I guess they would be disappointed. I feel kind of guilty about not telling them that I'm a lesbian. Someday I've got to tell them. . . .

As I begin my graduate studies at the University of Illinois, what I've learned the most from my college experiences is that constructing one's decolonized identity is not a one-step but rather a continuous process. The next step in my process of undoing internalized homophobia is to come out to my family in order to remove myself from the mask of half-truths I've told in order to be accepted and keep the peace. In my process of transformation, I've also learned (albeit slowly) that organizing with others is also necessary in order to change these conditions and that a transformation of my individual self alone will not alter the structures of society. I'm trying to challenge others to learn more about themselves and rethink the negative imagery of themselves, to challenge dominant groups on how they negatively relate to others, etc. In the process, I continue to learn more about myself as I continue down the road to self-empowerment.

"Are You Writing a Book?"

Jaimi Carter

The man whose turn in line it was ordered two Big Macs and fries and cokes for his wife and himself. He looked at me kind of queerly when I reached for his money, almost suspiciously. My hand stopped. "How do you say your name?" Oh, that was it; he was looking at my badge: "Great Service Guaranteed by Jaimi!" I told him. "Jay-mee." He smiled. Then he went on, "Can I ask you a personal question? You can probably guess what it is." Yeah, right. Anything from "Can-I-have-an-apple-pie?" to "Are you married?" But it was "You're not . . . Mexican are you?" The sidelong glances in case any of the Mexicans beside me heard were a bit much, I thought. But I answered in the negative so he was reassured. "Yeah, I didn't think so. I've got a feeling for that sort of thing." Funny. I always thought it was fairly obvious . . . "Well, what are you then? You're part black, huh?" Perhaps he was looking for an ally in this veritable sea of Hispanic faces, but "What" am I? "*What?!*" "Yes. My dad is black, and my mom is white." Again he beamed. "What a lovely combination you make." Would I be so lovely to him if I *had* been Mexican? I wonder. I wonder. And now he's thrown me back into the midst of some sort of identity crisis that I didn't know I had until I was nineteen and realised that I didn't know who half of me was.

"My dad is black," I'd said. True enough. Well, true in the sense that he planted the seed in my mother, and there his association as "dad" ended. He chose to leave before that union of father and mother, tadpole and egg, became external and real. So perhaps "father?" But "father" ended with the $50 a month that stopped two

24

months after I turned 18. Then "biological father?" Or perhaps "farmer?"

So when I was six and trying to pinpoint myself, to know me by knowing my parents, and I asked "J.C., how old are you?" was it any wonder that I'd said "J.C.," not "Dad?" His response was in the form of a Catch-22: "Are you writing a book?" I wasn't. I thought that should be clear. "Well, then you don't need to know." Oh. The next time I was more clever. I lied. "Yes." But he was even quicker than me: "Well, then that's one chapter you'll have to leave out."

When I was sixteen, I found I could get no further than the book, and whether it was or was not to be, it could not help me. I found that out when he accused me of lying and tricks and manipulation; said that I could not love and therefore could not be loved. So after sixteen years, I was told by my dad? farmer? that he didn't love me. And to my mother he said "I don't even believe she's really mine. Not the fruit of my loins."

But who else's could I possibly be? Not that I believed it. I look like him. Only lighter. And female. So I concluded he was a sadist and a liar and an asshole. A bastard that had spawned two bastards of his own, because he left before my elder brother and I could be made legitimate, real.

Not that I minded. He had, in effect, given me permission to stop trying to make him into my dad, and I stepped away. But I never got from him that side of me that I had been trying to find when I asked him his age, though at the time, I had forgotten that I had ever wanted to know.

Perhaps I didn't mind because I had always, since I could remember, had a "dad." To whom my mother teased us into saying "Thank you, Daddy Dwight!" after he had taken us all to dinner. (And whose name, by some ironic twist of baby-pronounciation was transformed into De-White.) I wonder if he noticed and felt something? In his house I grew up, with his sons, my half-brothers, who are just my brothers. So why does he encounter difficulty in describing me, in introductions? Again, the "who" is not the problem. "This is Jaimi." It is the "what." "Jaimi, my . . ." daughter? step-daughter? wife's daughter? How any of these, when he did not (would not? could not?) adopt, yet has lived with me for twenty-one years. "My daughter." Sometimes. Like in the "Father-Daughter Cake Bake" in second grade; or if I were to be married, and he had to give me away. "Step-daughter." Other times. Like when discussions about financial aid began . . . But always with the introduction, whichever he chose (chooses), the slight pause, the blush. So, like the man in McDonald's said: *"What"* am I?

I always solved that question by saying, "I'm me." True enough. Why should I be classified by father, absent or otherwise, or by colour? My mother solved it by saying, "You are a citizen of the world!" True enough. But isn't everyone?

So came nineteen, when I said "I'm me." And a voice inside me said, "but you know yourself only by half." And so came the crisis that the man in McDonald's had inadvertently stumbled upon. What is Jaimi? She is half of something, and that she knows. The mother, the grandparents, the relatives in England, the house in which she lives; the life she has lived. She is half something else, from a someone who would never tell.

So I wrote to his (the father's? the farmer's) grandmother in Mississippi, to ask. "He won't tell. Will you? I never thought I'd need to know, but I do. I do. Can you help me?" But the reply never came. That is, it never came to me. The father? the un-dad (I shall name him) mentioned not to me, but to my mother, a letter, "sent by my brother" to the great-grandmother in Mississippi. My brother knew nothing of any letter. Of course not. It was mine. How could such a mistake in the identity of the sender occur? Perhaps we are simply one, two half people that complete each other, and so the sender didn't matter. It didn't matter really, because no matter who was the sender, the eventual receiver was the un-dad, who would never tell.

So at nineteen, I discovered that I was bound not to know the un-dad side of me. And at twenty-two, I conclude that I will, I must, define myself out of a half-past, and a present. I am not a "*what*," I am a "*who*." I am Jaimi, who has a mother who happens to be white; who has a farmer, an un-dad, who happens to be black, or at least part black . . . I am a body of experiences and thoughts not restricted to (yet not excluding) the "*what*" that people seem to have such difficulty in defining . . . such a need to define.

I wonder if the man whose turn in line it was would have understood if I had said, "I am a citizen of the world." I wonder.

Flip-Flops

Perri Klass

I was in a little clothing store not far from my home when I heard a horrible noise out in the street—a crash of metal on metal followed by screams, automobile screeches, and general clamor. Without thinking, I ran out of the store and headed across the street; I had reached the island in the middle before it consciously occurred to me, *you're running to help because you're a doctor, you need to take charge.* Inevitably, I was wearing a tee shirt, ratty pants, and flip-flops; and I was particularly conscious of the flip-flops as I arrived at the crowd and pushed my way through. A motorcyclist had smashed into a pickup truck and been thrown far into the air; he lay now on the pavement with broken bones protruding through the skin of his wrists. I knelt down next to him and was relieved to see he was breathing, talking—he did not need cardiopulmonary resuscitation. What he was saying was this: "For God's sake, take my helmet off!" He gestured ineffectually with his wounded hands.

Helpful voices from the crowd immediately broke in: "He wants his helmet off, he said to take his helmet off." Someone else suggested that he be carried into the nearest shop, someone else that he shouldn't be moved.

I raised my voice. "I'm a doctor," I said, not sounding terribly convincing to myself. "I'm a doctor," I repeated. "The helmet stays on." I was shooing away a helpful bystander who was already working on the strap.

I had to say it maybe fifty times before the ambulance arrived. I didn't want to explain in detail, with this man already terrified and in pain, that a severe neck injury could be made worse if we moved his head, pulled off the helmet. I was also keeping an eye on his heart rate, on his breathing, on his general condition. And over and over I kept saying, "I'm a doctor. Please don't touch him. Please leave the helmet alone."

Do you know what I was wishing? Well, first and foremost that I wasn't wearing those flip-flops; they seemed to me to undercut my authority completely. But what I really wished was that I was six foot four, male, and an ex-football player, someone who could just bellow, "Stand back, everyone, I'm in charge here!" And, in my fantasy, everyone would immediately stand back, relieved to have someone in control.

Well, I did the right things. The ambulance arrived, and the EMTs splinted his broken bones and stabilized his neck, took him off to the hospital where X rays would show whether there was in fact an injury to his spinal cord. And I walked away feeling dissatisfied with myself, because I know perfectly well that you don't have to be an ex-running back to claim authority—when that authority is rightfully yours. You ought to be able to do it by force of character, manner, and self-confidence. But it isn't always easy.

Part of medical training is a rapid increase in authority; over a couple of years, you go from being a medical student—a novice in the hospital with no real power—to being an intern, a junior resident, a senior resident. You find yourself teaching medical students, supervising interns—you find yourself taking on, quite literally, responsibility for life-and-death decisions. And you have to come to terms with this authority. You have to accept it, learn to feel entitled to your own power. You have to develop a style for making decisions, giving orders, a style that works effectively with other doctors, with nurses, and with patients.

I've had a lot of trouble accepting my own authority over the past couple of years. It seems to me, in general, that women struggle with this whole question more than men do. Maybe men feel more entitled to power—or more unwilling to admit it if they are insecure. Also, there are time-honored styles of male authority in the hospital, and it often seems that men giving orders get immediate results—even if they aren't football players. But women may have to earn their authority, and it's just harder, in general, for women to use those commanding military tones that have traditionally gotten results for male doctors ("Scalpel!"). At the same time, women may not be easily forgiven for sounding brusque, or for taking control too assertively. We have to find our own way, develop our own special manner—and you can only do that if you feel entitled to your authority, if you are really ready to claim it.

In my training program, we have practice emergencies, situations where a group of doctors and nurses "resuscitate" a plastic dummy (the dummies come in baby, child, and adult sizes). At the beginning of my second year of residency, they told me it was my turn to run the resuscitation, give the orders. I said, quite honestly, that I wasn't ready, that I had no idea how to run a resuscitation. I knew how to follow orders—how to do chest compressions, give the "patient" oxygen, or start the IV, but I couldn't run the damn thing. "That's the point," said the supervising doctor, gently. "You need to hear yourself say it. You'll hear your voice saying, 'Why don't we give him some— some—some—*epinephrine!*' And there you'll be." Epinephrine, or adrenaline, is one of the drugs we give most commonly in resuscitations, since it acts as a cardiac stimulant. I had never ordered it before in such a situation. That night, I practiced saying it to my bathroom mirror. First I practiced Taking Control. "I'm in charge here, I'm running this resuscitation," I said firmly to the mirror. "Let's give him some epinephrine."

The next morning, at the resuscitation, a gang of interns and nurses looked at me expectantly, clustered around the plastic dummy. I heard my own voice, an octave higher than it had been when I talked to the mirror. "Why don't we give some—some— some—epinephrine!" I squeaked, and they did.

The authority of the "crash," the sudden life-and-death emergency, is the authority residents tend to fear most—a child will be found not breathing, and I'll be the only one there. Someone who was doing just fine will start to die before my eyes. But as residency moved along, I found that that authority did in fact come to me when I needed it. When I had to give those orders I gave them, though my voice still has a lamentable tendency to squeak. I find that I no longer automatically look around for a doctor when a sudden emergency occurs; it seems to have gotten through to me that I *am* a doctor. But there are other kinds of authority that may not loom quite so large, but which are even harder to assume, even harder to own. I remember once when a baby was brought to the emergency room essentially dead on arrival, a victim of sudden infant death syndrome, or crib death. We tried for half an hour to resuscitate that baby, not willing to admit that the small, perfect, still-warm body could really be beyond our help. But he was, and the senior doctor asked me to go out and tell the parents. And so I sat down with them and tried to explain, tried to give them answers they could believe, about a disease that nobody understands. I had to tell them, no, this did not happen because your apartment is too warm, no, it did not happen because you gave the baby a different brand of formula today—it *was not your fault.* I needed a particular mix of confidence, authority, and sympathy for that family, and I hope I found it.

As I have slowly claimed my authority as a doctor, I have worried that I may carry over some of those mannerisms into my life outside the hospital. I have learned to behave, in certain situations, as if I am the one with the final say, the one with the power. This does not go over particularly well on the home front. I have learned, when the going gets rough, to cut through the argument and give orders, make my choices, and accept the consequences. This is not a recommended technique for resolving arguments with one's significant other. The cliché of the surgeon's wife, who is constantly reminding her husband that he is no longer in the operating room, is relevant. Women cannot get away with this kind of behavior at home, by and large, and sometimes I think that the fear of sounding like I am trying to give orders has actually made me more wishy-washy in my personal life.

In a way, the most difficult authority for me to accept has been the responsibility in situations where I cannot help. A couple of months ago I was working in the newborn intensive care unit, it was the middle of the night, and a baby was getting sicker and sicker. I was working with the baby's nurse; together we did everything that could be done, increasing the help that the baby got from her respirator, adding one drug after another. It was becoming very clear that the baby was going to die, and I wondered whether I should wake up a more senior doctor and ask him to come help out. But the more I thought about it, the more I realized that there was nothing else he could do; I would be calling him in only so that he could be there to preside over our medical helplessness. The baby could not be saved. So I didn't call him. I just stayed there, with the nurse, doing what could be done. And toward morning, as I bent over the baby, I heard the nurse say, "You know, it's at moments like these that I'm really glad that I'm the nurse and you're the doctor." So I looked over my shoulder to see what doctor she was talking to—but there was no one else there. She was talking to me.

You're Short, Besides!

Sucheng Chan

When asked to write about being a physically handicapped Asian American woman, I considered it an insult. After all, my accomplishments are many, yet I was not asked to write about any of them. Is being handicapped the most salient feature about me? The fact that it might be in the eyes of others made me decide to write the essay as requested. I realized that the way I think about myself may differ considerably from the way others perceive me. And maybe that's what being physically handicapped is all about.

I was stricken simultaneously with pneumonia and polio at the age of four. Uncertain whether I had polio of the lungs, seven of the eight doctors who attended me—all practitioners of Western medicine—told my parents they should not feel optimistic about my survival. A Chinese fortune teller my mother consulted also gave a grim prognosis, but for an entirely different reason: I had been stricken because my name was offensive to the gods. My grandmother had named me "grandchild of wisdom," a name that the fortune teller said was too presumptuous for a girl. So he advised my parents to change my name to "chaste virgin." All these pessimistic predictions notwithstanding, I hung onto life, if only by a thread. For three years, my body was periodically pierced with electric shocks as the muscles of my legs atrophied. Before my illness, I had been an active, rambunctious, precocious, and very curious child. Being confined to bed was thus a mental agony as great as my physical pain. Living in war-torn China, I received little medical attention; physical therapy was unheard of. But I was determined to walk. So one day, when I was six or seven, I instructed my mother to set up two rows of chairs to face each other so that I could use them as I would parallel bars.

I attempted to walk by holding my body up and moving it forward with my arms while dragging my legs along behind. Each time I fell, my mother gasped, but I badgered her until she let me try again. After four nonambulatory years, I finally walked once more by pressing my hands against my thighs so my knees wouldn't buckle.

My father had been away from home during most of those years because of the war. When he returned, I had to confront the guilt he felt about my condition. In many East Asian cultures, there is a strong folk belief that a person's physical state in this life is a reflection of how morally or sinfully he or she lived in previous lives. Furthermore, because of the tendency to view the family as a single unit, it is believed that the fate of one member can be caused by the behavior of another. Some of my father's relatives told him that my illness had doubtless been caused by the wild carousing he did in his youth. A well-meaning but somewhat simple man, my father believed them.

Throughout my childhood, he sometimes apologized to me for having to suffer retribution for his former bad behavior. This upset me; it was bad enough that I had to deal with the anguish of not being able to walk, but to have to assuage his guilt as well was a real burden! In other ways, my father was very good to me. He took me out often, carrying me on his shoulders or back, to give me fresh air and sunshine. He did this until I was too large and heavy for him to carry. And ever since I can remember, he has told me that I am pretty.

After getting over her anxieties about my constant falls, my mother decided to send me to school. I had already learned to read some words of Chinese at the age of three by asking my parents to teach me the sounds and meaning of various characters in the daily newspaper. But between the ages of four and eight, I received no education since just staying alive was a full-time job. Much to her chagrin, my mother found no school in Shanghai, where we lived at the time, which would accept me as a student. Finally, as a last resort, she approached the American School, which agreed to enroll me only if my family kept an *amah* (a servant who takes care of children) by my side at all times. The tuition at the school was twenty U.S. dollars per month—a huge sum of money during those years of runaway inflation in China—and payable only in U.S. dollars. My family afforded the high cost of tuition and the expense of employing a full-time *amah* for less than a year.

We left China as the Communist forces swept across the country in victory. We found an apartment in Hong Kong across the street from a school run by Seventh-Day Adventists. By that time I could walk a little, so the principal was persuaded to accept me. An *amah* now had to take care of me only during recess when my classmates might easily knock me over as they ran about the playground.

After a year and a half in Hong Kong, we moved to Malaysia, where my father's family had lived for four generations. There I learned to swim in the lovely warm waters of the tropics and fell in love with the sea. On land I was a cripple; in the ocean I could move with the grace of a fish. I liked the freedom of being in the water so much that many years later, when I was a graduate student in Hawaii, I became greatly enamored with a man just because he called me a "Polynesian water nymph."

As my overall health improved, my mother became less anxious about all aspects of my life. She did everything possible to enable me to lead as normal a life as possible. I remember how once some of her colleagues in the high school where she taught criticized her for letting me wear short skirts. They felt my legs should not be exposed to public view. My mother's response was, "All girls her age wear short skirts, so why shouldn't she?"

The years in Malaysia were the happiest of my childhood, even though I was constantly fending off children who ran after me calling, "*Baikah! Baikah!*" ("Cripple! Cripple!" in the Hokkien dialect commonly spoken in Malaysia). The taunts of children mattered little because I was a star pupil. I won one award after another for general scholarship as well as for art and public speaking. Whenever the school had important visitors my teacher always called on me to recite in front of the class.

A significant event that marked me indelibly occurred when I was twelve. That year my school held a music recital and I was one of the students chosen to play the piano. I managed to get up the steps to the stage without any problem, but as I walked across the stage, I fell. Out of the audience, a voice said loudly and clearly, "Ayah! A *baikah* shouldn't be allowed to perform in public." I got up before anyone could get on stage to help me and, with tears streaming uncontrollably down my face, I rushed to the piano and began to play. Beethoven's "Für Elise" had never been played so fiendishly fast before or since, but I managed to finish the whole piece. That I managed to do so made me feel really strong. I never again feared ridicule.

In later years I was reminded of this experience from time to time. During my fourth year as an assistant professor at the University of California at Berkeley, I won a distinguished teaching award. Some weeks later I ran into a former professor who congratulated me enthusiastically. But I said to him, "You know what? I became a distinguished teacher by *limping* across the stage of Dwinelle 155!" (Dwinelle 155 is a large, cold, classroom that most colleagues of mine hate to teach in.) I was rude not because I lacked graciousness but because this man, who had told me that my dissertation was the finest piece of work he had read in fifteen years, had nevertheless advised me to eschew a teaching career.

"Why?" I asked.

"Your leg . . ." he responded.

"What about my leg?" I said, puzzled.

"Well, how would you feel standing in front of a large lecture class?"

"If it makes any difference, I want you to know I've won a number of speech contests in my life, and I am not the least bit self-conscious about speaking in front of large audiences. . . . Look, why don't you write me a letter of recommendation to tell people how brilliant I am, and let *me* worry about my leg!"

This incident is worth recounting only because it illustrates a dilemma that handicapped persons face frequently: those who care about us sometimes get so protective that they unwittingly limit our growth. This former professor of mine had been one of my greatest supporters for two decades. Time after time, he had written glowing letters of recommendation on my behalf. He had spoken as he did because he thought he had my best interests at heart; he thought that if I got a desk job rather than one that required me to be a visible, public person, I would be spared the misery of being stared at.

Americans, for the most part, do not believe as Asians do that physically handicapped persons are morally flawed. But they are equally inept at interacting with those of us who are not able-bodied. Cultural differences in the perception and treatment of handicapped people are most clearly expressed by adults. Children, regardless of where they are, tend to be openly curious about people who do not look "normal." Adults in Asia have no hesitation in asking visibly handicapped people what is wrong with them, often expressing their sympathy with looks of pity, whereas adults in the United States try desperately to be polite by pretending not to notice.

One interesting response I often elicited from people in Asia but have never encountered in America is the attempt to link my physical condition to the state of my soul. Many a time while living and traveling in Asia people would ask me what religion I belonged to. I would tell them that my mother is a devout Buddhist, that my father was baptized a Catholic but has never practiced Catholicism, and that I am an agnostic. Upon hearing this, people would try strenuously to convert me to their religion so that whichever God they believed in could bless me. If I would only attend this church or that temple regularly, they urged, I would surely get cured. Catholics and Buddhists alike have pressed religious medallions into my palm, telling me if I would wear these, the relevant deity or saint would make me well. Once while visiting the tomb of Muhammad Ali Jinnah in Karachi, Pakistan, an old Muslim, after finishing his evening prayers, spotted me, gestured toward my legs, raised his arms heavenward, and began a new round of prayers, apparently on my behalf.

In the United States adults who try to act "civilized" toward handicapped people by pretending they don't notice anything unusual sometimes end up ignoring handicapped people completely. In the first few months I lived in this country, I was struck by the fact that whenever children asked me what was the matter with my leg, their adult companions would hurriedly shush them up, furtively look at me, mumble apologies, and rush their children away. After a few months of such encounters, I decided it was my responsibility to educate these people. So I would say to the flustered adults, "It's okay, let the kid ask." Turning to the child, I would say, "When I was a little girl, no bigger than you are, I became sick with something called polio. The muscles of my leg shrank up and I couldn't walk very well. You're much luckier than I am because now you can get a vaccine to make sure you never get my disease. So don't cry when your mommy takes you to get a polio vaccine, okay?" Some adults and their little companions I talked to this way were glad to be rescued from embarrassment; others thought I was strange.

Americans have another way of covering up their uneasiness: they become jovially patronizing. Sometimes when people spot my crutch, they ask if I've had a skiing accident. When I answer that unfortunately it is something less glamorous than that they say, "I bet you *could* ski if you put your mind to it!" Alternately, at parties where people dance, men who ask me to dance with them get almost belligerent when I decline their invitation. They say, "Of course you can dance if you *want* to!" Some have given me pep talks about how if I would only develop the right mental attitude, I would have more fun in life.

Different cultural attitudes toward handicapped persons came out clearly during my wedding. My father-in-law, as solid a representative of middle America as could be found, had no qualms about objecting to the marriage on racial grounds, but he could bring himself to comment on my handicap only indirectly. He wondered why his son, who had dated numerous high school and college beauty queens, couldn't marry one of them instead of me. My mother-in-law, a devout Christian, did not share her husband's prejudices, but she worried aloud about whether I could have children. Some Chinese friends of my parents, on the other hand, said that I was lucky to have found such a noble man, one who would marry me despite my handicap. I, for my part, appeared in church in a white lace wedding dress I had designed and made myself—a miniskirt!

How Asian Americans treat me with respect to my handicap tells me a great deal about their degree of acculturation. Recent immigrants behave just like Asians in Asia; those who have been here longer or who grew up in the United States behave more like their white counterparts. I have not encountered any distinctly Asian American pattern of response. What makes the experience of Asian American handicapped people unique is the duality of responses we elicit.

Regardless of racial or cultural background, most handicapped people have to learn to find a balance between the desire to attain physical independence and the need to take care of ourselves by not overtaxing our bodies. In my case, I've had to learn to accept the fact that leading an active life has its price. Between the ages of eight and eighteen, I walked without using crutches or braces but the effort caused my right leg to become badly misaligned. Soon after I came to the United States, I had a series of operations to straighten out the bones of my right leg; afterwards though my leg looked straighter and presumably better, I could no longer walk on my own. Initially my doctors fitted me with a brace, but I found wearing one cumbersome and soon gave it up. I could move around much more easily—and more important, faster—by using one crutch. One orthopedist after another warned me that using a single crutch was a bad practice. They were right. Over the years my spine developed a double-S curve and for the last twenty years I have suffered from severe, chronic back pains, which neither conventional physical therapy nor a lighter work load can eliminate.

The only thing that helps my backaches is a good massage, but the soothing effect lasts no more than a day or two. Massages are expensive, especially when one needs them three times a week. So I found a job that pays better, but at which I have to work longer hours, consequently increasing the physical strain on my body—a sort of vicious circle. When I was in my thirties, my doctors told me that if I kept leading the strenuous life I did, I would be in a wheelchair by the time I was forty. They were right on target: I bought myself a wheelchair when I was forty-one. But being the incorrigible character that I am, I use it only when I am *not* in a hurry!

It is a good thing, however, that I am too busy to think much about my handicap or my backaches because pain can physically debilitate as well as cause depression. And there are days when my spirits get rather low. What has helped me is realizing that being handicapped is akin to growing old at an accelerated rate. The contradiction I experience is that often my mind races along as though I'm only twenty while my body feels about sixty. But fifteen or twenty years hence, unlike my peers who will have to cope with aging for the first time, I shall be full of cheer because I will have already fought, and I hope won, that battle long ago.

Beyond learning how to be physically independent and, for some of us, living with chronic pain or other kinds of discomfort, the most difficult thing a handicapped person has to deal with, especially during puberty and early adulthood, is relating to potential sexual partners. Because American culture places so much emphasis on physical attractiveness, a person with a shriveled limb, or a tilt to the head, or the inability to speak clearly, experiences great uncertainty—indeed trauma—when interacting with someone to whom he or she is attracted. My problem was that I was not only physically handicapped, small, and short, but worse, I also wore glasses and was smarter than all the boys I knew! Alas, an insurmountable combination. Yet somehow I have managed to have intimate relationships, all of them with extraordinary men. Not surprisingly, there have also been countless men who broke my heart—men who enjoyed my company "as a friend," but who never found the courage to date or make love with me, although I am sure my experience in this regard is no different from that of many able-bodied persons.

The day came when my backaches got in the way of having an active sex life. Surprisingly that development was liberating because I stopped worrying about being attractive to men. No matter how headstrong I had been, I, like most women of my generation, had had the desire to be alluring to men ingrained into me. And that longing had always worked like a brake on my behavior. When what men think of me ceased to be compelling, I gained greater freedom to be myself.

I've often wondered if I would have been a different person had I not been physically handicapped. I really don't know, though there is no question that being handicapped has marked me. But at the same time I usually do not *feel* handicapped—and consequently, I do not *act* handicapped. People are therefore less likely to treat me as a handicapped person. There is no doubt, however, that the lives of my parents, sister, husband, other family members, and some close friends have been affected by my physical condition. They have had to learn not to hide me away at home, not to feel embarrassed by how I look or react to people who say silly things to me, and not to resent me for the extra demands my condition makes on them. Perhaps the hardest thing for those who live with handicapped people is to know when and how to offer help. There are no guidelines applicable to all situations. My advice is, when in doubt, ask, but ask in a way that does not smack of pity or embarrassment. Most important, please don't talk to us as though we are children.

So, has being physically handicapped been a handicap? It all depends on one's attitude. Some years ago, I told a friend that I had
once said to an affirmative action compliance officer (somewhat sar-
donically since I do not believe in the head count approach to affirmative action) that the institution which employs me is triply lucky
because it can count me as non-white, female and handicapped. He
responded, "Why don't you tell them to count you four times? . . . Remember, you're short, besides!"

A Dictionary of Japanese-American Terms

R. A. Sasaki

Nihonjin [nē'hon'jē-n']

At the age of six, I thought "Americans" and "English" meant the same thing—"white people." After all, Americans spoke English. You have to understand, this was at an age when I also wondered why "onion" was spelled with an "o." It seemed to me that it should be spelled with a "u," except that would make it "union," which was a different word altogether.

I never thought about what I was. My parents referred to us as "*Nihonjin*"—Japanese. "*Nihonjin*" meant us. "*Hakujin*" (white people) meant them. Being *Nihonjin* meant having straight black hair and a certain kind of last name. The Chinese kids looked like us, but had one-syllable last names.

When I was in the first grade I got into a fight with Lucinda Lee because she claimed that she was American. "You're Chinese," I accused her. She started to cry. Later, I told my mother about the disagreement, and, to my outrage, she sided with Lucinda. It had never occurred to me that Lucinda was American. That I, too, was American. Other kids never asked me if I was American. It was always, "Are you Chinese or Japanese?"

That's how I found out that I was American—one kind of American. I still wasn't sure how I could be both American and *Nihonjin* (was I English, too? I wondered.)

Then a little girl who was REALLY *Nihonjin* moved in next door. Her father worked for a Japanese company, and the family had moved to San Francisco straight from Tokyo. Kimiko wore dresses all the time, even when she didn't have to. She covered her mouth with her hand when she laughed, and sounded like a little bird. When I stuck the nose of my wooden six-shooter in her back and called her a "low-down, dirty tinhorn," emulating my heroes on television westerns, my father, sitting in the next room, shot me a dark, warning look that made me quake in my boots. It was no good insulting Kimiko, anyway, because she wouldn't get mad and fight back. If Kimiko and I were both *Nihonjin*, well then, all I could say was that there must be different kinds of *Nihonjin*, too.

Jiichan [jē chăn]

I don't remember my grandfather.

Jiichan died when I was too young to remember him, but old enough to be afraid of death. He haunted my childhood by appearing in a nightmare so disturbing that I used to force myself to recall it every night before going to sleep so that I wouldn't dream it again. I believed that terrors could only get you when you were least expecting them.

In my dream, there was a large pile of laundry, mainly sheets, on the floor of the dining room in our house on 23rd Avenue. I was sifting through it with my sister, playing in the mountainous folds suddenly dropped into the midst of the usually neat order of my mother's house. We climbed the mountain; our feet sank into the soft mass. Suddenly I clutched a stiff hand. I screamed, and the dream ended abruptly; but I knew, without seeing the rest, that it was *Jiichan's* corpse in there.

My sisters, being older, had known *Jiichan* and did not have such dreams. They were not afraid of him. They remembered his quiet presence watching over them as they played in the back yard of the house on Pine Street. They remembered him tending his beloved cherry tree. I was the only one who needed to reconstruct him. I tried to do it by collecting facts—his name, for example, where he was born, that he had left Japan and come to San Francisco sometime around 1897.

But a part of me has always distrusted language, especially facts. We are so often deceived by them into thinking that we know something. Language is applied after the fact. It is a way of labeling an experience, and if we have never been to Wakayama, Japan, it means nothing that our grandfather was born there. Or if we were not alive in 1897, how can we understand what it meant to leave Japan at that time to come to America?

In 1975 I went to Japan to teach English. I didn't really know why I was going. Finding one's roots at that time was an expression which had been rendered meaningless by overuse. It was just that part of me that distrusts language, wanting to trade facts for knowing.

Other people don't seem to be haunted by the need to bring their grandfathers alive. Perhaps they remember their grandfathers, spoke the same language and heard their stories. If you know who you are and where you come from, or if you are accepted in American society at face value, you can forge ahead and never look back. My Asian face doesn't let me forget my origins. Everytime I start to forget, I will come upon that stiff hand, which will remind me. And if I don't know who my grandfather was, who I am, I will scream with terror. But if I know, then I will know that it is my grandfather's hand that I hold; and I need not be afraid.

osewa ni natta [o-sĕ'wă nē năt'tă]

I decided early on that it was hopeless; I would never be Japanese, so why try? There was too much to know, too much to be understood that could not be conveyed by the spoken English word. I would rather be forward-looking—American.

But much as I tried, I could never leave it behind. Someone would die. We always seemed most Japanese when someone died.

"We should go to the funeral," my mother would say. "Iwashitasan came to Pop's funeral." If someone had sent flowers, we would send flowers. If they had visited the house and brought food, we would do the same. *Koden*, funeral money, was carefully recorded and returned when the occasion arose. It seemed there was a giant ledger that existed in my mother's head that painstakingly noted every kindness ever rendered or received. How could I ever know or remember its contents? I couldn't keep track of my own life. A friend of mine was hurt once because I didn't remember staying at his sister's house in Minnesota. I felt awful about not remembering. It seems that there are whole periods of my life that have simply dropped from memory. Sensory overload. Am I busier than my mother was, or is there a Japanese gene that weakens in succeeding generations with increased Americanization?

Perhaps I was simply born too late. The youngest of four girls, I was the only one who didn't remember living in the old Victorian in Japantown where my mother grew up and my grandparents lived until they died. I was the only one who couldn't understand what my grandmother was saying, even when she was speaking English.

When someone talked about what a family acquaintance had done for us, I was the only one who didn't know who the person was.

This record-keeping and reciprocation did not revolve only around death. My mother would tell me one day on the phone, "The Noguchis are coming up from Los Angeles. They want to take Kiyo and me out to lunch."

I had never heard of the Noguchis, but it turned out that sixty years before, *Bachan* (my grandmother) had let them stay at Pine for a month after Noguchi-san lost his job. Noguchi-san had recently undergone surgery for cancer. "*Osewa ni narimashita,*" he had said. He had incurred debt. He wanted to repay it before it was too late.

The repayment of debt, then, apparently passes down from generation to generation. What will happen when my mother and my aunt Kiyo are no longer around? The ledger will be gone. How will I know to whom I am obligated, what debts to repay? One day in the future will I open the door to find a total stranger bringing me home-made sushi because of some kind act my grandmother did in 1946? Probably not. When I meet the grandsons and great-granddaughters of my grandparents' friends, who among us will know that our families were once connected? We will have lost the intricate web of obligation and reciprocation. The people who remember. This community.

Japanese-American [ja-pə-nēz' ə-mĕ'-rĭ-kən]

A Japanese-American is someone who has been trained in the Japanese ways of ultimate courtesy, but who has a quite independent and secret American sensibility locked into that pleasant and self-effacing exterior—like a *bonsai*. A tree trying to grow, but forced, through clipped roots and wired branches, into an expected shape. Like *bonsai*, a Japanese-American can be considered warped or deformed, or an object of uncanny beauty.

A Japanese-American is someone who, after a lifetime of being asked if she's Japanese or Chinese, or how long she's been in the States, or where she learned her English, will laugh when some white guy who has taken two semesters of Beginning Japanese tells her that she's mispronouncing her own family name.

Being Japanese-American means being imbued with certain values treasured by Japanese culture—values such as consideration, loyalty, humility, restraint. Values which, when exercised by white Americans, seem civilized; but they make Japanese-Americans seen unassertive, not willing to take risks, lacking confidence and leadership qualities.

Some sansei are like brash young redwoods, so new and naive. It's so clear why the nisei didn't talk. The nisei, whose psyches were wired like Japanese baby pines by the internment. They wanted the third generation to grow up American, like redwoods. They wanted them to shoot for the sky, tall and straight, to walk ahead like gods. To free themselves of the past like a rocket that discards its used stages as it shoots into space. Let go of the past; if you carry your spent burden with you, you will never reach the moon.

the story of when I was born
[thə sto'rē əv wĕn' ī wəz born']

When I was a little girl, and my mother put me to bed, she did not tell me stories about enchanted forests or beautiful princesses. I had seen "Sleeping Beauty." I knew "The Three Bears." These were not the stories I wanted to hear from my mother.

"Tell me the story of when I was born," I would say, mummified up to my chin by bedcovers. There were no magic wands or fairy god-mothers in this story. No poisoned apples or pumpkins that turned into coaches. It was a simple story, a sequence of mundane events, barely connected and sparingly described, peopled not by bad wolves or evil stepmothers, but sisters, my father, my mother of course, and friends of the family. The reason I wanted to hear that story, the reason I liked it so much, was because I was in it. It was real.

Life for me began just eleven short years after the Japanese dropped bombs on Pearl Harbor, precipitating events that would inflict on my family a kind of willed amnesia that would last for forty years.

As soon as he could after the war, my father moved us out of Japantown, into an orderly and integrated neighborhood where we had an Armenian grocery, a Russian delicatessen, an Italian piano teacher, and kind hakujin neighbors named the Freemans. The Richmond District of San Francisco, where I grew up, was always foggy. The fog would come in off the Pacific during the night, and when I woke up, I would hear the mournful dialogue of fog horns warning ships in the Golden Gate. Sometimes the fog would burn off by noon, and we would get a glimpse of the blue sky that California is supposed to be so famous for. But often the fog remained all day, or came back in the afternoon, so thick and low that it seemed like a white smoke. If we went anywhere else in the city, we must have looked like foreigners, just come in from Siberia, in our sweaters and coats and knee-high socks. We probably had an intensity, too, that outside people, people who lived in the sun, lacked. A seriousness. An introspection, come from too many days spent inside the house reading, or a range of options that did not include barbecues and lying on the beach.

In school we learned about the explorers, the Mayflower, the American Revolution. When we studied California history, we learned about Father Junipero Serra and the California missions. History, it seemed, focused on the conquerors, never the conquered.

The first time I went to Japan, I was twenty-two. My plane lifted off from San Francisco International, gaining altitude as it banked over the Golden Gate. Down below I could see the Richmond District, the geometrical avenues where I had spent my childhood. Then the plane entered the fog, and for a few seconds there was nothing but whiteness outside my window. For a few seconds, there was no east or west, no time. No memory. Suddenly, we were through. Above the floor of clouds, the sky was blue. The wing of the plane reflected pure sunlight. It was like all the time I was growing up, I thought. We were down there, under the fog, going to school and church and piano lessons—and all that time there was this blue sky, this glorious sun. And suddenly I hated that fog. I'm out of it, I thought, my heart leaping. I'm on this side now.

Going to Japan was like that for me—like breaking through the fog and seeing, for the first time, in full light, where I had come from. What my grandparents had left behind. What they had intended to return to, until circumstances intervened and they ended up staying in America. Until I went to Japan, I was a person without a past; I looked into a mirror and saw no reflection. All I knew was the little white house on 23rd Avenue, in the Richmond District.

It wasn't until I was much older that I realized that the house my mother returned to from the hospital, after she had me, wasn't that house. The school where my sisters had a Halloween parade that day wasn't the school that was just up the hill from that house. All those years, I had imagined the story, my story, in the wrong place.

Living in that fog-shrouded world perhaps made it easier for my mother and father to forget the past—America's lack of faith, the internment, the shame. To forget a heritage that cast suspicion on their loyalty. I didn't have to forget—I never knew.

In wartime, one must choose sides. But the price for doing so can be paid for generations.

Three Steps a Minute

Ruth Shigezawa

You sansei: coddled, soft. Listen to this. Think of rising at five, stumbling out the tent, the barracks, the boxcars. Those strawberry fields, stretch for miles, can't see no end. There you be, alone in section—picking, picking. Bend down, snap stems, put fruit in basket: gently, gently. No pay if you mash. Over and over. How long you think you could last, eh, kid? Eight hours? Hah, not hours, not even one. *You*—soft kid like you—I say two minutes. Then go nuts, that's what I say. You try it, come on, right now. Bend down, pick strawberries from floor, put in basket, search next plant. No pick green, no pay. No pick bug-eaten, bird-eaten ones. No pay. Pick-pick-pick. Come on, you! This foreman yelling at you—work faster. Eh! Not even thirty seconds. Eh, you squish one, no pay. You put inside basket too rough, mess up five berries underneath. No pay. This not salary job, you know. Piecework, pay by the basket. You never going earn your wages. How you going buy food? I timing you. How about that? Two minutes and you straighten up. Pretty smart, eh, for old man? No, I not laughing. (Two minutes, hee, hee). No, not laughing! Hey, packing your stuff? You going? Guess kid is mad, don't like old man show him up. Ok ok ok! Try wait. I polite now. I answer questions. Yes, be serious. Yes, serious job, your book. Oh, that's it—doc-to-ral dissertation. That mouthful sound like two-day meal of bad air. Ok,ok. Deadline when? Next year? Hooo, that a long time away. I know, I know. You told me, plenty times. Yeah, yeah, June 1970 you wanna graduate. Ok, ok! From now on—you ask, I answer. Sure, I wanna help. You gonna stay for dinner or something? I got tuna fish catfood to share—want some?

Your machine still on? Yeah? Ok. I serious now. Japanese name? Don't remember. You speak any Japanese? Too bad. I talk better in *Nihongo*. What for you study history then if you don't know language? Ok, ok, no need get pissed. Ben Inaba—that's all I gone by these last fifty-sixty years. Why so surprised? Don't remember my real name, nothing wrong with that. What's to be ashamed? Ben is good name. Short, sweet, something boss can say. See, there you go again. What the hell is wrong with having a name other people can say? It gets you jobs. Ok, next question.

What do I think about? What a question! Is that all you *sansei* college kids do, ask stupid questions? By time you *sansei*, third generation, come around, your mind soft. Ok, ok, I answer! I don't think about nothing. Now, don't go sour on me, I just joking around. You college kids don't know how to laugh either. Too busy protesting, growing long hair, wearing beads, waving flowers. Ah hah! You wonder how old man knows all about that. 1969, hoo, don't think I know that? You something else. You think I stick to this stinking room, all day, all night? I get around, I watch tv in stores on Broadway Aveenoo. Hear people talk. No, don't read English good. I hear people talk, ok? If you listen more, maybe you learn something.

Ok. What I think about? Think about walking. Yeah, how fast I walk. Used to be, I walk ten miles for nothing. I just do it. Used to be, I one strong sonuvabitch. Now, I use cane and walk slow, maybe three steps a minute, seems like. People huff behind me, brush past—I know what they thinking. See it in their backs. "Old man, get off sidewalk. Let us by, old man. We going places, there things to do. You finished. Done with, old man. We t'row you out."

Seem like forever to cross road out there. Car come around corner, maybe going knock me down, then in middle of the road, cars making left turn, scream at crosswalk and roar like animal. Stoplight always turn green for them when I halfway across street. I time myself by it. Three steps a minute. Old people take their lives casual when they cross streets.

You want facts, huh? Just facts. You sound like tv show. No, no tv now. Friend did once. In this place, even. We watch long time. "Let's Make a Deal," "Dragnet," "Dr. Kildare." Beats crossing streets.

Yeah, right. I know kids like you spit on tv—why I watch it then? What a question. To pass time. I deserve it. I passed time picking strawberries, picking peaches, picking grapes. In my old age, I deserve to sit and laugh a little.

Sour, today, aren't you? You always this sour? Professor don't like you? What he do? Give you B—? What so bad, it better than F, isn't it? Oh, graduate school different, ok. Professor treat you bad? Yeah, plenty things like that happen to me, all the time. What else happen? Oh . . . staring at you in street—high school kids make fun? What? "Ching, Chong, Chinaman, sitting on a fence." Heee, heee! That pretty funny! They can't tell apart Chinese and Japanese. What else? Yeah, that an old one, can you see anything outta those slanty eyes? All that happen to me, too. And more. Kids not the only ones who did it, that the problem. Me? Listen to this.

Japanese kicked in the balls in bars. Japanese run out of town. Ever hear of Turlock up north? Japanese cheated out of their pay. Herded to desert during war. Oh, you know about that? You study it? Ching, chong, Chinaman, nothing. You go to college, you study "ethnic studies," you have chances to make good. Why you complain? They don't give you respect? You gotta give it to yourself. Can't sit back and wait for them to give to you. They give you nothing and you going wait forever.

Spoiled, you *sansei* are. You have nerve asking why we *issei* didn't fight back at the camps? Some did. They got Tule Lake and then shipped back to Japan after the war. What that solve? Think they had an easy time of it, going back home, place they hadn't seen for years, wartime mess? If you lived back then, raised with same tough life, you only roll over and die.

Say something. You make me nervous. You want me to keep on with this, don't sit there like sack of rice. You and that puckered face. Tighter than a virgin's hole—that's you. Listen, have an idea. Ok, ok, listen minute. You teach me how run this machine and leave it. I tell stories my own way. Can't think when you tell me alla time speak in this pipe and ask stupid questions. Ok, ok. Teach me run this machine and I do it. Take it or leave it.

Hello, hello? Good, machine running smooth. Anything to get that kid off my back. Damn, he gonna hear that. Ok, so, no matter. Fill up tape, yeah, fill up tape. Talk about what? Too many things to do today. No time for foolishness. Bye, kid.

Hello, hello? Kid's on my back to fill up this tape. Ok, kid, I do it.

In *Nihongo*—Japanese. If you cannot understand me, you can find a translator. But you did want me to fill this tape fast and I can't do it fast enough in English. I'm very sorry. But I'm sure you'll find someone to tell you what I'm saying.

Today was the memorial service for my best friend, Takada-san. He had no family here, so we old men chipped in for an urn. One of the others will dump the ashes and all into the ocean, off the pier. My friends are all dead now, what do you think of that, kid? Anyway, all are dead. I remember this friend of mine, when he was young, he'd

say, "Inaba-san, someday we shall go back to Japan so rich, we'll
have all we want to eat, we'll eat 'til we're sick and then we'll have
girls, too." We did have a good time when we could eat all we wanted.
We were making twelve to fifteen dollars a day. That was good money
at that time. We thought the money would last forever. We were
young, strong, willing to work. We didn't think about tomorrow. The
Big Time—that's all we wanted—make lots of money, spend lots of
money.

They're all gone now. Only friend I have now is The Tube, that cat,
toilet-water gray, comes in here every once in awhile, shares what I
eat, pet food and tuna fish, share and share alike. You've seen him,
I'm sure. No one else. My faucet drips, my lights dim brown in sum-
mertime. The hot plate shorts out. The management would take my
hot plate away if they knew I had it: fire hazard. It's better not to eat
in summer anyway, when it's hot like this.

I remember, my friend and I, not eating for days when we were
young. Not because of the heat, but because we had no money. For
days, we wouldn't eat. We'd cinch our belts and bend our backs and
we'd pick that lettuce, the strawberries, the tomatoes. We'd even eat
a few bug-eaten berries when no one was looking. We worked winters for railroads—Montana, Wyoming, Colorado. Summers in California, picking crops. I'll wager you didn't know I went to college, too.
Sure, kid, four years, I studied in the winter, picked crops in the summer. I studied to be a CPA. Graduated, too. Then no accounting firm
would hire me, so it was back to following the crops.

I looked around today, all around this hotel, and, for the first time,
I've begun to see it the way you do, kid. Sweaty lobby downstairs and
old Rick asleep at the front desk. Torn flowers in the carpet on the
stairs, threads hanging out at the center of each step. The hall smells
like burnt toast—hotplates working until they short out—and the
whole place smells like sour bodies and piss. Real dim out there, that
hall. Naked light bulbs jut out from the ceiling like an old whore's
tits, burnt out, useless. Garbage sits in corners and flies buzz around
oily dog food cans. Ripped up shopping bags filled with green wine
bottles, tuna fish cans, bread wrappers. Yeah, it looks like Ben Inaba
has seen better days.

Sometimes, here in my room, I can reach out, I can touch the opposite walls from where I sit. Once I slept on a bunk no wider than
a shelf. In snow country. With a single blanket. In a bunkhouse
where the snow flurries blew in. Thinking about that, this place is
luxury. I don't feel so bad now, remembering those days.

Oii, kid? Want to hear something funny? Probably not. But I'll tell
you anyway. I'm a year younger in America than in Japan. When a

baby's born in Japan, we celebrate the new baby's birthday once on the day of birth and once on the next New Year's day. I was born in the twelfth month, December. When January came around, I became one year old. Now in America, I shed that year, because Americans like to keep young. I used to tell employers in the city, as I got older, that I was a year younger in America than Japan and I would joke about it, "America keeps me young." They'd laugh and say "Ben Inaba, you're a card," and give me gardening work. I was shedding years like winter clothing to get work. Younger and younger until one day it didn't work anymore—I was sixty-five and looked it. The years stuck to me after that like flaking dry skin I couldn't brush off me. I just couldn't peel anymore layers.

Now is the time in my life that I should go back to Japan. They honor the old people there. But too late. My home's here. I feel funny talking to spinning wheels, to a humming machine. No one answers me.

Kid, I'll tell you another story. I was riding a bus once: all the way to the beach and back. Hooo, that Santa Monica is nice: green, cool, blue. I wanted to get out of this place. It took a long time to ride out there and back, but I liked the bus ride. The air became cooler the closer we came to the beach. At the end of the line, at the beach highway, I got off to breathe a little and it was ten degrees cooler than downtown. If I had a room in one of those old apartments near the pier—things would be better if I had a room at the beach. Well, maybe, maybe not.

Anyway, before I got off the bus, I was sitting in front of this woman who talked about her entire life at the top of her voice. Nothing was secret with this woman. NOISY. It seemed everyone was getting off a stop earlier if only to get away from her noise. She was loud but no one heard her. I stayed on the bus. I know how it is to talk and no one hears you. She was still sitting there when I got off finally. I sneaked a look at her through the bus window. But she caught me looking and started to get off the bus, too. I can't walk fast, but I hustled. She plumped down again in a different seat by another window and I saw her face from the sidewalk before the bus drove away. Through the window, her mouth still moving, she was staring at me. No one was hearing her, not even me.

More questions. On list this time. Notice I speaking English now? Pretty good, eh, two languages? More languages than you. And you have nerve telling me what I been saying not useful. Maybe you got da kine wax in your ears—cannot hear me good. So! Can't find interpreter in that college of yours? Shoot, must be around somewhere. And you have nerve: "What about dinner?" you say. "Of course, I'll

pay," you say. Why not? I asking myself. Know damn well why not.
Ben Inaba, you paying price for all this. Spill guts, old man. Kid pay-
ing this meal. Dance to kid's tune. But, what the hell, I go with you.
Tired of tunafish. Good steak hits the spot.

You college kids, wear crummy clothes, you. T-shirt with holes size
of quarters, sleeves ripped up. Blue jeans, no, white jeans, only junk
sandals, no socks. But you wear good-looking wristwatch and all
those beads. How can people take you serious? I pick out college kids
on Hill Street downtown every time.

"Read the questions on the tape and answer." What this gonna win
me, third curtain on TV show? Apartment at beach?

"1. In your opinion, what was the impact upon your life of the Immigration Act of 1924, namely, the Exclusion of 'Aliens Ineligible for
Citizenship,' or specifically Japanese immigrants to the U.S.? How
did this law affect your ability to find a wife? What other instances
of prejudice can you name?"

Holy Jeezus. Can't even figure the question let alone answer.
What this, eh, kid?

"2. In which internment camp were you situated during World
War II? How long were you forced to remain there? What feelings of
bitterness did you harbor upon release? Do you believe there should
be restitution and if so what kind?

"3. Please answer the questions in the space below to the best of
your knowledge. I reiterate that your answers will be kept strictly
confidential."

Hear me, kid? I reading these questions over your machine so you
know I read them. Hear this? List of questions squashed up, thrown
out. That my answer. What jobs you have? Where you live? Answer,
old man, answer! Talk about your sex life, old man. Count the times
you been to whore houses. How many kids you got, you who not married? Ever bang a white girl? A black girl? Hell, I'm not a man to you,
I'm a damn sta-tis-tic. Who needs it?

Last time I talking with you, kid. Sorry, no dinner. No worry, old
Rick downstairs watching your machine after I leave. Evicted, kid.
They tearing down this building. Condemned. Simple as that. No
fussing about it. No asking me to stay in your apartment. No feeding me. I take care myself. I been in pretty tight spots. It wasn't all
women and good food, you know. But I got through. I going look for
room in Santa Monica, small one, maybe share. No worry, I always
get through.

Got something for you. Call it going-away present. I answer one
question on your list. How I came this country. I tell you that.

Some friends—remember Takada-san, who had funeral? He was

one and there were two others. We landed in Mexico from Japan, this after 1924, Maybe that Exclusion Act you talking about. We couldn't land in America. We headed for border and plan to cross desert then sneak over to California. We hike by night, sleep by day, sleep in shade by tumbleweed. Hoo, hot enough to fry your brains and then some. Mountains we had to climb, the land rolling, rolling forever, heat melting the air. We wanted to see better living than at home, and that made us take one more step and one more.

Stupid. We so stupid. Didn't bring enough water or food. We got weak 'til one of us collapsed. Leave him or carry him? Draw straws to see who do the job if we leave him. Someone got to kill him so no suffering. Other friend say, "He can suck a piece of cactus." He lived. We crawl over border, dead night, tired out, dried out. After that, we so grateful to be in America, we say we make good, we make lots of money, work hard, go home rich.

What happened? Yeah, we make lots of money. We got rich, all right. But we spent all, then later no jobs. After that, we struggle just to get by. You know, I never done anything I didn't want to do. Everything came to me like I ask for. What can I tell you, kid? You feel sorry for old Ben, living here, eating cat food, riding buses to the sea. Don't. You don't know what kind of life I was headed for at home, in my village, nose in the dung, rice prices way down. A farmer's life no better.

The days we work hard, nights we whore it up. Maybe the other one still at it. Maybe. Or maybe he dead, too.

What the— Oh, just the cat, he jump up on your machine. No worry, not breaking anything.

Gotta go, kid. Listen, don't believe everything you hear. I can take care myself. I walk slow, sure, but I still walking.

Listen, take care my cat, will you? I hear landlords no like pets in Santa Monica.

How I Got to Be Jewish

Erica Jong

News of America travelled quickly around the Euro-
pean shtetls. Word was that even if the streets of the
"Golden Land" weren't paved with gold, at least a
Jew had a chance.—Jeff Kisseloff, You Must Remember This (1989)

The older we get, the more Jewish we become in my family. My
mother's father declared himself an atheist in his communist youth,
so we never belonged to a synagogue or had *bat mitzvahs*. But we
wind up in Hebrew homes for the aged and in cemeteries with Hebrew letters over the gates. Thus does our heritage claim us—even
in America, our promised land. In my family, if you're still protesting
you're Unitarian, you're just not *old* enough. (I refer, of course, to one
of my ex-husbands, who having married a *shiksa*, worships at the local Unitarian Church. That will change, I predict.)

My father, on the other hand, sends money to Israel and carries
around a card that supposedly will expedite his admission to Mt.
Sinai Hospital, and after that Heaven, identifying him as a Big
Donor. This is the sort of thing he would have done riffs on in his
vaudeville days. Now my daughter *Molly* does those riffs. The young
are cruel. They *have* to be to supplant the old. The old are such a burden, so territorial, so inclined to hold on to their money. The young
have to be tough to make it at all.

After all, what does the ritual of circumcision say to a Jewish son?
"Watch out. Next time I'll cut off the whole thing." So Jewish boys are
horny, but also full of fear about whether their cocks will survive
their horniness. Alexander Portnoy is the archetypal good Jewish

boy. The good Jewish boy and the bad Jewish boy inhabit the same skin—if not the same foreskin. Jewish girls are luckier. Their sexuality is less damaged—whatever those jokes about dropping emery boards may imply. Girls are allowed to be sexual as long as they keep it inside the family. Marriage is sacred as long as you marry an oedipal stand-in. Jewish adultery is an oxymoron. We read Updike for that. Jewish men who cheat end up like Saul Wachler or Woody Allen. In big trouble. Even Jewish lesbians are required to have silverware and bone china from Tiffany's. Jewish lesbians are required to fall in love with women who remind them of their mothers. And, in today's feminist times, are doctors or lawyers.

How did I get to be Jewish?—I with no religious training? Jews are made by the existence of anti-Semitism—or so says Jean-Paul Sartre, who knew. And despite myths to the contrary, there is *plenty* of anti-Semitism in America (otherwise we'd be saying, "Next year in Oyster Bay or Grosse Pointc" instead of "Next year in Jerusalem"). But American anti-Semitism takes the clever form of class snobbery. Let me show you what I mean.

We say that America is a classless society, but really it is not. It's just that our class distinctions are so much subtler than those of other countries that sometimes we don't even see them as class distinctions. They are uniquely American class distinctions and they follow us all our lives. We go happily into the Hebrew Home for the Aged, having learned that where aging and death are concerned, only our own kind *want* us. When we're young and cute, we can hang out with *goyim*—but as the sun goes down, we revert to *knishes* and *knaydlach*. We do *mitzvahs*—of the sort that I have done by getting my aunt into the Hebrew Home.

When I was growing up in a New York that seemed dominated by Jews whose parents or grandparents had fled from Europe, I never consciously thought about Jewishness. Or about class. And yet invisible barriers ruled my life—barriers which still stand.

Even in childhood I knew that my best friend Glenda Glascock, who was Episcopalian and went to private school, was considered classier than me. We lived in the same gloomy Gothic apartment house near Central Park West. We both had parents who were artists. But Glenda's name ended with *cock* and mine did not. I knew that names ending in *cock* were intrinsically classier.

What was my name anyway?

My father was born Weisman and became Mann. My mother was called Yehuda by her Russian Jewish parents when she was born in England, but the intransigent Englishman in the registry office had changed it first to Judith and then to Edith ("good English names")—leaving the resultant impression that Jews were not even allowed to keep their own names. The dominant culture around our (mental) ghetto required names that did not *sound* Jewish or foreign. That left a strong impression too.

There were categories of Americans in our supposedly egalitarian country and I did not belong to the better (as in "better dresses") category. Glenda did. Her last name bespoke this. Even her nickname— Jewish girls did not have nicknames like Glennie then—bespoke this. And yet we were close as twins, best buddies, in and out of each other's apartments—until we took a bath together one day and she accused me of making peepee in the bathwater because that was "what Jews did." I was outraged, having done no such thing. (Unless my memory censors.)

"Who says they do that?"

"My mother," said Glennie confidently.

So I reported this conversation to my parents and grandparents and mysteriously my friendship with Glennie cooled.

She went off to private school. I did not. I was in some "Intelligently Gifted Program" at P.S. 87 on 77th Street and Amsterdam Avenue—a great Victorian pile in those days, with girls' and boys' entrances. There I discovered other class stratifications. The closer you lived to Central Park West and the "better" your building, the more classy you were. Now I had status. Below me were poorer Jewish kids whose parents had fled the Holocaust and lived in lesser buildings further west, Irish kids who lived in tenement side streets, and the first sprinkling of Puerto Rico kids to arrive in New York. They lived in other tenements on West Side Storyish side streets. In the forties, New York was far from being racially integrated. I did not meet black kids from Harlem until I went to the High School of Music and Art where talent, not neighborhood, was the qualification. The only African-Americans we met—called Negroes then—were servants. In childhood, my word was Jewish, Irish, Hispanic—with Jews lording it over everyone else.

The WASP kids were, by this time, off in private school meeting their own kind so they could run the CIA, go to Yale, and rule the world (like George and Barbara Bush). Jewish kids did not go to private school in *that* New York—unless they were superrich, had disciplinary problems, or were orthodox.

I figured out pretty soon that in my school I was high class, but that in the world I was not. The kids on television shows and in reading primers did not have names like Weisman, Rabinowitz, Plotkin, Ratner, or Kisseloff. Certainly not Gonzales or O'Shea. There was another America out there in televisionland and we were not part of it. In that other America, girls were named things like Gidget and boys were named things like Beaver Cleaver. Our world was not represented—excepted when the credits rolled by.

Kept out of this *proper* America, we learned to control it by reinventing it (or representing—as in agent). Some of our parents already did this as actors, producers, or writers, so we knew this was
a possible path for us. Others were businessmen, or artists-turned-
businessmen—like my father. The point was: We were outsiders
longing to be insiders. In those days, we knew that Princeton and
Yale might not want us unless we were rich enough. We knew our
initials were ICM, not CIA. We knew we were not born into the ruling class, so we invented our own ruling class. Mike Ovitz, not
George Bush. Swifty Lazar, not Bill Clinton.

How much the world has changed since the forties! And how *little*! Except for Henry Kissinger, who has changed these laws of class
and caste? Not even Mike Ovitz. What you see your parents do is
what you think *you* can do. So are we defined, designed. Since my father was a songwriter-musician turned importer, my grandfather a
portrait-painter, my mother a housewife and portrait-painter, I just
assumed that I would do something creative. I also just *assumed* that
I would graduate from college, and live in a "good building" forever.
I also assumed that I would never turn out to be anything like those
American families I saw on TV.

My family was fiercely proud to be Jewish, but not religious—unless our religion was buying new English Maryjanes at Saks and
English leather-leggings, and velvet-collared Chesterfield coats at de
Pinna. We were dressed like little English princesses and I understood that this was the class to which we aspired.

Dress tells you everything about aspiration. I hated the damned
leather leggings but had to wear them because Princess Elizabeth
and Margaret did. How did *they* get to be Princesses of the Jews? Better not ask. It was tacitly understood just as it was understood that
Glascock was a better name than Weisman (or even Mann).

I smile writing all this. I am trying (clumsily, I fear) to re-enter
that world of 1940s New York with its "air-cooled" movie palaces
(complete with towering matrons and wrapper-strewn children's sections, its striped awnings on apartment buildings in summer, its bus
transfers, its candy stores, its big marble lunch counters that sold
the most delicious bacon lettuce and tomato sandwiches and fresh-
dipped ice cream cones).

Gone, gone forever. But just as sunlight on a series of paving
stones or the taste of tea-soaked cake returned Proust* to his hal-
cyon childhood, I sometimes stop on a streetcorner in New York and

---

*Note to reviewer. Of course I am not comparing myself to Proust. I know
my place. If I don't, I'm sure you'll remind me.

am taken back to the forties. The smells do it. The mouths of the subway stations still, on occasion, blow a blast of cotton candy/bubble
gum breath, mixed with sweat and popcorn, with piss and (its pre-
cursor) beer—and inhaling deeply I am taken back to being six years
old, standing in the subway, staring at a forest of knees. In childhood,
you feel you'll never grow up. And the world will always be incom-
prehensible. First you are all mouth, then you have a name, then you
are a member of a family, then you begin to ask the hard questions
about better/worse which are the beginnings of class-consciousness.
Human beings are naturally hierarchical beasts. Democracy is not
their native religion.

It was in Junior High that my world opened up beyond 77th Street
and the West Side. Because my parents and I were both terrified of
the violence of the local junior high, I went to private school—a deli-
ciously comic place where the paying students were mostly Park Avenue Jews and the scholarship students mostly WASPs from Washington Heights whose parents were professors, clergy, missionaries.

The teachers were genteel and Waspy like the scholarship students, and they had proper American-sounding names like the TV
people. The school had been started by two redoubtable New England ladies named Miss Birch and Miss Wathen who were probably
lovers—but in those days we called them spinsters. One of them
looked like Gertrude Stein, the other like Alice B. Toklas. They pro-
nounced "shirt" as if it had three i's in the middle, and they pro-
nounced poetry as if it were poy-et-try. I knew this was classy. I knew
this was WASP.

At Birch-Wathen, most of the Jewish kids were wealthier than me.
They lived on the East Side in apartments hung with expensive art
and some of them had German names. They went to Temple Emmanuel—my nephews now call it Temple Episcopal—and took dancing and deportment—what an old-fashioned word!—at Viola Wolf's.
Again my sense of class was up for grabs. With my Russian grandparents and my West Side bohemian home, I didn't fit in with these
kids either. And the scholarship kids all stuck together. I thought
them snotty—though now I realize they must have been scared to
death. The paying students got bigger allowances—and some of
them came to school in chauffeured Cadillacs, Lincolns, or Rollses.
That must have seemed daunting to kids who rode the subway. It
seemed daunting to me. Cliques splintered us. The Park Avenue kids
stuck with their own kind. The scholarship kids did the same.

I floated between the two groups, never knowing where I belonged,
now shoplifting at Saks with the rich kids (the richer the kids, I
learned, the more they shoplifted), now wandering up to Columbia
with one of the scholarship kids (whose parents were professors).

I felt I belonged nowhere. Ashamed that my father was a businessman, I used to wish he were a professor. If you couldn't have a name that ended with cock, you ought to have a Ph.D. at least.

When High School began, I joined still another new world—a world that was racially mixed and full of kids from the ghetto. Chosen for their talent to draw or sing or play an instrument, these kids were the most diverse I'd ever met. Their class was talent. And like all insecure people, they shoved it in your face.

It was in high school that I began to find my true class. Here the competition was not about money or color or neighborhood but about how well you drew or played. At Music & Art, new hierarchies were created, hierarchies of virtuosity. Was your painting in the semi-annual exhibition? Were you tapped to perform in the orchestra, or on WQXR? By now we all knew we did not belong in televisionland America—and we were *proud* of it. Being outsiders was a badge of merit. We had no teams, no cheerleaders, and the cool class uniform was early beatnik: black stockings, handmade sandals, and black lipstick for the girls; black turtlenecks, black jeans, black leather jackets for the boys. Stringy hair was requisite for both sexes. We experimented with dope. We cruised the Village hoping to be mistaken for hipsters. We had found our class at last.

Many of us rose to the top of it. I count among my high school classmates pop singers, television producers, actors, painters, novelists. Many are household names. A few earn tens of millions of dollars a year. Most went to college—but it was not finally a B.A. or a Ph.D. that defined our status. It was whether or not we stayed hot, were racing up the charts with a bullet, were going into syndication, on the bestseller list, into twenty-five languages. Even the professors envied *this* status: money and name-recognition level all classes in America. Hence the obsession with celebrity. Even in Europe you can pass into the "best" circles, though the rules of class are quite different there.

Having done my time with the Eurotrash set, I'm always amazed at how an aristocratic name still covers a multitude of sins in Europe. In England, in Germany, a lord or ladyship, a gräf or gräfin, a von or zü, still carries weight. Italians are more cynical about titles. The classiest friends I have in Italy may be *contesse, marchesi,* or *principi,* but they're too cool to advertise it. They'd rather be famous for a hit record, or a big book. But, go to the chic watering spots—St. Moritz, for example—and membership in the best clubs still goes by family, not by individual achievement. Walk into the Corviglia Club and say you're Ice T. or Madonna. Honey—you won't get in, while any old Niarchos or von Ribbentrop will.

Many of my European friends still inhabit a world where name and old money can become a positive *bar* to achievement. There is so much *more* to do than merely work. If you have to be in Florence in June, in Paris in July, in Tuscany in August, in Venice in September, in Cologne in October, in New York in November, and St. Bart's in January, in St. Moritz in February, in New York in March, in Greece in April, in Prague in May—how on earth can you take (*let alone* hold) a job? And the fittings. And the balls. And the spas. And the dryings out! As a husband of Barbara Hutton's once asked: "When would I have *time* to work?" True class means never even having to *talk* about it. (Work, I mean).

Americans are intrinsically unclassy—so the Jews almost fit in. All we talk about is our work. All we want to do is make our first names so recognized we don't even *need* a last (Ms. Ciccone is the ultimate American here). We believe in change as fervently as Europeans believe in the status quo. We believe that money will buy us into heaven (with heaven defined as toned muscles, no flab at the chin, interest on interest, and a name that cows maitre d's). Once that's accomplished, we can start to save the world: plow some money into AIDS research, the Rain Forest, political candidates. Maybe we can even run for office ourselves! (Witness Mr. Perot.) In a society where pop name recognition means everything, celebrities are more equal than everyone else. But celebrity status is hell to keep in shape (just like an aging body). It needs a host of trainers, P.R. experts, publishers, media consultants. Plus you have to keep turning out new product—and new scandal. (Witness Woody Allen.) Maybe the reason celebrities marry so often is simply to keep their name in the news. And maybe—whether they know it or not—they create scandal to hype their movies. (Again, witness Woody Allen, né Alan Konigsberger.)

Ah—we are back to the question of Jews and names. Can we keep our names? As long as we keep them *hot*. Otherwise, we also have to change them. We may have, as political theorist Benjamin Barber says, "an aristocracy of everyone," but not everyone can be hot at once. Thus, the drive for class becomes as relentless and chronic in America as the diet. No matter how hot you are, you're always in danger of growing old.

It's a lot like mortality, isn't it? No wonder *carpe diem* is our motto. This is what makes America such a restless country and her top-class celebrities so insecure.

Ah friends, I long to be born into a membership in the Corviglia Club. But I suspect I never would have written any books.

Did you ever wonder why Jews are such relentless scribes? You may have thought it was because we are people of the book. You may have thought it was because we come from homes where reading is stressed. You may have thought it repressed sexuality. Yes, yes—all that is true. But I submit the *real* reason is our need to constantly define our class. By writing, we reinvent ourselves. By writing we create pedigrees. Some of my heroines are West Side, New York Jewish girls like me. But the heroines I love the best—*Fanny* in *Fanny Hackabout-Jones*, and Jessica in *Serenissima*—are to the manor born, good little equestriennes, and you can bet they have high cheekbones. Fanny grew up at Lymeworth, Lord Bellars' country seat. Jessica grew up on the Upper East Side of Manhattan, in the Golden Rectangle. Her pedigree was very gin and country club. Why does a West Side kid like me invent such heroines? Am I trying to escape from my *schmearer-klesmer* class? Interestingly enough, my heroines always escape too. Fanny runs away from her aristocratic upbringing, becomes a highway woman, a whore in a brothel, and a pirate-queen. Jessica leaves the Upper East Side for Hollywood! And both of them come to regret it, and find their final happinesses back in their own backyards. The heroines who are *apparently* more like me—Isadora Wing and Leila Sand—change their status, or else establish it, through creative work. I guess my writing tells me something that I didn't even consciously know about myself: I write to give myself a class, to invent my name, and then to leave myself a country seat!

I suspect the process is not so different with other writers—however uninvolved with class their books may seem. Saul Bellow's heroes start out as drifters and end up professors. But his very best picaresque hero, Henderson the Rain King, is a WASP to the manor born who goes to Africa and embraces his multiculturalism, thereby finding his true identity. Philip Roth's heroes are equally concerned both with questions of class and with questions of Jewishness. Though they themselves are almost always Jewish, they aspire to fuck their way into WASPdom—a familiar gambit for American Jewish (male) creators. We could call it the Annie Hall Syndrome. Surely Woody Allen defined it forever when his autobiographical hero, sitting at Annie Hall's midwestern dinner table, amid the WASPs, suddenly sprouts *payess* and a big black hat.

The archetypical Jewish American fear! If we eat *trayfe*, we may suddenly grow payess! Perhaps the reason Jews in America have adopted Thanksgiving as their own special holiday is that we hope by claiming the Pilgrims as our fathers, we will fool the rest of America too!

Howard Fast is a perfect example here. His best books, the fictional *April Morning* and nonfictional *The Jews*, are oddly connected. They both chronicle rootless people. They testify to the fact that Americans, like Jews, must constantly define themselves.

A Jew may wander from Egypt to Germany to America to Israel, picking up different languages and hair and eye color, but he remains a Jew. And what is a Jew? A Jew is a person who is safe *nowhere* (i.e., always in danger of growing *payess* at inopportune times!) A Jew is a person who can convert to Christianity from now to Doomsday, and still be killed by Hitler if his mother was Jewish. This explains why Jews are likely to be obsessed with matters of identity. Our survival depends upon it.

Americans, too, are obsessed with defining identity. In a melting pot culture, where aristocratic titles are considered laughable (witness Count Dracula or Count Chocula, as kids are introduced to him—a breakfast cereal), we must constantly test the limits of identity. Andy Warhol's remark that in the future everyone will be famous for fifteen minutes, delineates the quintessential American dilemma. We can become famous, but perhaps not *stay* famous. And once having known that fame, how will we live out the rest of our lives? More to the point, how will we ever get into the Hebrew Home for the Aged?

Many American lives seem doomed by Warhol's definition. Remember George Bush struggling to stay president against the historical tide? Or Stephen King aspiring to top all three bestseller lists at once? Or Bill Clinton wiring the White House to become its own media network? American can never rest. They can never join the Corviglia Club and amuse themselves skiing down into the picture-book village. The grace of their skiing is *never* enough in itself enough. They must always climb back on the chairlift and do it again, do it again, do it again.

I see that the Corviglia Club has become my symbol of aristocratic *sprezzatura*—a lovely Italian word which means the art of making the difficult look easy. Perhaps I select that image because it evokes a world of blessed people who do not have to *do* anything, they only have to *be*. I long for such status as only an American Jew can. How nice to have an entrée into the world that cannot ever be revoked. How nice to be *born* into an identity.

My yearning is real even though I know dozens of people born into such identities who use them as excuses to become drug addicts and drifters. I know it is not easy to be noble and rich. Yet, like F. Scott Fitzgerald, something in me insists: "The very rich are different from you and me." Fitzgerald tested that hypothesis in Gatsby, showing the carelessness of the very rich to life, limb, and love. And yet the longing *remains* in American writers. Perhaps that's why that this rather slight, beautifully written American novel has become a bona fide classic. It embodies the American dream of identity and class.

The jumped-up bootlegger, Jay Gatz, dreams of a world where he wouldn't have to *work* to be Gatsby. And that is still the primal American dream. Even lotteries play to it, promising houses and yachts. Rootless by definition, we dream of roots.

American novelists are usually good examples of this. The first thing they do after a bestseller is to buy a house and land. Alex Haley bought a farm in the south. He didn't become a slave-owner, of course, but he became a landowner. Gore Vidal settled in a villa in Ravello fit for an Italian aristocrat. Arthur Miller bought a Connecticut farm for a Connecticut Yankee. So did Philip Roth.

I'm no different. After *Fear of Flying*, I bought a house in New England. Believing that when writers died and went to heaven, heaven was Connecticut, I bought a piece of that literary state. To a writer, used to making up the world with ink and a blank piece of paper, roots and gentrification are the same thing. And you get them both with *words*.

Rootless people always gravitate to those fields of endeavor where class has to be repeatedly self-created. Perhaps that's also why creativity flowers during periods of great social turmoil and often among former underclasses. Perhaps that's what draws Jews to the word and the image. If you think of the vitality of Jewish-American writing in the fifties and sixties, the vitality of women's writing in the seventies and eighties, the vitality of African-American writing in the eighties and nineties, you see that there is a clear connection between change of status and productivity. As a group becomes restless and angry, it produces writers.

I may dream of what I would have done with my life if I had been born on a plantation with plenty of coupons to clip, but probably my literary ambitions would have never blossomed. Perhaps I would have written inscrutable poetry, readable only by advanced graduate students. But most likely the anxiety and aggression needed to finish a whole book would have been denied me. For writing is not just a question of talent with words, but of drive and ambition, of restlessness and rage. Writing is hard. The applause never comes at the end of the paragraph. The rotten tomatoes often come at publication time. And given the hours put in, the money isn't all that good. Counting taxation and time spent, most writers make less than dental hygienists.

But we don't do it for the money. We do it to give ourselves a class.

When I finished college at Barnard, I went on to graduate school, simply because I couldn't think of what *else* to do. I knew I wanted to be a writer, but I wasn't yet sure I had the *zitsfleish* to sit down and write a whole book. While I waited to mature a little, I studied English literature. Somehow I knew it would come in handy.

But the period I studied—the rollicking eighteenth century

engraved by Hogarth—was the one that saw the birth of America, of women's rights, and of the novel. The novel started as a low-class form, fit only for serving maids, and it has been the only literary form where women distinguished themselves so early with such excellence that even the rampant misogyny of literary history cannot erase them. Ever wonder about women and the novel? Women, like any underclass, depend for their survival on self-definition. The novel permitted this—and pages could still be hidden under the embroidery hoop.

From the writer's mind to the reader's there was only the intervention of printing presses. You could stay at home, yet send your book abroad to London—the perfect situation for women. In a world where women are still the second sex, many still dream of becoming writers so they can work at home, make their own hours, nurse the baby. Writing still fits into the interstices of a woman's life. Through the medium of words, we have hopes of changing our class. Perhaps the pen will not always be equated with the penis. In a world of computers, our swift fingers may yet win us the world. One of these days we'll have class. And so we write as feverishly as only the dispossessed can. We write to come into our own, to build our houses and plant our gardens, to give ourselves names and histories, inventing ourselves as we go along.

Dear Aunt Nanadine

Alexis De Veaux

Dear Aunt Nanadine,

As much as I love to write, I've never written you a letter. And
"What do we need with letters?" you say. "We live in the same city, a
bridge and a subway apart." Well, yesterday I took from the back of
my closet that red three-piece walking suit you gave me. "Too fat to
wear it now," you said, pushing it in a Macy's bag. "Take it."

So this letter is to say I used to admire you in that red suit; how
it colored your light handsome beauty. And made you look so rich, so
pockets full of freedom and loose change. Red, you instructed me,
was a color *I* should *never ever* wear. I was absolutely "too dark."
"Whose little black child are you?" you'd tease. "Who knows who you
belong to?" Did you know then that your teasing mirrored my own
apprehension? *Who did I belong to?* Who does a dark-skinned child
belong to in a family where lighter skin is predominant, in a society
where dark can't mean anything positive? It's not supposed to. Who
do you belong to and who do you trust?

Should I have not trusted you then when I was eight years old?
Not listened when you advised me at ten that not only reds but certain bright pinks, yellows, blues and oranges were also off limits to
me? And to other girls my color, like Cheryl Lynn Bruce, who grew
up on the South Side of Chicago (grew up to become an actress).
Cheryl was ten, and dark, and recalls: "I remember going to my
grandmother's house one day (she taught piano). I put on a red out-
fit—red coat, red dress, red shoes, red everything. I was fascinated
with the color red. And off I went to my grandmother's house. Well,
my grandmother gasped when she saw me, and called my mother,

63

and sent me back home. My mother opened the door, grabbed me inside and said, "Take off all that red. You are too dark to wear all that red." I hadn't understood there was a construct that decided what colors a dark girl could wear. I was ten at the time. Red is such a vibrant color. It calls attention, and it was calling attention to my skin. After the red incident, I felt there was a search to find a color I could wear that would not draw attention to my color. Mother dressed me in navy blue a lot because it was a neutral color. I became very conscious of how colors affected my skin.

Quite frankly, Aunt Nanadine, I was a little surprised when you gave me the suit. On the train, I wondered if you still thought I was "too dark." Was I lighter to you now? More acceptable? Had your feelings changed after some twenty years? At home, I stuck the suit in the closet of my writing room. I never wore it. It waited among my piles of complete and incomplete ideas, filed away, an unfinished draft of an old story. One day I would get back to it. But I could not sincerely thank you. And the next month, rummaging through some old notebooks, I came across this fragment of story: *I am a little girl. I am in the third grade. I come home from school. I run all the way today. My favorite dress—the navy one with tiny white polka dots— is torn at the sleeve and neck, with buttons missing and Lord, it's so dirty. There are dried tears on my face. My hair stands all over my head. I am pissed-as-shit. I know my mother is going to kill me. I bust through the apartment door.*

"Girl, what happened to you?" she say.

"Had a fight."

"Fight 'bout what?"

"Livia and them keep calling me Blackie—"

"I send you outta here to go to school and learn something. Not to fight, miss."

"She started it. Callin' me Blackie and Lil Black Sambo."

"Well the next damn time she do, you tell her YOUR MOTHER says sticks 'n' stones might break your bones, but words will never harm you. Hear me?"

BULLSHIT, BLACKIE AIN'T MY NAME, I want to say. It hurts. It's painful. It's embarrassing, Momma. Livia is dark as me. Why everything Black got to be evil, everything dark got to be ugly? I say nothing. I learn the bravado of strike back. Incorporate the language of segregation: "inkspot," "your Momma come from Blackest Africa," "tar baby tar baby," "Black nigga." I say it in (great) anger to others on the block. This is a skill. It is a way to hurt another deeply. We all practice it. In 1956, nobody wants to be a "Blackie" or a "darkie" or no other kind of African nothing. Africa to (most of) us is Tarzan 'n' Jane: uncivilized life on the "Dark Continent," half-naked cannibals

on TV. Africa was something to be ashamed of. The closer we are to
that which symbolizes it, the greater our potential for shame.

Reading and rereading the story, I wondered if anyone, any Black
person, ever dared to call you Blackie, Aunt Nanadine, you with your
elegant, light skin. And what would you have done to them if they
had? What would you have done if *your* grandmother anointed elbows and knees religiously every Sunday with Pond's Vanishing
Creme, to keep away the ashiness of "dark"?

I am not ungrateful for all the things you did teach me about my
color: how to use Nadinola bleaching cream as a foundation under
makeup; to buy my stockings in a shade of off-black; how to assimilate and integrate to survive; to *fade in* as much as possible (however
ridiculous, at times); to "act my age and not my color." All the ways
you penetrated the interior of my feelings, where you and I lived, I
believed then, in a separation of shades; where our different colors
wedged between us like a yoke. Separated and politically bound us
to the psychological and psychic brutality that was American slavery. *That still binds us to generations of self-hatred*, a hatred of our
darkness. Hatred for the overwhelming, monumental, lynching pain
attached to it.

"Color has made extremely deep scars in Black people," says Sandra Ross, a good friend. (You might have seen some of her work, Aunt
Nanadine. She's a freelance lighting designer in theaters around the
city.) "It has affected what we do with our lives, what we *think* we
can do or accomplish. It has shaped our self-esteem and sense of personal and group power. In my family, color wasn't mentioned. We
talked about Black and white, but we didn't talk about light and
dark." The neighbors did, though indirectly: "She's pretty for a Black
child, smart for a Black child," they would say.

Is it just circumstantial that we are blood kin, women, products of
America, descendants of heroines and slaves, that we have shared
family crises and skeletons, but never talked intimately or honestly
about skin tones and color? That I have never said to you: I like my
color. I want to be even darker, blacker, still.

"I'm glad I'm as dark as I am because there is a certain point beyond which I can't compromise, beyond which I can't assimilate,"
Cheryl Lynn said to me over the phone. "I like to wear a lot of colors
and bells and stuff to remind me that *I am different. I am an*
African. And all the stares I get on the street and in the subway,
even from my own people, are a healthy sign because we all need to
be reminded that Black *is* beautiful, inherently beautiful, and we
can enhance that beauty or twist it into something grotesque when
we hide it."

When we deny it. When I am wrong *just because I am darker than you*. When my color *and* my sex are considered heavy deficits in the outside world. When, like Sandra, I cannot see myself as attractive for a long time, because I am, society says, repugnant and exotic: with my large breasts, my period, my pussy. "Just a dark, nappy girl." And as such, I must never call attention to myself. Never want it.

And never deserve it; because a dark girl was also unfeminine, unworthy, ignorant. *Neither ambition nor achievement was expected of me.* I could be propositioned by Black men, old enough to be my uncle. Rubbed against by a strange man in the subway on the way to school. I could be trespassed against in any number or variation of social ways, simply because, after all, I was only a Black girl. What a sad thing it was to learn that *a dark girl meant an ugly girl*. That my people had no standard for judging colored beauty. That within our race we judged ourselves by outside criteria. That there was no beauty underneath the nappy, unruly hair I was taught to fry and radically alter; no grace to my African buttocks squeezed into panty girdles at fifteen. Could I ask my mother if she thought I was beautiful? Could I demand to know if colored people had the *right* to be beautiful? If all the Sojourner Truth in me, all the Harriet Tubman, the Ida B. Wells-Barnett, all the Hatshepsut Queen of Egypt, all the dark, handsome history of my smell, talk, dreams, would not, indeed, one day rot inside the choking rope of

> *if you light you all right*
> *if you brown stick around*
> *if you Black git back*

Can you see how your red suit in my closet would make me see red? That to open the closet door daily was to open a Pandora's box of racism between us? Because we are in the closet too. A color closet we cannot get out of. It is too personal, too much a knife in a never healing wound. There is nowhere inside my color, inside your color, to be objective. No way to fade in. No way not to be dark. *And what color is dark? Who is dark? Compared to what, compared to whom? Is a dark woman in a darker skinned family light or dark? Is a light woman in a high light/mulatto family dark? Will we end the racism or shall we perpetuate it?*

"What do you think?" I say to Cheryl Lynn, taking notes. She replies: "I've seen so many ranges of color since I became conscious of my own color that sometimes it seems pointless to make any distinctions between dark and dark. I've seen navy-blue people and dusty-gray ones and some a sandy, translucent black. Is an eggplant person darker than a maroon person? What does it mean, beyond that?" Some of us are darker than others but, Aunt Nanadine, we are all dark peoples.

That's what the sixties taught me. In the red, black, green artifacts of my African heritage, I could *learn to love* the dark me that was the Civil Rights movement here in America. The dark me that was the independence movement in Africa. That was an outside shade of brown. When I went on those marches and stood on those demonstration lines and chanted against our oppression, *I felt Black*. And the natural Black was beautiful to express. And it was as beautiful to express my anger as it was to express my natural, nappy hair; to express my skin by painting it. I celebrated every ritual that celebrated my darkness: Kwanzaa, nose piercing, braids, nationalism. I wanted American saturated with the henna on my lips. I wanted color: I wore reds and yellows and greens in provocative African combinations. *I wanted the freedom to be dark*; I could not get dark enough. In the summer, I disappeared on the beaches for days at a time. "Stay out of the sun," you warned me. "It's just making you dark and oversensitive." "There's nothing wrong with being dark," I defended myself. Remember?

I remember *believing*, in the sixties. Many others do too. Like Carole Byard: "When we chanted 'Black is beautiful,' we were very assertive because we were *involved* in turning history around," she reminisced. "But some of the young people are not as aggressive as we were at their age. For many of them, it seems as if the sixties never happened. They are culturally embarrassed. There seems to be more of a willingness to merge, and not to assert cultural identity, particularly if it relates to Africa. Maybe they feel less threatened [than we did] by involvement with white cultural things."

I remember believing I wanted to judge myself from then on against *my own* darkness. And the darkness of my history. The sixties gave me a solid foundation, a bridewealth of "Africanity." Taught me to carry cultural beauty in my hair, my clothes, the words in my mouth. Taught me that while there was a "cultural Blackness" (artifacts), there is a "genetic dark," an *inside dark*, I must learn to love. *Learn to love the dark and trust it* because there are schools, clinics, governments, families, freedom, art to build between us.

But the sixties were only a beginning. And while it released some of our racial tension, it did not free us from our own color prejudices. When our slogans and anger no longer served us, when government and social backlash teased our spirit in the seventies, and Black was defined by Madison Avenue instead, some of us forgot that *our struggle did not begin in the sixties* and would not end there. Some of us mistook the invisibility of our darkness as the end of it.

Maybe that's not the stance to take at all, Carole disagrees,

"Maybe the way we went about it is just no longer necessary. Maybe that's the difference between this decade and the last ones. Maybe we who were active in the sixties are like generals from another war. Maybe it's a *different* war, with different equipment for fighting it. Maybe it's not all gone, just different."

Different, but the same. Whether in Brooklyn, Baton Rouge, or Baltimore. Whether in Africa, the Caribbean, or America; at the core of our struggle lies an ugly pattern of color consciousness between family, strangers, friends. Lies deceptively, and hides, beneath our global view, like a pain. Or a journal entry:

After dinner, Margo and I lay on her bed. Her quilt is a weave of cloth from the Ibo of Nigeria. We talk about her master's thesis topic: "The Impulse to Love in the Narratives of African American Slave Women." We smoked a good joint. Margo is a light-skinned Black woman. Her 'fro is big, but not kinky. Margo has African facial features. She's attractive. I am much darker. I have a short kinky 'fro. I have African facial features. I'm attractive. I was born in Harlem. Margo was born in Mississippi. She attends a prestigious Ivy League school. We live in Boston. Margo is very, very intelligent. Her mind is mercurial. When Margo smokes reefer she is aggressive. She sees how tall she is, how tall I am not. Wrestles me on the bed: "Let's play," she says. Punches me: "Let's fight." "No," I say. "Stop." When Margo's nose gets clobbered she cries, turns red. "You Black bitch," she spits. "I didn't mean to call you that," she says later. "Forget it," I say. Margo is my friend. We were lovers once. I quit her after that.

Aunt Nanadine, it is the impulse to love that does not quit. To love my history sex skin. Not in spite of it but because of it. *To love myself.* As Carole says, "We must deal with the internal aspects of 'Black is beautiful.' Work on a stronger sense of self to make the whole group stronger by caring about our family histories, our health, our spirit, what kind of people we are. Our self-love. *If I love myself then I have to love you too.*"

And I have to love the visibility of mass protests that created the sixties, transformed lives forever, Africanized me. And still love it now, as it regroups underground; as today's fashions and the current national politics turn back the clock—turn our 'fros to Geri Curls and our cornrows to "extensions." "We have to evolve to a point of caring about contributing to the whole," Carole is quick to encourage. "It's a personal thing. Something each one of us has to do. In the sixties there was a lot of emphasis on mass health, mass healing, but now we have to strengthen the individual parts. We have to remember that the whole is equal to the sum of the parts."

Remember that in these ugly times, there *is* something to fall back on. Remember that it is the impulse to love that comes between the silence between aunt and niece. Comes in this letter saying I love you. Comes, as I write, struggling to internalize beauty, because *color is still a critical issue between our people.* We still discriminate against our own. The darker ones against the lighter ones. The light ones against the dark. Little kids on the street today still call each other Blackie as a way to hurt each other deeply. And yet we cannot afford that "luxury." Or any other "luxury" of segregation that diminishes our numbers. We cannot afford to believe that we have been defeated; that "Black is beautiful" is dead. That dark is ugly. I am not dead and I am not defeated. I am beautiful. Black is in my heart, blood, work; in the eyes of my dreads, in the amber/cowrie of my tongue.

So Aunt Nanadine, I have taken the red suit out of my closet. I am going to the cleaners with it. Then to the mailbox to drop this letter. Please get in touch with me. I'd like to know how you feel about all this. Perhaps I can come see you soon. Next week I will give a talk on "Writing as Activist Art." I will wear our red suit. Thank you for giving it to me. I have always loved it.

> Take care.
> Moving forward to freedom: Your niece,
> Alexis
> Brooklyn, 1982

PART 2

THE IMPORTANCE
OF WORK

THE IMPORTANCE OF WORK

In a testimony to the importance of work in our lives, Freud is reported to have said that maturity is the capacity to work and to love. Indeed, if work and love are broadly defined to include both task-oriented and people-oriented behavior, nearly all of our life experiences could be included within these domains. Work and love are also overlapping and interactive as our "work" may deal with people, and our relationships may require as much work as our occupational obligations. And like the relationships in our lives, the work that we do, whether paid or volunteer, not only structures our lives, but contributes to defining who we are. Indeed, an answer to the question of "Who am I?" is often in terms of one's work ("I'm a pilot, teacher, construction worker," and so on).

From a developmental perspective, the capacity to work and how we see ourselves in relation to work changes over time. Erikson (1963) for example, identified the late childhood stage of industry versus inferiority as the period when a work orientation begins to develop: "To bring a productive situation to completion is an aim which gradually supersedes the whims and wishes of [the third stage of] play" (p. 259). While learning to be productive occurs in late childhood, adolescence and young adulthood are exploratory periods when young men and women consider and test the career and work options available to them. Changes that occur in one's worklife extending beyond young adulthood, and the growing phenomena of midlife career changes and post-retirement careers, can be attributed to a combination of individual developmental trajectories and societal-level changes. For example, midlife adults who take stock of their situation, accomplishments, and life to date, may discover that they have never found their work fulfilling; this assessment could lead to a dramatic career change. On the other hand, being "downsized" or terminated in a corporate merger may lead to the same midlife adult preparing for a different kind of work—work that will be a source of steady employment until retirement age.

The literature on occupational choice and career development contains several well-known models of career development such as those proposed by Super (1986), Levinson (1978), and Holland (1992). By and large, these models assume a continuous career pattern and thus have worked better for men than for women. In Levinson's (1978) model, for example, there is a trial stage of from 15 to 25, a stabilization stage (25 to 45), a maintenance stage (45 to 60) and an adjustment to retirement stage occurring sometime after 60. Bee (1996), however, makes the point that "it is probably time-in-job rather than age that is the more critical variable" (p. 269). Regardless of chronological age, any worker beginning a new job will have to learn about the job before there is some comfort (or "stabilization" in Levinson's terms) with the demands and expectations inherent in the new situation.

The social context of work at a specific historical time, as well as individual factors of race, class, and gender combine to shape the nature of any individual's work experience. With regard to historical time, the early Christian belief that "work was punishment for original sin" was supplanted by the Calvinistic notion that "work was the will of God." In a contemporary Western perspective, "work does not serve God so much as it serves the psychological development and enrichment of the individual" (Rohrlich, 1980, p. 31). As we enter the twenty-first century, work is being increasingly defined by the so-called global marketplace. In this framework, the value of sustained economic growth, competitive free markets, corporatization and privatization, technology and globalization are taken for granted. Workers compete for jobs that go to overseas vendors, or are "outsourced" to consulting firms and telecommuters, organizations are downsized, mechanized, and hierarchies are flattened into work teams and skeletal structures. Traditional modes of selecting an occupation as well as models of career development seem to have little relevance in today's fast-changing work environment.

That race, class, gender, and other factors affect job selection and career development is not new, although perhaps more attention is being given to these variables through today's discussions of workplace diversity, equal opportunity, sexual harassment in the workplace, and so on. Class, for example, has always been a major determinant of job selection and preparation. From Willis's analysis of this phenomenon in his classic study of *Learning to Labour: How Working Class Kids Get Working Class Jobs* (1977), to recent research on occupational choice and class (Bee, 1996), it is clear that the major social institutions of family, community, and school act in concert to reinforce class distinctions and status. Regardless of academic performance, for example, middle class students are more likely than working class students to attend college, thus resulting in better-paying, higher-prestige jobs which in turn perpetuates their middle class status.

Gender, especially as it interacts with race and ethnicity, is also a major variable in shaping the worklife of today's adults. While increasing numbers of women are entering the workforce, they are still being socialized into "women's jobs" or "female occupations." The sex-role socialization of women into lower-paying and lower-status jobs can be related to stereotyped notions of women's abilities, strengths, and weaknesses. For example, women are directed toward jobs that draw upon their so-called nurturing nature (nurses, teachers, helpers as in clerical support), and discouraged from physically challenging or managerial positions. Sex-role socialization interacts with class as working class families are more likely to reinforce gender-based stereotypes. Sex also interacts with race and ethnicity. Bee reports on a study by Amot and Matthaei (cited in Bee, 1996, p. 258) comparing the job status of Puerto Rican, Filipina, Japanese, Chinese, African American, Chicanas, and American Indian women with that of European American men. The study shows that "Asian American women, along with European American women, have moved more into the traditionally male higher-level jobs than have either Chicanas or African American women. But in every one of the ethnic groups, lower-level jobs are dominated by women."

The selections in this section on work consist of two short stories and one poem each of which illustrates some aspect of the role of race, class, gender and/or disability in shaping the work experience and the developmental concerns inherent in that experience.

Learning to Work by Dale Brown gives us some insight into how a learning disability affects job performance. The author vividly describes her first job as a waitress and how much trouble she had taking orders, filling them in the proper sequence, using the cash register and remembering prices: "I couldn't memorize the prices, despite studying the menu during breaks and even taking one home to work on it. I kept forgetting where the plates, silverware, and tools were located." Subsequent jobs present similar problems; however, once her problem is diagnosed she learns various strategies for coping, such as requesting extra training.

Sweetheart by Molly Martin is a humorous story of sexual harassment on the job. Bev is a four-foot-eleven truck mechanic who won her job after lodging a complaint with the Fair Employment Office. So, not only is she in a traditional male occupation, she is short, raising the question of whether she could even do her job, should she be hired. Once hired and eventually demonstrating her competency to the grudging satisfaction of the other men in her shop, she has to deal with an employee who insists upon calling her "sweetheart" instead of her name. In her humorous rendition of her encounter with "Harry the Hulk," she captures many of the issues women face in trying to be treated as equals in the workplace.

The final selection in this section is a poem by Mona Adilman titled, "Piece Work." The setting is a garment factory where working class immigrant women work "hunch[ed] over their machines" dreaming of their homelands. The factory floor is contrasted to the show room which is air conditioned and where the presumably male designer and the boss work. The women feel "lucky to be working, and live in fear of seasonal layoffs." Again, this poem captures the sex, ethnicity, and class segregation of the workplace. Having no support to pursue other types of work, these women become like the machines they are operating; they are separated and alienated not only from more nurturing experiences, but from their own inner selves. Little if any development can be fostered in this environment.

In summary, the centrality of work in people's lives is a critical factor in their development and definition of self. Being forced to work in situations largely because of one's sex, race, class or some combination of these factors stifles personal growth to the point of not feeling alive. Although the contemporary workplace is beginning to attend to issues of diversity and global consciousness, more needs to be done to foster work environments where *all* have an opportunity to develop their capacity to engage in meaningful work.

Learning to Work

Dale Brown

My First Job

My first day of my senior year in high school, I eagerly applied for jobs. A drugstore manager hired me as a waitress. I was very excited. Two dollars and sixty-five cents an hour seemed like a fortune to me. And I was thrilled to have my first job. I did not know at that time that I was "learning disabled."

My first impression was of noise and brightness. Cash registers clattered. Dishes crashed. Silverware clanged. We picked up our large white aprons from a hook next to a steel steaming sink. To one side of a narrow aisle was a shiny counter where the customers ate. On the other side was the grill, the bins of food, the soda machines, and the silverware and dishes.

Pam, a slender, young woman explained the system. "First, you take the order." She handed me a green pad. "Put it in your pocket. We're each assigned a section. You can help me with my section today, because it's a training day. Anyway, my section is here." She gestured, but I didn't know where she was pointing. "OK, just watch me." She approached a customer and said, "May I take your order please?" The customer told her and she wrote it down. I leaned over her shoulder to watch but she pushed me gently away. I didn't see what she did.

"One hamburger," she shouted to the cook.

"Now we have to make the tuna salad. Here's the scoop. You put the lettuce on the plate like this, then put the tuna on top. Then you put the tomato here."

Pam and I had to lean close to the counter to avoid being hit by a man carrying trays and the other passing people. I tried to watch her as she put the order together, but could barely follow.

"Show me how to do the tuna salad again?" I asked. "I don't remember how to do it."

"I can't until we get another order for it. Now, we clean up the counters by putting the dishes down here. Roy takes them later . . ."

She spent the day talking to me and telling me detail after detail. I tried to listen to her, but the other conversations, the sizzling of the grill, and the rushing of water distracted me.

"How do you take an order again?" I asked.

"It's easy," she replied. "All you have to do is to write down what they say and then get the prices."

The next day, my own section was assigned to me. Fortunately, my shift began at 2 P.M., which was "off hours" and there were only two customers. A man and a woman were waiting expectantly. The man asked for a hamburger and coke. The woman asked for a tuna salad and rootbeer. I wrote down the order, but didn't know the prices.

"How much is a hamburger?" I asked Pam.

"Eighty-five cents."

"How about a Coke?"

"Was it large or small?"

"I didn't ask."

"Better find out."

"How much is a tuna salad?"

"45¢. Look at the menu, next time. It has all of the prices."

I went to make the tuna salad. I couldn't find the scoop and had to ask Pam for it. The plates had disappeared. Again, I had to interrupt her. I laid down the lettuce, but it wouldn't lie flat. Then I couldn't scoop the tuna. I tugged into it with the rounded scoop, but didn't know how to press the handle to let the tuna out in a ball. So I ended up spooning it on the lettuce and hoping it was enough. Then I gave the woman her tuna salad.

I checked my list and brought their drinks, using the first paper cups my hand encountered. I couldn't easily see the difference between large and small, and by now I had forgotten Pam's reminder.

"Where's my hamburger?" asked the man.

"Oh, I'm sorry, I forgot to tell the cook," I replied."One hamburger," I shouted to him. Fortunately, there was already a hamburger next to him, so I took it and gave it to my customer. I was feeling quite proud of myself for serving my first order and relaxed for a moment.

"Listen, don't steal my hamburger again," said Pam.

"What do you mean?"

"You know what I mean! The cook made that hamburger for my customer, yours is just now being made! Don't do that again!"

I approached two other customers to take their order. They both ordered hotdogs and tea.

"Where's our check?" asked the first man I had served.

I gave him the check. He looked at it thoughtfully. "How much are we supposed to pay?" he asked.

"I don't know," I said and took the check back. Panic hit. How much were the cokes? I made up a price of 30¢, then concentrated on adding them up.

"You owe us $1.90," I told him, handing him the check back.

"Where are our hotdogs?" asked one of my customers.

"And my order?" said another person.

I ignored them.

"You overcharged us for the cokes," said the man. "They cost 25¢."

"O.K.," I said.

"We owe you $1.80," he said.

I approached the huge-looking cash register. I had forgotten how to work it.

"Pam, you need to show me how to work the cash register."

"I showed you that yesterday."

"Sorry, you need to show me again."

She rang up my order, without telling me what she was doing. When the numbers $1.90 came up, I said, "I'm sorry. I made a mistake. I overcharged them for the Cokes. They're 25¢, but I didn't change it on my order form."

She glared at me. "Now we have to make a void slip." She turned on a small microphone. "Mr. Connors, please come to the counter. Mr. Connors, to the counter."

I waited. "Dale, don't you have any other orders to take?" she asked.

I nodded. I had lost the order slip. I checked my pad, my pockets, the floor around me, I would have to ask them again. But who were they? I couldn't remember their faces!

"Dale, come here," said Pam. Mr. Connors was working at the cash register.

He looked at me sympathetically.

"You'll catch on soon," he said. "It's only your second day." He showed me how to use the cash register and said, "Try not to make too many voids."

I reached into my pocket and fortunately, the order slip was there.

"Dale, your customers are building up. I'm going to take care of those two and you finish your order," said Pam.

How did she do it, I wondered. She moved efficiently and effortlessly, taking orders, preparing food, and ringing things up.

I brought the hotdogs to the next customers.

The first few days were a blur of confusion and errors. Other employees were kind to me at first, but rapidly grew impatient as I constantly asked questions. I couldn't memorize the prices, despite studying the menu during breaks and even taking one home to work on it. I kept on forgetting where the plates, silverware, and tools were located.

"Where's the scoop?" I asked Pam once.

"Right in front of your nose," she replied. She pointed to it, and suddenly it appeared. Today, I know that this is a typical symptom of visual figure-ground problems, but at that time I didn't understand why things disappeared and then, suddenly, reappeared.

Preparing food was difficult, even after learning how to do it. For example, to fix a coke, one took a paper cup and pushed it against a knob under the nozzle. It required a lot of seltzer water and a small amount of coke syrup. I couldn't tell the difference between the knob for seltzer water and the knob for coke syrup. The left knob and the right knob seemed the same and so did the two labels. My only choice was to squirt a little bit of liquid into the cup, check and see which it was. Then if it was coke syrup, I had to remember to only put a little bit of it and a lot of seltzer water. Since the coke syrup looked like a coke, it was easy to serve a lot of syrup with a tiny bit of seltzer water. The customers would comment on my funny tasting cokes!

I never figured out the sequence of putting an order together. Now, it seems clear that you start with the cooked items and work on your other food while they are cooking. With my inability to conceive of time properly, it was not obvious, and nobody told me. So I always served my customers their food at different times.

I had trouble walking back and forth in the small space between the counter and food preparation area. I often bumped into other workers or dropped things. Once, I dropped and broke a tray of glasses.

Because of difficulty in seeing and remembering faces clearly, I often confused customers' orders. I concentrated hard on each face. Sometimes I would count and write the number of stools from one end. Unfortunately, I often miscounted or skipped one of the stools. Once, I wrote down "blonde hair and blue eyes." The customer laughed when she saw that. A few times, I went down the aisle and said, "Who ordered the hamburger and coke?" Someone always took them.

Gradually, I mastered the cash register, although I had a tendency to punch the wrong numbers and end up with $13.80 instead of $1.38. The tax table print was so small that I sometimes guessed the tax or forgot it all together.

My favorite job was going to the stockroom to get ice. The other waitresses hated it. I loved it and got almost all of the ice. I would walk downstairs holding two buckets, one in each hand. Then, I'd sit on a carton for a few minutes to calm myself. Then I'd fill each bucket with a scoop, enjoying the rhythm of the ice hitting the bucket. When they were full, I took them upstairs and poured one into each icebin.

I was cheerful and most of my customers were sympathetic. Whenever they pointed out my errors, I apologized and immediately corrected them before going on to my next orders. I asked them to find the prices on the menu. I'd often ask, "Have I forgotten anything? Can I do something else?"

Due to my cheerfulness, reliability about coming in on time, and obvious eagerness to please, the manager liked me. Sometimes, Mr. Conners kidded me about all of my void slips, but he was very patient. My coworkers, on the other hand, had to constantly answer my questions and correct my errors. Even though I took care of some of the unpopular jobs, they found me difficult and were undoubtedly glad when I had to leave, due to a change in bus schedule.

Later, I had many jobs. I was a salesperson in a department store during Christmas rush. You can imagine the problems! At Pitzer College, I woke up at 6 A.M. to clean the dormitory kitchens. I loved that job, because I worked alone and at my own pace. After transferring to Antioch College, I became a cafeteria worker and served food, washed dishes, and helped the cooks. I did each job better than the last.

DISCOVERING MY LEARNING DISABILITIES

As I worked, I often wondered why I had to try so hard. Everyone else could do the work so easily. They picked it up quickly, not needing as much training and attention from the supervisor. If I concentrated hard and did everything correctly, I was accused of being too slow. On the other hand, when I went faster, I made errors. Other people could do the job correctly and at the right speed. No one else had to work during the breaks or worse, punch out then return to complete undone tasks.

The answer to that question came after working at an electronics factory during a work-study quarter. There, I realized that I must have some kind of specific problem. My productivity was very low. For example, we had to strip wires, cutting one layer of wires with a razor blade, without cutting into the next layer of plastic. I had trouble using the right amount of pressure. Either, I'd cut into the next layer of wires or not cut through the first layer. Sometimes the thin copper wires broke as I twisted them. I often cut my fingers.

One day my supervisor asked me to strip "eighty" wires. I was doing the job, when she said, "Dale, it's taking you an awfully long time to strip those eight wires."

"You said eighty wires," I replied, surprised.

"I said eight."

"No, you said eighty."

"I said eight!"

"I heard eighty," I replied. What was it? Was it my hearing? It had been tested several times and was considered good. Yet, there was no question that I often misheard instructions. I knew about my clumsiness and difficulty in seeing correctly. But I had assumed my hearing was fine.

After leaving that job, I visited a counselor who told me that my mistakes were similar to those of children with something called learning disabilities. She sent me to the library to read about the topic. At that time, learning disabilities were assumed to be outgrown in early adulthood. My research was revealing. My handicap had a name! There was a reason for all that extra hard work! Each problem was actually a symptom of a disability. If only someone had recognized all of that extra effort. For a few weeks I felt sorry for myself and wished for the praise that was deserved, but never received.

Basically, however, information about my learning disability was very useful. Weaknesses, I realized, could be worked on systematically. For example, many learning disabled people can't use one side of the body well. In my case, I dropped things because the muscles of my right arm would suddenly relax. So I decided to carry items with the weight of my left arm. That solved that problem.

My knowledge of my learning disabilities was particularly essential during my first job after college graduation, working as a court reporter. Obviously, this was not the right job for me. However, during the recession of 1975, there were very few jobs, and I was lucky to get one, even as a court reporter. I had been searching for five months when I applied for the job. Helen, who directed the company, showed me a large black box, which stood as high as my hip.

"Can you lift that?" she asked.

I picked it up, keeping a straight face and hiding my breathlessness.

She nodded. "There will be two of these and you will have to carry them all over the place." She told me that I would be responsible for taping the trials so that the typist could produce an accurate transcript.

Listening to her, I wondered if I could do the job. Clearly, I'd go right up against my learning disabilities. With inaccurate hearing, vision, and touch, it would be a challenge to do the job correctly. But

I needed a job! So I enthusiastically sold myself during the interview. They chose me.

On my first work day, they assigned Paul to show me how to use the equipment. Now that I could realize that it was impossible for me to learn it all the first time, I relaxed and absorbed as much as possible. . . .

When Paul took me to a trial where he was recording, I watched carefully and asked questions. At the end of the day, I still did not understand what to do, although the major points were becoming clear.

"I'm sorry, but I still don't feel ready to work on my own," I said. "Can I spend tomorrow watching another reporter?" He asked Helen, who let me have several extra training days.

Our training paid off. While it took me longer to record trials, the transcribers told my boss that they liked to receive my work because it was easy to follow. And, once, a judge requested me.

MEETING OTHER LEARNING DISABLED PEOPLE

But my hunt for a more appropriate job continued. Finally, a professional association hired me as an office manager. This job also required overcompensation. My work week was about sixty hours long. The business manager jokingly threatened to charge me rent because I was there so often.

During this job, I often felt lonely. I had finally found a professional job in which I could succeed and advance. But the price was spending most of my time in the office. Was life only work? I decided to seek out other people with disabilities. Since the handicap is invisible, forming a self-help group seemed the only way to meet others. Thus, I started the Association of Learning Disabled Adults (ALDA). Meeting other learning disabled people made me realize how severe our handicaps are. Many people in ALDA couldn't even hold a job. Either they couldn't find one or they were frequently fired.

We had no access to help from professionals, since we supposedly outgrew our disabilities. Our problems were considered minimal. We were told that we weren't trying or that we were being careless. The help we could give each other was our only chance. But that should not have been. We deserved the help that people with visible handicaps received.

I decided to look for work in an organization that dealt with disabled people. There, I could learn about the field and tell other people about learning disabilities. . . . One group that interested me was the President's Committee on Employment of the Handicapped. I visited them and read a tall stack of publications from their stockroom. One was by Bob Ruffner, their Director of Communications. I wrote to him and complimented him on his article. He responded by arranging to meet me and have me interviewed by the Committee's magazine, *Disabled USA*. . . .

A job opened up at the Committee. I filled out form after form, and after five months of being interviewed, of waiting, or refilling forms, of competing against many other qualified men and women, I got the job! Today, I am on the Committee staff, promoting opportunities for disabled people through writing, public speaking, and special events. I enjoy the work, doing things that I'm good at. My job can be done in a reasonable amount of time.

It has not been easy for me to find my place in society as an LD adult. It took hard work, self-discipline, and positive thinking. I had to demand the training that was needed in each situation. . . .

On the other hand, I was born with many advantages. My family was warm and supportive. They paid for my college education. It was always clear to me that blue-collar work was temporary. What happens to people with these disabilities who are raised in factory towns? Or those who cannot afford a college degree? Or those who are not intelligent or emotionally stable? What happens if you are not qualified to be a professional, but can't do entry-level jobs either? These are the people we must help. I hope my story gives some clues as to how.

Sweetheart

Molly Martin

I was doing pretty good on this new job. See, they didn't want to hire me. Said four foot eleven was too short to be a mechanic. The trucks are put up to a certain height they said and I wasn't tall enough to reach them. But after I complained to Fair Employment, they decided it was okay for me to use a ladder.

So here I am on my little ladder under a diesel changing the oil. The roll-up doors on the garage are all open so I'm kind of on display. And I'm the first woman so I'm a curiosity. They all make detours past the maintenance shop just to see me on my ladder. As if I was a two-headed snake or something. Strange how their minds work. Or they'll come in with some "problem" just to get a look at me. Sometimes they'll walk past and make comments, sort of muttered under their breath, but I know they mean for me to hear. I try not to, though. I concentrate on my work and try to ignore them. They're chicken, anyhow. I say, you don't like somebody, you just tell 'em to their face. I'd have more respect for them if they talked right to me.

One time I thought I heard the word bitch but when I turned around the guy was gone, out the door. Now I don't know if it really happened or if I was just paranoid. I decided it doesn't really matter one way or the other, whether I hear it or not. They're trying to get my goat. They're letting me know they don't want me. Well, you do that to me, it's like waving red in front of a bull. No way am I quitting now. The more they bug me, the harder I dig my heels in. Besides, this is the best money I ever made. Beats waitressing any day.

So anyhow, I'm standing there under this truck and I hear from across the yard kinda sing-song but loud, "Hey sweetheart, how ya doin' today?" I squint out into the sun and see this big old red-faced

85

guy waving his arms at me. His belly looks like a hundred pound sack of flour slung over a farmer's shoulder. His waving arms cause the sack of flour to jiggle and expose a rim of pink flesh above his belt. His head looks like an engine block, hair shaved into a military flat top. He must be a teamster, I think. No neck.

I gotta admit my first impulse was to laugh at this fool. Next I wanted to punch his lights out. Now I know some women don't mind being called sweetheart or honey or any of those sugar-coated names. Men will tell you women think it's a compliment—especially older women. Then they look at me as if I should understand. You know, I'm not that old, but it seems like I hate this name calling more the older I get.

I decided if I ignored this joker maybe he'd get the point and leave me alone. Wouldn't you know, that tactic only encouraged him. Every time he'd see me, he'd yell, "Heeeeey sweeeetheart" at the top of his lungs so everyone could hear. One day he came right up and introduced himself, friendly as can be. "Hey," he says, holding out a grimy hand, "I'm Harry. Harry the Hunk they call me." I'm like, is he kidding? Harry the Hunk! Is he putting himself down? I had to hide a smile. I wanted to appear serious, intimidating if possible.

"My name's Bev," I scowled, "and I'd appreciate it if you'd call me that."

"Okay, sweetheart," he leered, and walked away.

Well you can imagine, that got my dander up. I fumed about that all week. It got so every night I'd be beating up Harry the Hunk in my dreams. Now I've never been one to criticize any woman for how she chooses to survive in a job. We each pick our own battles. God knows you can't take on every one that comes along. You'd be wrung out like a dishrag at the end of every day. Some insults are better ignored, but some if they were water wouldn't even slide off a duck's back. So I determined to take on Harry the Hunk or my mind would never be set at ease as long as I worked on this job.

By this time I've been on the job a while and I've gotten to know the crew of mechanics in my shop. They turned out to be a pretty good group after all. Dave struck me as a Hell's Angel type at first glance. Kinda scruffy, his beard half grown out. Yeah, I know that's in style now, but believe me on him it looked scruffy. Skinny as a cotter pin and at least six three. Drives a Harley. He's the first to talk to me. "Don't let 'em get to you," he says. "I know what you're going through. My wife's a sheet metal apprentice."

I'm like, no kidding. We were instant friends.

Well, that broke the ice. The others might have been a little jealous of Dave, or they might have decided I'm no more different from any of them than they are from each other. Two are immigrants, from Ireland and El Salvador. The rest are blacks, whites, and Chicanos.

We circled around each other for a while, testing limits. I had to tell one or two not to call me girl or honey. Had to thank them for their offers of help, but let them know I've got two arms, I can carry things just like taller people. Maybe better, 'cause I'm closer to the ground.

I did almost get into a scrape with the foreman, Fernando, a very proper Catholic gentleman who let me know in so many words he thinks women belong at home and not in a garage earning a man's wage. In his world women don't leave their children to go to work, they don't wear pants, and they don't swear.

Now all my friends know I can cuss a streak as blue as any longshoreman. I let the guys know swearing doesn't bother me at all. So I'm starting to feel real comfortable in the shop, and one day I'm shooting the breeze with Fernando trying to tell him I deserve a good job, I've got three kids to support just like him, when I guess I let a four-letter word drop. Well, he gets this look on his face all kind of furrowed and scrunched. I swear the corners of his mouth drooped more than his mustache. His eyes turned into little black ball bearings under his bushy brows. Then he draws himself up and says, "Dear, I don't see any reason to use that word."

'Course I know this is not true, since I hear the guys say it all the time. What he means is he has a different standard for women and men. Well, you know I'll fight for a lot of things, but my right to swear at work is not first on my list. "Okay, Fernando, I'll make a deal with you. I'll never swear in front of you again, if from now on you call me Bev instead of dear." He thinks this is an honorable agreement, and we even shake on it, though I suspect he doesn't think women ought to shake either.

Turns out Fernando took me seriously. Called me by my name from then on. I've kept my part too, ever since, and our truce stood me in good stead in my ongoing battle with Harry the Hunk. Fernando could see what was going on. So, after that, when Harry would come through the shop, before he could even get his big mouth open, Fernando would yell at him, "Heeeey sweeetheart."

This should have been enough to make any grown man blush, but Harry just took it in stride. He'd smile sheepishly and go about his business. But he wouldn't stop calling me sweetheart.

Then one day I hear Harry lay the same trip on Dave. "Hey, hippie," he says, "when are you gonna get a haircut?" Harry's smiling the whole time, but I can tell Dave doesn't think it's funny. Dave just keeps his mouth shut and concentrates on his brake job.

Harry keeps smiling at me, too, and I start to figure out the only way he knows how to be friendly is harassing people. But I decide I don't care, I never liked being called names and I'm not gonna get used to it. If he wants to make friends he's got to at least learn my name.

One day I put it to him. "Harry," I say, "why do you keep calling me sweetheart when you know I hate it?"

"You hate it?" he says. "But I call my wife sweetheart and she loves it."

"Harry, I'm not your wife, I'm your coworker, Bev. I'm not your sweetheart." Now I'm thinking this guy is thick. He really doesn't get it. This is gonna be harder than I thought.

A while later he brings in his truck for emergency work and I'm the only mechanic available. "Come on," he says, "hop to it, sweetheart. I gotta get this baby back on the road."

"Harry," I say, "either you never learned the mechanics' law or you forgot it."

"Mechanics' law, what's that?" he says.

"Very basic," I say. "The law says you treat your mechanic right, you got a smooth running truck. Treat your mechanic bad and your truck never gets out of the shop. Harry, if you don't stop calling me sweetheart, you could be a permanent pedestrian."

"Okay, okay," he says, "if it means that much to you. I really need my truck . . . Bev."

I could see his mouth had great difficulty forming the word, but it was a start. After that, he seemed to try harder. He'd bolt into the shop in his usual back slapping, shoulder punching way and yell, "Hey, Swee . . . Bev." This was a great improvement, and I told myself I'd made progress, but Harry seemed to be having a hard time making the transition. I couldn't tell whether his harassment had taken a new form or his mind just wasn't making the connection.

Now that we're "friends" Harry thinks he can take new liberties. One day he lopes over, yells, "Hey Swee . . . Bev," and wraps his arms around me in a bear hug. I duck, but not soon enough, and he gets me in a headlock.

I growl at him, "Harry, what are you doing?"

He looks hurt. "Just saying hello."

So after that whenever he sees me he holds his arms outstretched as if to hug me and gets this sad teddy bear lost puppy look on his face. God, I think, I've created a monster.

"Jeez, Harry, go hug an I-beam."

Harry finally learns to say my name without having to stop and think every time. Natural as can be, he comes in and says, "Hey, Bev, how ya doin'?" We chitchat about our kids, I ask him how his wife puts up with him. He tells me she's really a liberated woman. I start to actually like the guy, but as soon as I let him know that, he thinks all the rules are off. He thinks he can call me whatever he wants and I'll go along with the program.

I run into him as I'm hurrying across the yard on my way back from lunch break. "Hey, sweetheart," he grins, arms outstretched as he walks toward me. I can see if I keep walking I'll head right into his grasp, so I have to stop and move sideways like a crab to avoid him.

When this happens, I frown, cross my arms, look him straight in the eye and say something like, "Harry, go drive your truck off a cliff." I'm trying to let him know I'm not playing, but to him this is the game.

One day he walks into the shop with a woman. I should say amazon. This woman's gotta be six feet tall. Built like a linebacker. Her skin is the color of Colombian coffee. Her black hair is knotted up under a red kerchief and she's dressed in work clothes and boots, so she's got to be working here. Another woman in the yard! I'm thinking, who is she, what does she do, when Harry brings her right over to introduce me.

"Sweetheart," he booms, "I want you to meet my new partner, Pam." He's grinning so wide, his teeth take up half his face.

Now people say I'm easygoing. I'm known for my high boiling point. But I swear when Harry says this I feel like an engine overheating. Smoke must be coming out of my ears. I have to hold my arms next to my sides to keep from strangling him, and I start yelling all the words I promised Fernando I wouldn't.

"Aww, come on," he whines, "I was only kidding."

"Harry," I hiss, "don't call me sweetheart. It's not funny, it was never funny, and it's never gonna be funny."

When he turns around and walks out of the shop I hope I never see the jerk again. I also hope Pam doesn't think I'm a total nut case. I do want to talk to her. But a little while later Harry slinks back in, alone this time, and stands beyond punching distance from me, head hanging, and says in a low voice, "Bev, I'm really sorry. You know I didn't mean to make you mad. I was just showing off to my new partner. I promise, I'll never do it again."

"Right," I say, and jerk my socket wrench so hard I take a slice of skin off my thumb knuckle when it hits the block.

By this time I don't trust Harry the Hunk for a minute, and I tell myself I'm never gonna get set up again. So I just try to avoid him and be real busy whenever he comes by. He still acts friendly and says hi and I try to be civil. He always calls me Bev, still yelling as loud as ever. And because I'm not a person who can hold a grudge, I loosen up and let my defenses down some. Pretty soon we're back to our old routine. But he's never called me sweetheart since.

One day he stops by and gives me a hand with a generator I'm trying to move. "Thanks," I say. "I don't care what they say about you. You're okay."

"Hey, Bev," he grins, "all that work paid off. I turned out okay, huh."

"Yeah, Harry," I say, "and it only took me five years."

Piece Work

Mona Elaine Adilman

The knot of women,
heat-shrivelled,
hunch over their machines—
piece work puppets
manipulating bits
of fabric, the whir
and hum of technology
stinging the air
like a giant wasp.

Steam iron in hand,
the girl from Barbados,
soaked in sweat,
dreams of the sea.
The hissing iron distorts
her crested vision
with a vaporous
river of sound.

Dialects in Greek,
Portuguese and Italian
are savory fruits
in the sweltering
factory heat.
Conversation rises
like yeast

in the industrious
oven of humanity.

Pockets, collars, sleeves,
in rainbow streams,
flow from each
punctuating needle.
Buffeting
buttonhole machines
bite sharply
into polyester tissue.
Precision speaks
with geologic force.

The factory is canopied with
plastic-swathed garments,
candy-cane copies
of haute-couture originals.
Operators, cutters,
pressers, shippers
scurry across
the room, hunchbacked,
ducking under 4 foot high
metal pipes
supporting parades
of dresses and slack suits,
labelled, tagged,
inspected,
ready to be shipped.

In the show room,
air conditioners
articulate
a comforting chill.
Buyers
finger the goods,
and eye the models.
The designer
is all smiles.
The boss has
order forms
at the ready.

The season looks
promising.

In the factory,
the odor of sweat
mingles with the smell
of steaming garments
and dry-cleaning fluid,
but the women
are lucky to be working,
and live in fear
of seasonal
layoffs.

The needle trade
marches on,
populated by
its human machines.
Immigrant women,
shapeless
in sleeveless smocks,
are mechanical tools,
overexposed film

      hemming, pressing, basting,
      threading, cutting, stitching.

The fashion treadmill
goes round and round
on the laws of
supply and demand.

Production
is an adrenalin flow,
a cover-up for
yesterday's cop-out,
today's emptiness,
the lost look of tomorrow.

Piece work is the
name of the game.

Pieces of soul.

Pieces of bone.

Pieces of sinew.

Pieces of gut.

Pieces of Pride.

Pieces of pain.

Pieces of flesh.

Pieces of people.

Pieces of profit . . .

PIECE WORK.

PART 3
INTIMACY

INTIMACY

Relationships sustain and define us throughout our lives. As infants, we rely on the connection with a primary caretaker for our survival. Our ability to make friends and get along with others is important both in childhood and adulthood. In grade school we are evaluated on how well we play with others and as adults in the work world, we are encouraged to be team players, cooperative and committed to each other for the good of the organization. From family relationships, to casual friendships, to intimate relationships, these connections vary in depth and intensity and help us cope with the demands of everyday life. We are sisters, brothers, mothers, partners, best friends, co-workers and neighbors, and learn more about ourselves and others as a result of our connections.

Psychologists have noted the importance of love and intimacy in human development. Freud believed that to be a successful human being, one must both work and love. In his hierarchy of needs, Maslow (1968) proposed that once people moved beyond physical and safety needs, they progressed to love and belongingness needs where they socialize with others in order to be accepted and feel a sense of belonging. Erikson (1980) asserted that after achieving a sense of identity, people grappled with the psychosocial stage of intimacy versus isolation learning to fuse their identities with another or risk isolation. Carol Gilligan (1982) argues that relationships with others help women define themselves.

Scholars have further analyzed love. Sternberg (1987) proposed that there are eight varieties of love which vary in degree of commitment, passion, and intimacy. He defines intimacy as feelings of closeness or connectedness. Passion includes longing for the person and sexual union. Commitment means staying with the person over a long period of time. Types of this love include infatuation defined as passion without intimacy or commitment, romantic love which has passion, and intimacy without commitment and liking where intimacy exists, but passion and commitment don't. Everyone experiences these types of love, but factors including class, education, and sexual orientation affect our intimate relationships.

In *The Linden Tree,* Giulio and George, a gay, interracial couple who have been together fifty years, exemplify companionate love which is passionless, but intimacy and commitment are present. The author notes, "In the early years there had been passion, but now they were just a couple who had grown old together." As Giulio slowly succumbs to a heart ailment, George recollects their life together. He remembers, "Life had always been strangely easy for them. They had been incapable of acknowledging affronts, even when they were refused lodgings or openly stared at on the street." Giulio does not want to die and is consumed by thoughts of "worms and bones." At night each holds the other's hand for comfort.

Lewis (1960) looks at love from the categories of affection, friendship, Christian love (agape), and passion (eros). Affection is the bond between parents and children (Lewis, 1960). Friendship requires equality between people with common interests. Agape is a self-sacrificing, unconditional type of love that is best demonstrated by people such as Mother Teresa and Martin Luther King, Jr. (Lewis, 1960). Eros is sexual love and is probably the most "popular" love.

Agape, or Christian love, is shown to the main character of *Church.* Langston, an African American, returns to his hometown after being diagnosed with AIDS. He goes to the church he attended as a boy and notes the lack of class distinctions. Langston narrates, "This was a place where the well-to-do and the can-hardlies mingled and shook hands with equal pretense." He is invited to speak in front of the congregation and admits his long absence from the church and that he "has a kind of cancer." He writes, "I had so many things to get off my chest and out in the air that I almost didn't know where to begin. But then I remembered where I was and who all was listening." He is accepted by the church. He says, "And I cried, 'I'm gay! Praise God! Hallelujah!' And I heard the congregation say, 'Amen.'"

Eros is the driving force for the main character in *Is This the Reward of a Catholic Girlhood?* as she slowly recognizes her passion for women. She talks of her erotic feelings when she says, "Mary sat for a long time on the edge of my bed and then kissed me on the neck . . . I was overwhelmed. I wanted to be kissed again but was too shy to say so or to kiss her." Despite their Catholic school upbringing and societal prohibitions against being attracted to the same sex, the author writes, "We had both had such repulsively successful careers as Catholic schoolgirls and devout young women that we ought to have been guilt-ridden, but somehow we escaped the tortures of a bad conscience."

In addition to examining love, scholars have also defined and looked at intimacy which is a component of love (McAdams, 1989). Maslow says intimacy is "gentle, delicate, unintruding, undemanding, able to fit itself passively to the nature of things as water gently soaks into crevices" (Maslow, 1968). The intimacy of friendship involves such qualities as self-disclosure and helping. Friendships have qualities of intimacy, trust, sharing, acceptance, caring, and enjoyment.

Intimacy knows no bounds. Attachments occur between people of similar and different races, ethnicities, sexes, and classes. For example, some women prefer the company of gay men because they don't want to cope with the tension of a possible sexual encounter. They feel more appreciated as people rather than sexual objects (Nahas & Turley, 1979). These relationships between women and gay men are defined as "marginal relationships" (Nahas & Turley, 1979, p. 127). Such is the case with the protagonist in *Between* whose relationship with Paulo, a gay, male friend, and Tim, her boyfriend leaves her confused about what type of intimacy she wants. She and Paulo are roommates and friends who "play at being married" and "lament the cruelties of dating." She is unsure of Paulo's feelings toward her and says, "Why does Paulo bring me to a [gay] bar? I'm not sure. Sometimes I think it's because he loves me. Other times I think it's because I'm a fashion accessory." She admits, " I want him just for me." She recognizes her protectiveness of Paulo and feels strange going on vacation with Tim alone after the three of them have lived together for eight months. She also recognizes that when Tim speaks of future plans they seem "far-flung." On the vacation she realizes Tim is jealous of Paulo and that she and Tim are drifting apart. Tim warns her, "[Paulo would] leave you if he found the right person." The main character is left at the end of the story without the intimacy she craves from either man.

We are often attracted to those who are like us and differences cause challenges. For the young couple in *First Love,* class and educational aspirations create a chasm between two young lovers of Japanese descent. George Sakamoto is a sixteen-year-old, motorcycle-riding immigrant from Japan. Joanne Terasaki ("Jo") is a third generation Japanese American "brain" who "was a product of the middle-class, ethnically mixed Richmond District." Her mother graduated from the University of California—Berkeley in 1939. Jo's dating George violated the "unspoken law of evolution which dictated that in the gradual march toward Americanization, one did not deliberately regress by associating with F. O. B.'s [fresh off the boat]." To Jo's family, "George . . . was a shock." George's family was thrilled with Jo. Jo goes off to college and George attends a community college. George's embarrassing visit to Jo's college precipitates their breakup.

In summary, we are defined by our connections with others. Passion, intimacy, and commitment vary between relationships which create different kinds of love. As with everything else, relationships are affected by race, class, and educational aspirations among other things. These differences between people may create problems and/or opportunities for growth. One thing is for certain, connections to others are necessary for life.

The Linden Tree

Ella Leffland

In the early years there had been passion, but now they were just a couple who had grown old together. The last twenty years they had owned a rooming house, where they lived contentedly on the ground floor with their cat, Baby.

Giulio was a great putterer. You could always see his sweeping the front steps or polishing the doorknobs, stopping to gossip with the neighbors. He was a slight, pruny man of sixty-eight, perfectly bald, dressed in heavy trousers, a bright sports shirt with a necktie, and an old man's sweater-jacket, liver-colored and hanging straight to the knees. He had a thick Italian accent and gesticulated wildly when he was excited.

George was quite different. Everything about him was slow and solid, touched by grandeur. Though he was a Negro from the Midwest, he spoke with an accent that sounded British, yet not exactly. He was seventy-four, but looked much younger, with a hard body and a hard face with only a few deep fissures in it. Giulio was a neat dresser, but George was attired. His perfectly creased trousers, his crisp white shirt, smoothly knotted tie, and gray sleeveless sweater seemed out of place in the stuffy little flat.

A home is usually the wife's creation, and so it was in their case. The doilies, the vases with their wax flowers, the prints of saints hanging among gaudy floral calendars—all these were Giulio's. George's contribution was less concrete but more important. He made their life possible, dealing with the rents and taxes, attending to the heavy chores, ousting tenants who drank or brawled. If Giulio were to run the building he would soon come to grief, for he had no real sense of work, and as for the rents, it was all he could do to add

101

two digits together. In addition, he was fussy and fault-finding, so that he often took a dislike to perfectly good tenants, yet countenanced glib bullies.

They were a nicely balanced couple, and for years had been happy. When they were young they had had their troubles—living quarters had been hard to find not only because of George's color, but because of their relationship. In those days Giulio had had fetching ways, too obvious to be ignored. But gradually he passed into a fussy dotage, and now people thought of the pair merely as two lonely old men who lived together. George's color no longer presented problems now that he had proved what was not necessarily demanded of those who asked for proof: that he was a responsible man, an asset to the neighborhood. His building was the best kept on the block, his rents reasonable, his tenants, for the most part, permanent. He would not rent to the fly-by-night element that was slowly invading the district.

The tenants consisted of a pair of raddled, gadabout sisters, a World War I veteran with one leg, and a few clerks and students. Giulio regaled George with facts about these people he gleaned by snooping through their rooms in their absence, and George put him down for this, even threatened him, but it did no good. And in any case, the tenants did not seem to care; there was something so simple about Giulio that his spying was like that of a mouse or a bird. They called him Aunty Nellie (his last name being Antonelli), and the younger ones sometimes invited him into their rooms so that his teeth might be enjoyed. These were ill-fitting, too large for his mouth, and clicked through his speech. When he grew excited, they slipped out of place, at which he would pause in a natural, businesslike way to jam them back in before going on.

Giulio was forever dragging the carpet sweeper up and down the halls, looking for an ear to gossip in. George, on the other hand, talked very little. Only tenants who had lived there a long time got to know him at all, when, once in a great while, he would invite them in for a glass of sherry when they came to pay the rent.

In his flat, the tenants found George to be a different man, less aloof and forbidding. Sitting there with Giulio and Baby, the cat, he had something patient, indulgent, altogether loving in his face. Giulio looked with pride at him, glancing now and then at the guest, as though to say: Isn't he wonderful? Sometimes he would go so far as to confess, "I no good at the paper work, but George, George, he *smart*." Or, "We live together fifty years, never a yell, always happy." And George would give him a look to show him that he was saying too much, and then Giulio would sulk and refuse to rejoin the conversation. But the next day he would be the same as ever, whirling creakily around the steps with his broom, or around his garden with a green visor clamped to his head.

He had a shrine in the garden, with statues of the saints standing in sun-blanched profusion. He was an ardent Catholic, and there was no one with a greater collection of religious objects—rosaries and crosses and vestments, which he kept in his bureau drawer and brought out to enjoy their varied glass, wooden, and satin richness. But religious as he was, he would not divest his beloved garden of one fresh bloom for his saints. It was a skimpy garden, heavily bolstered with potted geraniums, and he was so proud of each green shoot that struggled through the hard ground, and attended its subsequent flowering with such worried care, that it was only when a flower had finally begun to wither on the stem that he would pluck it as an offering to his statues.

George understood this attitude and was properly grateful when once a year on his birthday he received a sacrifice of fresh daisies and marigolds. He was amused by Giulio's niggardliness toward the saints. He himself did not care about them. He, too, was a Catholic, but had become one only so that he and Giulio might be buried together. Two fully paid-for plots, side by side, awaited them under a linden tree in Our Lady of Mercy Cemetery just outside town. Whoever was the first to go, George because he was older, Giulio because he was frailer, the other would join him in due time. Giulio had vague visions of an afterlife. The older man did not. He had had a good life, everything considered, and he would be content to die and be done with when the time came, and have his bones rest by his friend's forever. Sometimes he thought of the linden tree and gave a satisfied nod.

But lately George had noticed something strange about Giulio. His large red ears seemed to have grown less red.

"Giulio," he said one day, "your ears don't seem to be as red as they used to be."

Giulio touched his ear. When he was young he had been sensitive about their largeness. "Nothing wrong with my ears," he said defensively.

"I'm not criticizing you, Giulio. I think it's just strange." And now he realized that some definite change had been taking place in his friend, but he could not put his finger on it. It was as though he were a little smaller. The jacket seemed to hang lower than it had.

Ah, well, he thought, we're both getting old.

A few days later, as Giulio was raking the leaves in the garden, he complained to George of shortness of breath, and there was the faintest touch of blue in his lips.

"Why don't you go to the doctor for a checkup?" George asked as casually as he could.

Giulio shook his head and continued his raking.

That night, as Giulio was turning on the television set, he suddenly stepped back and dropped into a chair with his hand spread across his chest. "Help!" he shouted into the air. "Help!" and when his friend ran to his side, he gasped, "I gotta pain. Here! Here!" And his hand clutched at his heart so hard that the knuckles were white.

The next day George took him to the doctor, and sat by his side through all the tests. Giulio was terrified, but when it was all over and they came out of the doctor's office he seemed restored.

"See," he said, "I'm okay. The doctor he say no worry."

George's face did not reflect Giulio's good spirits. "I know he says not to worry, but . . ."

"He say no worry," Giulio repeated cheerfully.

But from then on Giulio was visited frequently by the paralyzing pains. He would stop what he was doing and crouch over, his eyes darting frenziedly in their sockets. If George was there he would hurry to his friend's side, but at these moments Giulio seemed totally alone even though his hand grasped George's arm. When it was over he would be stripped of his little ways; he would wander slowly around the room or stand for long moments looking at nothing. Patiently George would wait, and eventually the old Giulio returned. Uneasily, fretfully, he would say, "I no understand. Looka me, I never hurt a fly in all my life, and this pain, he come and scare me. It's not right."

"Well," George would venture soothingly, "if you'd just eat fewer starches and stop worrying, these pains would go away. You've got plenty of years ahead of you . . ."

"Plenty years?" Giulio would break in sharply. "I *know*, I *know* I got plenty years ahead. The pain, he no *important*, he just *scare* me."

In an effort to distract him, George broke a lifelong precedent and invited Myrna and Alice Heppleworth, the two aging sisters who lived on the third floor, down to the flat for the evening. He himself did not like women, but Giulio did, in a way that George could not understand. Giulio loved to gossip with them, and afterward delighted in describing their clothes and manners, which he usually found distressing. He was more interested in the Heppleworth sisters than in anyone else in the building, and always pursed his lips when he saw them going out with their rheumy escorts, and could never forget that he had once found a bottle of gin in a dresser drawer ostensibly given over to scarves and stockings.

The Heppleworth sisters came, drank all their wine, and turned the television set up as high as it would go. George grew rigid; Giulio went to bed. The sisters were not asked again.

It seemed to George that Giulio failed daily. His ears were as pale as his face, and this seemed particularly significant to George. He found himself suddenly looking at his friend to check his ears, and each time they looked whiter. He never discussed this with Giulio, because Giulio refused to speak about his fears, as though not daring to give them authority by acknowledging them.

And then one morning Giulio gave up this pretense. As he was getting out of bed he had an attack, and when he recovered this time he let out a piercing wail and began to weep, banging his head from side to side. The rest of the day he spent immobile, wrapped from head to foot in a patchwork quilt.

Toward evening George made him get up and walk in the garden with him. George pointed to the flowers, praising them, and gently turned his friend's face to the shrine. The white plaster faces looked peaceful. Even he, George, felt it, and he realized that for weeks he had been in need of some comfort, something outside himself.

"Look," he said, and that was all, fearing to sound presumptuous, because the statues belonged to Giulio and the Church—he himself understood nothing of them.

Giulio looked without interest, and then, forgetting them, he took George's arm and his eyes swam with tears. "What can I do?" he asked. "What will happen?"

As they walked slowly back to the house he drew his lips back from his big false teeth and whispered, "I'm gonna die."

"No, no, don't think that way," George soothed, but he felt helpless, and resentful that his friend must go through this terror. And now that Giulio had said the words, his terror would grow, just as the pain of a bad tooth grows when you finally acknowledge the decay and are plunged into a constant probing of it with your tongue.

When they came back inside Giulio went straight to bed. George stood in the kitchen and looked at his face in the little mirror that hung on the wall. He feared Giulio would die this very minute in the bedroom as he was removing his carpet slippers, and he wanted with every muscle to run to him. But it would not do to become as hysterical as Giulio, and he stood still. Presently the sound of the bedsprings released a sigh from his throat. The flat was silent. He looked again at his face in the mirror. It was as though he were one person and the reflection another, and he was uneasy and embarrassed, and yet could not look away. He felt deeply aware of himself standing there, staring, and it seemed he was out of place, lost. He whirled around, catching his breath. He had felt entirely alone for the first time in fifty years.

The next day he decided to call for Father Salmon, the young priest from the neighborhood church Giulio attended. Father

Salmon dropped in for friendly chats now and then, and Giulio liked him very much, so much, in fact, that the priest often had to silence him when he got carried away with intimate gossip.

A few days later the priest knocked on the door. He was horse-faced, with thinning hair and rimless glasses, and he was quiet and pleasant.

Giulio was wrapped up in his quilt in the armchair. He did not greet the priest with his usual beam of pleasure; he did not even smile.

"Well, Giulio," the priest said, "how are you feeling? I haven't seen you at church lately."

Giulio said at once, "Father, I'm dying."

"What is the trouble?" the priest asked gently.

"It's my heart," Giulio shot back, his hand scrounging around his shirtfront and fumbling with the buttons until it was clutching his bare chest. He looked as though he were prepared to pull the heart out for inspection. His eyes pleaded with the priest to set it right. The priest sat down next to him.

"What does your doctor say?" he asked.

"Oh, Father," Giulio moaned, "the doctor is a stupid. He never tell me one real thing. In and out and all around, around the bush. He no understand, but *I* understand—this heart, he gonna kill me. You think so, Father? What do you think? You think so?"

"Surely, Giulio," the priest replied," you must accept the doctor's word. If he says there's no reason to fear . . ."

Giulio looked away, black with melancholy.

The priest sat silently for a moment, then began again. "Giulio, death is as natural as birth. Think of your flowers out there in the garden, how they grow from little seeds and then fade and fall—what could be more natural? God has been with you all your life, and He will not forsake you now . . ."

But Giulio, his eyes shutting tighter and tighter as the priest spoke, got up from his chair and crept into the bedroom, dragging his quilt behind him.

Afterward he said to George, "I no wanna see Father Salmon again."

"Father Salmon is trying to help," George told him.

Giulio shook his head, his fingers rubbing the area of his heart.

What a strange person he is, George thought, looking at him closely. All these years he has been immersed in the church, and now, suddenly, the church means nothing to him. He recalled a conversation he had overheard a few days ago as he was fixing a faulty burner in the second floor kitchen. Two of the students were going down the hall, talking. One had commented on Giulio's bad health. The other had replied, "Don't worry, Aunty Nellie could never do anything so profound as to die."

George had bristled, as he always did whenever anyone made fun of his friend—but it was true that Giulio was not profound. He liked pretty things, and the church gave him its rich symbols; he liked intimate conversation, and the church gave him patient Father Salmon; he liked the idea of an afterlife, and the church gave him that, too. He loved the church, but when you came right down to it, he believed only what he could see with his own two eyes, and he could see only his blue lips and wasted face in the mirror. This oddly realistic attitude explained his stinginess toward the saints; they were, after all, only plaster. And yet when Baby had once jumped up on the shrine and relieved himself on St. Francis's foot, Giulio had screamed at the animal until the neighbors hung from the windows.

All these amiable contradictions in Giulio had been known to George for fifty years, and he had always believed that they would sustain his friend through everything. Now the contradictions were gone. All that was left in Giulio was the certainty of death. It made George feel forlorn, on the outside. He sensed that nothing could be set right, that Giulio would live consumed by fear until he died consumed by fear, and the linden tree would not mark two intertwined lives, but forever cast its shadow between two strangers.

They had met for the first time in front of the Minneapolis train station in the first decade of the century. George sat in the driver's seat of a Daimler, in his duster and goggles. His employer had gone inside to meet one Giulio Antonelli, just arrived from Calabria, nephew of the head gardener. When he emerged he had in tow a thin boy of eighteen dressed in a shabby suit and carrying a suitcase that looked like a wicker basket. He wore cherry-colored cigar bands on his fingers, and had a shoot of wilted wild flowers stuck through the buttonhole of his jacket. His eyes were red-rimmed; apparently he had been crying all the way from Calabria. Delicate and terrified, his cigar bands glittering hectically in the sunlight, he crawled into the Daimler and collapsed in a corner.

George had worked as a chauffeur and handyman on his employer's estate for five years, but was originally from an isolated Finnish farming community where God knows what fates had conspired to bring his parents, a bitter, quarreling, aloof, and extremely poor black couple. George became friends with only one thing native to that cold country, the stones that littered the fields. He could not say what attracted him to them, but he felt a great bond with them. When he was ten he built a wall of the stones. It was only a foot high and not very long, and there was nothing in the world for it to guard there in the middle of the empty field, but he knew he had discovered the proper use of the stones, and all his life he had the feeling he was that wall.

In Minneapolis, on the estate, he kept to himself. He liked the Daimler, which he drove with authority, and the appearance of which on the streets caused people to gawk with admiration. He picked up his employer's speech habits, and this, combined with the Finnish accent he had absorbed, gave a peculiar, unplaceable ring to his words, which he relished, because it was his alone.

The Calabrian boy turned out to be a poor gardener, not because he was listless with homesickness, for that soon passed, but because he made favorites of certain flowers and would have nothing to do with the others. The tulips, for instance, he apparently considered stout and silly-looking, and he made disparaging faces at them. He liked the wild flowers that cropped up in odd corners.

George was fascinated by Giulio, although he did not like him. He reminded him of a woman. Women had never respected George's wall, at least a certain type of woman had not—the bold Finnish farm girls, some of the hired women here on the estate. He was well favored, and maybe there was something in his coloring, too, that attracted women, something tawny, reminiscent of the sun, here, where everyone else looked like a peeled banana. In any case, they were always after him. He was not flattered. He felt they were not interested in him as he knew himself, proud and valuable, but in some small part of him that they wanted for their own use, quickly, in a dark corner.

But Giulio, though girlish, had no boldness in him. He would leave the garden and lean against the garage door where George was polishing the Daimler. *"Bella, bella,"* he would murmur, and his face shone with a kind of radiant simplemindedness. There was no calculation in him—sometimes you could see him cocking his head and singing before the wild flowers in the garden. Watching George, the boy spoke foreign words rich in their tones of admiration, and his quick, glittering fingers—he had bought flashy rings with his pay—seemed anxious to catch the sun and make a present of it to the tall, mute figure in the gloom of the garage.

Two months after his arrival Giulio was fired. George, filled with fear for himself, feeling a great chasm opening before him, quit his job, and the two of them, with hardly a word between them, took the train to San Francisco, where Giulio had another uncle. All during the trip George asked himself: "Why am I doing this? Why am I going with him? I don't even like him. He's a silly, ridiculous person; there's something the matter with him."

They got off at the San Francisco depot, and before George was even introduced to the uncle, who stood waiting, he picked up his baggage and, without a word of farewell to Giulio, walked quickly away from him.

First he found odd jobs, and finally he wound up on Rincon Hill with another Daimler. On his half day off each week he would wander around the city, looking at the sights. Whenever he saw a quick, thin figure that reminded him of Giulio his heart would pound, and he would say to himself, "Thank God it's not Giulio, I don't want to see him again." And then he found that what had begun as a casual walk around the city was turning into a passionate weekly search. The day he caught sight of Giulio sadly and ineffectively constructing a pyramid of cabbages in a vegetable market, he had to restrain himself from throwing his arms around him.

Giulio's face had blanched with surprise when he looked up, and then his eyes had filled with a dazzling welcome, and he had extended his hand to his returned friend with a tenderness George never forgot.

They were together from then on. In time they bought a vegetable stand, and as a result of George's frugality and common sense he was able to save in spite of Giulio's extravagances. They worked and invested, and in thirty years they were able to buy, for cash, the old apartment building they now lived in. Life had always been strangely easy for them. They had been incapable of acknowledging affronts, even when they were refused lodgings or openly stared at on the street, and the last twenty years in the security of their own flat had been free from problems, satisfying in all ways.

Now Giulio moaned, "Oh, I gotta pain, I gotta pain."

George would take his hand and say, "I'm here, Giulio, I'm here."

But Giulio would look through him, as though he did not exist.

"Don't we *know* each other?" George finally exploded one day, causing Baby to speed under a table with his ears laid back. "Are we strangers after all these years?"

Giulio closed his eyes, involved with his fear.

George sighed, stroking his friend's hand, thin and waxy as a sliver of soap. "What are you thinking about now, this very minute, Giulio? You must tell me."

"I'm thinking of my dog," Giulio said, after a silence.

"What dog was that?" George asked softly.

"I had him in Nocera."

"And what about him?"

"He died, and my father he dug a hole and put him in." His lips turned down. "I dug him up later, I was lonely for him."

"What a foolish thing to do, my poor Giulio."

"His own mother wouldn'a wanted him. Bones and worms . . ."

"Hush, Giulio."

"Gonna happen to me."

"But your soul . . ."

"What's my soul look like?" Giulio asked quickly.

"Like you, Giulio . . . it's true . . ."

Giulio cast him a look of contempt George would not have thought him capable of.

"The little hole, the bones and worms," Giulio moaned.

"But you've *had* a life!" George suddenly cried with exasperation. "Do you want to live forever?"

"Yes," Giulio said simply.

From then on George felt a fury. In the past all Giulio's little fears had been bearable because he, George, could exorcise them, like a stevedore bearing a small load away. But this final cowardice excluded him. And there was nothing, no one he could turn to. He went halfheartedly to church, but got nothing from it. He began making small overtures to his tenants, but his sociability was stiff with rust. He looked with curiosity at the black people on the street, and thought there were more of them than there used to be. When a young black couple stopped him on a corner one day he listened attentively as they talked of civil rights. He accepted a pamphlet from them and read it thoroughly. But afterward he threw it out. He felt no connection with the problems it presented.

He cursed Giulio as he had cursed him fifty years ago when he had walked away from him at the train depot, and he wished for the oneness with himself that he had known in the empty fields of his youth.

In the daytime he was angrily helpful, like a disapproving orderly, but at night, as they sat in the small living room with Baby flicking his tail back and forth across the blank television screen, he went to Giulio and mutely pleaded with him. Giulio sighed abstractedly; he seemed far away, deep inside himself, listening to every heartbeat, counting every twinge, with a deep frown line between his eyes.

George moved the twin beds together, and Giulio allowed his hand to be held through the night. From then on they slept that way, hand in hand. George slept lightly, waking often. It was almost as if he wished to be awake, to enjoy the only hours of closeness he had with his friend as he held his hand. And also, in the back of his mind was the fear that if he drifted off, Giulio would be released into the arms of death. And so he lay quietly, listening to Giulio's breathing, to the wind in the trees.

Then gradually the bedroom window would turn from black to gray, and the breeze that ruffled the curtain carried in the scent of early morning. Dawn brought him sleep; the rising sun gave him a sense of security. Bad things never happened in the daytime—at least one felt that way. And so his fingers grew lax in Giulio's hand as he trusted his friend to the kindness of the dawning day.

But when he awoke later it would be with a sharp sense of foreboding. Quickly he would turn to look at Giulio, his eyes narrowed against the possible shock. But Giulio would be breathing evenly, his blush lips parted over his gums, his teeth grinning from a water glass on the bureau. Giulio's clothes were neatly laid out, his liver-colored jacket hung over the back of a chair. How lifeless the jacket looked. George would shut his eyes, knowing that the sight of that empty jacket would be unbearable when Giulio was gone. He shook the thought from his head, wondering if life could be more painful than this. Then Giulio's eyes would open, George's face take on a formal nonchalance. And so another night had passed. Their hands parted.

"How do you feel?" George would ask shortly.

Giulio would sigh.

They took their breakfast. The sun shone through the kitchen window with a taunting golden light. George snapped at Giulio. Giulio was unmoved.

One summer morning George persuaded Giulio to sit outside in the backyard. He hoped that watching him work in the garden, Giulio might be persuaded to putter around again. He settled his friend into a chair and picked up the rake, but as the minutes wore on and he moved around the garden in the hot sun, raking the leaves together, Giulio showed no sign of interest. George stopped and put the rake down. Not knowing if he wished to please Giulio or anger him, he suddenly broke off the largest marigold in the garden and held it out.

Giulio shaded his watering eyes with his hand; then his eyes drifted away from the flower like two soap bubbles in the air. George flung the flower to the ground, staring at Giulio, then strode to the shrine and stood there with his hands in fists, blindly determined to do something that would shake his friend open, break him in two if need be. He grabbed the arm of the Virgin Mary and lifted the statue high, and heard Giulio's voice.

"George."

"That's right," George growled, replacing the statue and breathing threateningly through his nostrils. "I would have smashed it to bits!"

"Smash what?" Giulio asked indifferently, and George saw that under the awning of his thin hand his eyes were closed.

"Were your eyes closed?" George thundered. "Didn't you *see* me?"

"You no care that I can't open my eyes—this sun, he hurt them. You *mean*, George, make me sit out here. Too hot. Make me feel sick. I wanna go inside."

"I was going to smash your Virgin Mary!" George cried.

Giulio shrugged. "I wanna go inside."

And then George's shoulders hunched, his face twisted up, and he broke into a storm of tears. Turning his head aside with shame, he made for the back door; then he turned around and hurried back, glancing up at the windows, where he hoped no one stood watching him cry. He put his arm around Giulio and helped him up from his chair, and the two old men haltingly crossed the garden out of the sun.

"Humiliating," George whispered when they were inside, shaking his head and pressing his eyes with a handkerchief. He slowly folded the handkerchief into a square and replaced it in his pocket. He gave a loud sniff and squared his shoulders, and looked with resignation at his distant friend.

Giulio was settling himself into the armchair, plucking the patchwork quilt around him. "Time for pills," he muttered, reaching next to him, and he poured a glass of water from a decanter and took two capsules, smacking his lips mechanically, like a goldfish. Sitting back, he looked around the room in his usual blank, uninterested way. Then a puzzled expression came into his eyes.

"Why you cry then, George?"

George shook his head silently.

"I do something you no like?"

"You never talk. It's as though we're strangers." And he broke off with a sigh. "I've told you all that before—what's the use?"

"I got big worry, George. No time to talk."

"It would be better than to think and think. What do you think about all day?"

Giulio slowly raised his eyebrows, as though gazing down upon a scene. "Bones and worms."

"Giulio, Giulio."

"Big worry, George."

"You'll drive yourself mad that way."

"I no mad at you. Just him." He lay one thin finger on his heart, lightly, as though afraid of rousing it.

"I don't mean angry . . ."

But Giulio was already tired of talking, and was plucking at the quilt again, ill, annoyed, retreating into sleep.

"Giulio, please, you've talked a little. Talk a little more—stay."

With an effort, his eyes sick and distant, Giulio stayed.

But now that he had his attention, George did not know where to begin, what to say. His mind spun; his tongue formed a few tentative words; then, clubbed by an immense fatigue, he sank into a chair with his head in his hands.

"I'm sick man," Giulio explained tonelessly, closing his eyes. After a silence he opened them and looked over at George, painfully, as though from under a crushing weight. "Tonight I hold your hand in bed again, like always. Hold your hand every night, you know that."

"You hold *my* hand?" George asked softly, lifting his head.

"In daytime," Giulio said slowly, his eyes laboriously fixed on George's attentive face, "in daytime only the bones and worms. But in the night . . . in the night, I see other things, too . . ." He was silent for a moment until a twinge had passed, then spoke again. "See you, George. And I hold your hand. Make you feel better . . ." His eyes still fixed on George's face, he gave an apologetic twitch of the lip as his lids closed, and slowly he nodded off to sleep.

Church

G. Winston James

Eerie. That's what it was. Eerie walking into that church after all those years. It was like hearing myself say, "Why do I gotta go to church, Mama?" all over again. It was like hoping that it wasn't first Sunday this Sunday and praying that if I had to be there, at least the Gospel Choir would be singing. I felt, walking out of the bright light of the summer morning and into the calm dim of the chapel, that I was stepping into the past. The past of a family and friends and a Jersey town I'd left long ago for a bigger life that could contain this young boy's grownup dreams.

It was all Black people. Black women mostly. Dressed to the teeth. I'd almost forgotten what it meant to go to a Black Baptist church. This was the place where the well-to-do and the can-hardlies mingled and shook hands with equal pretense. And it was beautiful to see, even when I was a child. Though I never could stand those old women pinching my cheeks and mussing my hair. The church was a place where you could witness the Black family defining itself: the faithful wife, the obedient children, the disappearing older children and the often absent husband. Every Sunday was an experience, though each was painfully similar to the one before it. I'd chosen to leave it all behind, mostly because I thought that too much of anything just couldn't be good for you. And I'd stayed away because I realized I was right.

But here I was coming back. Following behind my mama, as she ushered my niece and nephew to their seats. All I could think as I walked was how the intervening years seem to slip away when you come face-to-face with something you were accustomed to. Some of the backs of the heads were the same today as they were ten years ago. The stained-glass windows were just as stained and no more or less allegorical than they had been when the Pastor had interpreted them for us years before. This was Sunday, all right. So I left my family, as I always did, and sat where I used to sit and talk with my friends, though they weren't here today. Today I would simply go over our old conversations and hope that none of the congregation noticed my lips as they mimed the past.

"Good morning, son!" I felt a hand on my shoulder. "We ain't seen you in such a long time."

"I know," I said. "I've been away, Sister Bailey." She smelled strongly of a perfume applied by hands that had long ago forgotten the meaning of enough.

"Well, you welcome back," she said. She lightly pinched my cheek, then patted my face and looked at me with her head slightly tilted to the side, her white handkerchief dangling from her palm. The wrinkles in her face and her deep-set eyes made me think of gentleness and grandmamas, even though I never knew mine. "Such a handsome boy," she added. "You enjoy the service. OK." She smiled broadly. "The Lord's got a message for us all."

"I will, sister," I said, as I remembered all the sermons I'd slept through when my friends weren't there to keep me company. I thought about Sister Bailey. About how old she was, and how old she had always been. I decided to give the church its due; it had a way of giving some people the what all to keep going on.

It was third Sunday, I believed. I picked up my bulletin and quickly flipped through it just to check if this was the Sunday the Gospel Choir would be singing. Sure enough, it was, and I saw happily that some things just don't change. It wouldn't make a difference what the Reverend had to say, as long as I could feel that music mixing with the marrow of my bones.

Oh yes. Oh yes, I could remember Almetra singing, "One Day at A Time, Sweet Jesus." I recalled how Sunday after Sunday it would move me to tears. Singing. Singing. And I could see Grace, born to a name that defined her and guided her to open her mouth in the service of the Lord. She sang. Yes, she did. "God Is." It was "God Is" every time she stood up in front of the choir. Every time she gospelled, "He promised to lead me, never to leave me. He's never ever come short of His word," dear God, she was joined by the chorus and the Holy Spirit as it worked on even the least holy of the holies in the congregation. Yes, this was Church!

But even the most holy of them were hypocrites. No matter how many times the Lord bent them low, and made them holler, "Save me, Jesus! Save me, my God. I'm a sinner," I could still see the flames of self-righteousness licking at their heels. I always thought that I must have been the only one that God didn't give shoes, because I felt the fire. So I walked slowly—so as not to stoke the flame—away.

I was lost in recollection during the processional hymn, so I sort of missed the ushers walking down the center aisle—the way they fanned out as the Preachers climbed those short steps to the altar. We had all sat down before I came to. And there he was, Reverend Rollins up in the pulpit. He had never been a fiery Preacher—though at times he tried—but he was a well-respected man in the Baptist community and in the city. In his way, he sort of resembled Martin Luther King. It was in the roundness of the face, I think, and the little moustache. I'd always thought that perhaps one person too many had spoken of that resemblance, and that that had left the right Reverend feeling that he had naught to do but to achieve more than he was able to dream. When he entered city politics, and then allowed city politics to enter the church, he lost much of the credibility he had as my Preacher. I found that I would sooner trust him with my vote than with my soul. Unfortunately, I was still too young to vote.

I found myself scanning the congregation and not paying too much attention to what was going on at the front of the chapel. I was trying to locate those schoolmates of mine who had never left our hometown, and who never would for fear that there was something more out there to be taught, let alone learned. In a sense, I was still bitter, because I used to hate them all for fitting in so well. Then I would get angry at myself because I'd learned that hate was a sin. It was many years and many miles before I appreciated the amazing usefulness of the word *dislike*. But now I only watched for them at the edges where our separate worlds slid across one another. And I marvelled at their ability to become an integral part of such an old and oft-forgotten town.

We were more than halfway into the service before I admitted to myself that I really wasn't there. I was doing more wondering and surmising about things than I was doing participating. Even as I came to that realization, I was wondering whether all the "uh-hums" and the "yeses" from the congregation weren't actually these other people inadvertently affirming conclusions they'd come to in their own private wonderings. Speaking responses aloud to questions they had silently been thinking. Then I started asking myself if maybe church wasn't mainly about this: bouncing your own ideas about life, love and religion off the walls and the ceiling of the chapel in hopes that maybe one or two of them will come back and hit you squarely in the face, and maybe make you moan.

When the Deaconess called for the welcome of visitors and announcements, it dawned on me that I had indeed come into church today for a purpose. To be among family. As she stood up in front of the pulpit, it reminded me of the time when the Pastor had stood by my side in that same spot and had asked the church whether they would second and ratify the motion from the Deacon Board to allow me to become a member of the church.

He said, "All in favor say aye." And I bowed my head for fear that he would be answered with a chorus of nays, but he wasn't. I was put on that path that led to baptism in the cool waters in the pool up high at the back of the chapel, above the altar. He'd whispered, "Hold your breath." I did, but not long enough. When he dipped me into the water, I suddenly felt that his strong arms wouldn't be enough to hold me and keep me from drowning in the knee-deep water. I let go and the holy water filled my nostrils and my eyes. He lifted me snorting and gagging to my feet before the congregation. They chanted "Amen" and I breathed. Relieved. Reborn.

"Are there any visitors?" the Deaconess asked. "If so, please stand and state your name."

I rose to my feet. Away so long. Now as a visitor in my own home. "Good morning, Calvary," I said. "My name is Langston Ambrose, and I am a member of this church, though I've been away a long time."

"Well, welcome home," she said. "It's good to see you. All grown-up." She smiled.

"Thank you. I'm very glad to be back."

I was about to take my seat when Reverend Rollins rose to his feet in the pulpit and went to the podium. He dropped his pastorly demeanor for a moment and said, "Langston Ambrose, come here," as he motioned with his arm. Then he said, "Praise the Lord that the lamb never strays far from the fold."

This was actually what I'd expected. To be called to the podium and asked to account for all the years of my absence. I went smiling. I shook his hand, felt his still steely grip, and wondered again what he might be trying to prove with it.

"It's been a long time." He smiled, still holding my right hand and gripping my left arm with his other hand.

"Yes. It has," I replied.

"Now, did you graduate already?" he asked. I sort of chuckled then, hoping that he would remember all the years that had passed, so that I wouldn't have to embarrass him. But he didn't recall, so I said, "Yeah, Pastor Rollins. Ten years ago."

"Ten years!" he exclaimed, grabbing my shoulders as though I were a runaway child that had only just returned home. "Time," he said. "Our young ones are growing up. Praise the Lord." He held me out from him, as if appraising his young son, then asked, "Now, you went to that school in . . ."

"New York," I finished for him. "New York University. I graduated in 1982."

"Amen," came the response from the congregation. For a young black man to go to college, let alone graduate, was a reason for celebration.

"What'd you get your degree in?"

"I earned a bachelors degree in Latin American Studies," I said.

"Well, amen. And what have you been doing?"

"Well, a lot of things, Reverend Rollins," I said, smiling, knowing that he and the rest actually cared. "I worked for a couple of years here and there doing international relief work with people like Save the Children and CARE before setting off to travel on my own. I've, uhmm, even written some books—"

"Praise the Lord," he interrupted. "We've got an author. Heh, heh," he laughed. "What kind of books?"

"Books of poetry, a collection of short stories, and one novel." I felt as if I were divulging childhood secrets. There I was confessing publicly from the pulpit about my writing when no one in my family had ever seen any of my work. I'd been writing and being published for a long time, yet it still seemed like such a private act, the fruit of which I shared with particular people at particular times. My parents never could understand why I never shared my writing with them, but I had my reasons. Aside from some of the obvious ones, ever since I was a child, I never really thought they appreciated the things that I did that were art, especially when my particular art tended to be so revealing.

"When are we gonna see these books?" the Reverend asked. "You're gonna give us some copies to put in the church library, aren't you?"

"Sure," I laughed. "I hadn't thought about it," I lied. The fact of the matter was that I knew that it would be a long time before there was room on Calvary's shelves for my books. But standing up there, I thought just maybe.

"So where have you been that you couldn't come to church every once in a while?"

"Well, I've been a lot of places. I've lived in Venezuela, Brazil, Angola, Mozambique, Switzerland and England." I took a deep breath. "I don't stay put much." A few people in the congregation simultaneously "uhmmed."

"Well, no, you don't," the Reverend answered. "You're a man of the world, huh?" He patted my shoulder.

"I guess."

"So how long are you gonna be with us? You back to stay?"

"Yes. I'll be living here for a while."

"That's good. So we'll see more of you."

"I think so."

"What made you decide to come home, Mr. World Traveler?" Reverend Rollins asked. "You seen it all or you just back for a change?"

"Well, not really, Reverend Rollins," I said. I hesitated a moment. "No, I've got a reason. You see, I'm dying. I wanted to come home to die. Ain't no use in dying someplace where only a few people even know your whole name."

In that moment, I tried to recall if I'd ever heard such silence in that church. Tried to remember if I'd ever stood this close to a man and not heard him breathe. For a while I was trapped in the vacuum I'd created. "I've got a kind of cancer," I breathed. "It's eating me up inside. That's why I came home. And in a way that's sort of why I came to church, Reverend Rollins—hoping that you would call me up here. Because I've got something to say."

"That's all right," Sister Bailey crooned. "Tell us."

I looked to Reverend Rollins and he nodded his assent to let me continue. Strangely, I wondered then about the structure of the Church. I couldn't quite figure out where the hierarchy started after the Trinity. Right then I thought that it just had to be the Deaconesses who sat most close to God. But what would Sister Bailey have said if my cancer had been showing all over my face, instead of on my legs and all tied up in my intestines? She probably wouldn't even have dared to touch me, I bet. But there was no point in thinking about it, asking people to accept more than they can fit into their world.

"I've only lived a short time," I began. "But as you've all heard, I've lived a full life. And I'm not afraid to die."

"The Lord is thy shepherd," someone shouted. "Amen. Amen."

"I don't want to die. Don't get me wrong, Reverend Rollins. I feel like there's still so much to do. So much more to see. But it doesn't do any good to complain, does it?" I tried to laugh. To lighten the mood. "But one thing I've lived with for as long as I can remember has been weighing on me lately. And I've just got to get it out."

"What is it, son?" asked Sister Bailey. She was standing in her place. I thought to myself how beautiful her spirit was and how today she was the church for me.

I had so many things to get off my chest and out into the air that I almost didn't know where to begin. But then I remembered where I was and who all was listening, so I decided to let most of those sleeping dogs lie right where they'd grown so fat over the years. I figured there wouldn't be any use in talking if everyone decided not to listen. So I chose the only thing that was really close to my heart, yet seemingly benign enough that it could tell my story without really touching on the facts of my life.

"It's my love for children, Church," I said. "I've never had any, so I've never had the chance to raise any, but I love them just the same. I see too many of them wasting their lives being angry the wrong way. Being rebellious in a pitiful way."

"I know it," someone said.

"We've got to teach them, Reverend Rollins. We've got to teach them what it means to live. Dying isn't hard. I can tell you that. Hell, I've been doing it for a long time. But, now, living. That's another question."

"Yes. Uh-hum."

"Reverend Rollins, promise me that when you tell the church that they won't know the minute nor the hour, that you let them know that it's not just for God. When you're staring death in the face, you've got to come to terms with yourself and your life before you ever set eyes on God. Tell them that it's all right to go out there and fall and get hurt. God made bones to heal. And tell them that the world is a big place and that there's somewhere out there where they'll be happy, and that they shouldn't stop looking until they find it. Or they shouldn't stop struggling 'til they build it."

I looked over at Pastor Rollins, and was suddenly ashamed for making him "Johnny-on-the-spot" this way. His face said in a thousand ways that this was not what he'd planned for this Sunday's service.

"I'm sorry," I said. "I guess I'm just being selfish, taking up all this time."

"No. You're not," Reverend Rollins said. "You're saying what you feel like saying. Who am I to say that it's not the Lord speaking through you? I prepared a sermon. It's true. But maybe so did He." Then he turned to the congregation. "Can I hear amen?"

"Amen."

"Can I hear a hallelujah?" he asked.

"Hallelujah!" they yelled. "Hallelujah."

"Thank you, Calvary," I said. "I've seen so much death in my life— you just don't know! Children starving, senseless wars, stupid drugs, AIDS. People just dying all over the place. So young. I've stood by too many bedsides. Listened to too many stories about what they would've done and what they wish they could do. There can't be much worse, Reverend Rollins, than to realize when you're just about to die, that you haven't really lived. So tell them to live."

"God grants them the gift of life," Reverend Rollins said. "It's not for any man to tell God's children how to live."

"I'm sure," I said. "But He also gives them other gifts and talents that they can choose to use productively or not. I'm just asking you to tell them to really use this one." I smiled. "It's probably the most important of all."

He looked at me for a moment. Sizing me up, it seemed. Then he said, "Oh course, I'll tell them." I guessed he'd decided that he didn't want a public debate.

"Now, are you really OK?" he asked. "If not, you've got the whole church family to help you.

"Yeah, I'll be OK," I said. "I've just got one regret." As I thought about what I was about to say, a lump formed in my throat. And I stood there in silence, wondering is this was the place to do this.

"What is it, Langston?" the pastor asked.

"I just—" I stopped to fight back a sob.

"That's all right," someone said. "Take your time."

"Well, it's something I guess I never outgrew. I saw my mother cry once. She'd told me to hurry back from playing outside, and I'd said something like 'Ah, Ma' before I went out. When I got back she gathered my brother and one of my sisters and me around her. She lowered her head, then she said softly, 'Do you all hate me too?' Then she cried. One of my sisters had told her she hated her because she corrected her about something. I've felt since that day that maybe if I had said something like 'Of course, Mom. I'll be back,' maybe she wouldn't have had to cry. I promised myself then that I would never hurt my momma again. I never wanted to see her cry again."

I took a few deep breaths as the tears started rolling down my cheeks. "And now I'm gonna die. And my momma's gonna cry." I couldn't hold back the grief. "She's gonna cry. Cry again because of me." I started to sob.

Then I looked up to see her. My momma. Someone was holding her, trying to console her. But she was struggling against them. Fighting to get up, even as my niece and nephew slept on. She cried, "That's my son. That's my baby." And she bolted from her pew and carried all her sixty years running to the front of the chapel. The whole way she was shaking and screaming, "That's my son! Oh, my God, that's my baby. Can't no AIDS just take my baby! Lawd Jesus, I love him too much!"

Before she reached me, the congregation lit up with the Holy Spirit. Two women and some man jumped up from their seats and fell in the aisles, convulsing. They were just shaking and kicking. Some people were screaming, "Praise God!" And others were just wailing.

I heard Sister Bailey try to start up a chorus of "Swing Low Sweet Chariot," but her "coming forth to carry me home" was drowned out by all the hollering. Then as my mamma grabbed me up in her arms and pulled me against her breasts, I got lost in my childhood. I think I dreamed that a sweet soprano voice cut through the hysteria—

floating from the back of the chapel, from in front of the doors. The voice sang, "One day at a time, sweet Jesus. That's all I'm asking of you." I whispered, "Almetra" because I thought I saw her. She'd just walked into the chapel. In my dream, her voice seemed to attract the Holy Spirit like a magnet. It lifted the holiness from the congregation and it travelled on her every note. Then the Gospel Choir rose up behind me to accompany her.

When my sobs woke me from my dream, the choir was up. They were singing the final verses of "Hush, Somebody's Calling My Name." The music gave the congregation some focus again. As we all recovered and softly sobbed together, Reverend Rollins asked that we stand and pray. And we did. Then he asked the choir to render a selection.

As the choir prepared, my mother and I started for our seats. I felt ashamed. Not because I'd cried in front of a whole bunch of people, but because my momma had loved me enough to declare my affliction when I had been too frightened to do it. While we walked, I looked around at the chapel, and thought to myself, "This is Church." I felt my momma's arm around my waist, and knew, "This is family." I cried my tears, and witnessed, "This is love."

Then I turned around and looked at the altar. I wondered, teary-eyed, those three truths notwithstanding, whether there actually was a God. That's when I saw Grace stepping out from her place in the choir. I thought "God Is." But when she began, she was singing something different. It was "Better Than Blessed." She sang and I thought, "Well, goddamn, what a Black woman can do to a song!"

She sang, "I've got God, the Father above me. And I've got Jesus Christ, His son, walking beside me. I've got the Holy Spirit within me. All of God's angels, all around me. And I am blessed. Better than blessed. Thank you, Lord."

I thought then that she was singing about more than God. Walking with my momma, and crying with my niece and nephew, I knew that she was singing about family. She was singing about the Church family. The Black family. Even in its weakness, it was stronger than all tribulation.

Grace was singing, "I used to complain that I had no shoes, then I saw a man who had no feet to use. And I am blessed. Better than blessed. Thank you, Lord."

I realized that that's just what I was talking about. Realizing how slight most of our limitations really are. Then I found myself wishing that I could believe in more than just gospel music. I wanted to believe in God because of how good that burning in my heart felt at that moment. So I thought about the verses Grace used to sing. I remembered "God is the joy and the strength of my life." And I won-

dered if maybe God wasn't whatever made you truly happy in life.
Then I looked up at the ceiling of the chapel. I threw my question to
the beams. As Grace was singing, "I am blessed" one more time, my
question bounced off the ceiling, fell down and slapped me to the
floor. And I cried, "I'm gay! Praise God! Hallelujah!"

    And I heard the congregation say, "Amen!"

Is This the Reward
of A Catholic Girlhood?*

Margaret Cruikshank

My coming out story is unexciting. If I were to fictionalize it, I would make it sexier and funnier, and assign myself a younger age than 26 and a less staid personality. The other woman, Mary, could keep her real age of 23; that's a good age for coming out.

I met her a few months before her 23rd birthday in a literary criticism class at the midwestern Jesuit school where we were both graduate students who had National Defense Education Act grants to get Ph.D.'s. Our educations contributed nothing to the national defense, of course; and it was certainly not the intention of the male bureaucrats at H.E.W. to bring young lesbians out of the provinces and into big cities, where they could meet, fall in love, and oppose the Vietnam war together. Left in the small towns where we grew up and dependent only on private enterprise, Mary and I might never have felt free enough to love each other, or any other woman. From my failures to care deeply about a man, I would have concluded that I was not a caring person or someone who belonged in an intimate relationship.

That at least was my suspicion after an experience with a man in 1965, several months before I met Mary and got her to stop sitting in the front row of lit. crit. class like a pious Catholic schoolgirl and sit with sloppy indifference next to me in the last row. A male friend from my hometown, whom I had met at the Graduate Record Exam (I hope young lesbians are finding each other these days at the GRE), called

---

*From Kate Millet's *Sita*.

to announce that he had that day passed his doctoral comprehensives and could now attend to other business—would I marry him? Confused as I was about love, men, and my future, I saw at once that there was something ludicrous about putting emotional life second to intellectual life. But what to say? I didn't love him, but I knew women were supposed to want marriage. Why didn't I? Awkwardness was the main emotion I felt. As potential mates, Frank and I had lumbered along in a way that reminded me of the Herbert Spencer-George Eliot romance; and, ironically, his dissertation was to be on Spencer, mine on Eliot. I said on the phone that I would send my answer by mail. I remember going to the library to do the letter, probably because I felt safe in libraries and no doubt also because the letter would be like an assignment. With a directness and honesty I hardly ever attained in those days, I told Frank that I couldn't marry him because I was not physically attracted to him. Thinking of the letter today I feel frustrated because, although I had correctly diagnosed the problem with that relationship, I was blind to the implications of the letter, which seem so obvious now: 1) no man would be sexually attractive to me, except in a casual/temporary way; and 2) I was attracted to women.

Not understanding these crucial facts about myself in 1965, I had no expectation at all, when I began to spend time with Mary, that I could love her. How could I have been so ignorant of this possibility, I wonder now, when two years before the call from Frank, one of my roommates had fallen in love with me. I obviously couldn't connect one experience with a woman to another. I was attracted to Kathi, the roommate, an Irish Catholic from Iowa with a background much like mine. I remember walking by myself one day and getting a thunderous message from my brain *she loves me* which made me stop suddenly as I was crossing the street. But my attention was focused so much on her dilemma (poor Kathi—what a rotten thing to happen to her) that I never asked myself what my response might be or thought in any general way about women loving women. Soon I had persuaded myself that I was crazed from studying too much—Kathi didn't love me. But one night she came to my room late at night, sat on my floor, and looking very embarrassed she said that Marge, the third woman in our apartment, had been making fun of her for loving me. She hoped I would not be angry with her. I wasn't, but I couldn't have been very sensitive, either. All I remember is that our conversation was short and awkward. In the days that followed, although I did not feel love for Kathi, I did want some physical contact with her, but I was too inhibited to touch her. One night we got a little drunk together and sat next to each other on the living room couch with our arms around each other. Marge, who was with us but sober, said: "Goddamned lesbians!" I remember thinking, smugly,

No, absurd, if we were goddamned lesbians we would have to be doing this in some secret place; we couldn't be hugging right out here in the living room in the presence of another person. This spectacularly false assumption was one I suppose I had to accept: to question it would have led me to uncomfortable thoughts about the significance of all my attachments to women.

The early weeks of close friendship with Mary gave me no clues about what was to follow. We tossed a football around in the park, hung upside down from the jungle gym, and studied hard. After our long talks late at night, I'd walk her back to her apartment and then she'd walk me back to mine. That pattern should have been a clue. The first Superbowl was also her birthday. We watched together in high spirits and then our friends came for a surprise party. I had never liked a woman well enough to plan a party for her, and no one had ever given a party for Mary. Those clues were lost on us, too. Although she asked me to move in with her when her roommate left, we were so far from knowing what was happening between us that we invited a third woman to share the small apartment with us.

Within a month after the move, I realized I cared for Mary very much, but had no idea that my feelings were the appropriate ones for the beginning of a love relationship. I took my two new roommates to a Clancy Brothers' concert on St. Patrick's Day and during the concert I held Mary's hand in the dark. I had never had that experience before. The raucous Clancys must have loosened me up. Later that evening as Mary and I were taking off our coats in our big walk-in closet, we stood for a long time with our arms around each other. I felt scared and excited at the same time. Hugging a woman through her winter coat is not very satisfying, I now realize, but for someone like me who had hardly ever been able to touch another woman (or a man or a child), this closet cuddling was a great step forward. One night not long after St. Pat's I was sick in bed. Mary sat for a long time on the edge of the bed and then kissed me on the neck (I think she was aiming for my cheek) and ran out of my bedroom. I was overwhelmed. This was even more exciting than holding her hand or feeling her coat. I wanted to be kissed again but was too shy to say so or to kiss her. But one night when she was reading I sat on the floor at her feet and leaned against the chair she was sitting in. She lifted me into the chair with her and we kissed and laughed for about four hours. That we both liked prolonged physical contact was a great discovery. We must have known vaguely that we were doing a forbidden thing, but whatever guilt we bore did not keep us from doing what felt good. We had both had such repulsively successful careers as Catholic schoolgirls and devout young women that we ought to have been guilt-ridden, but somehow we escaped the tortures of a bad conscience. In all their vivid descriptions of the sinful, secular, atheistical world into which they were reluctantly sending us, those of us not good enough to want to imitate them and become nuns, our teachers never mentioned that feeling sexual attraction for another woman was an abomination. At Mary's college, the "mulier fortis" was much lauded (the valiant woman), and at my school, her counterpart was the "dynamic Christian woman." But we were never told that a mulier fortis must refrain from passionately kissing a dynamic Christian woman. Maybe that's why the sin button didn't flash red the night I sat in Mary's lap kissing her and knowing that I loved her.

The rest came only gradually. Once when we were doing our Beowulf lesson together, while sitting on the floor not too close to each other, we began to kiss and somehow got wound around each other on the couch, neither of us sure what to do with our bodies. Mary knew enough the next time to touch me with her hand, and I was amazed by the pleasure she could give me. But I was too frightened and self-conscious to touch her until two weeks later when she came home late one night and demanded that pleasure for herself. I was too surprised to refuse (she was not at all a demanding person). After that, our love-making was less inhibited, although often furtive, because of the third woman in our one-bedroom apartment. Luckily she taught an early morning class. As soon as she walked out the door, I would bounce on her bed on my way into Mary's bed. Those were exuberant mornings, and it pleases me to recall that we got the highest grades on the Beowulf exam, too.

We lived together very happily for three years, the last two in our own apartment. During summer vacations we had wonderful times traveling in Mary's Volkswagon. We saw the iron mines in northern Minnesota and walked around on Isle Royale, and watched the Little League world series in Pennsylvania. We got thrown out of a pet cemetery for laughing at the inscriptions on the tombstones, and another time we were stranded in a small town in Scotland and had to sleep in the local jail.

During the school terms we helped each other with teaching (we had the same classes) and with studying. I might not have been able to write a dissertation without Mary's constant reassurances and good suggestions. And for six terrible weeks in 1969 when I was fighting with my department over my dissertation, she plotted my strategy with great cunning, helped me figure out the moves against me, and once when I cracked and decided to go right to the chairman's office and curse him, she literally barred the door and kept me home. She even stood at my side for 2-1/2 hours while I xeroxed the required number of copies of my dissertation for the slippery misogynists who were to sit in judgment of it.

Those days were idyllic. Neither of us pretended to be looking for men to fulfill us. And yet we did not see ourselves as lesbians—the word had vile connotations—as women who had made a conscious choice of a woman to love. I told myself that the person I loved happened to be a woman, and she must have said the same thing to herself. In any case, we had no conversations about lesbians or lesbianism. Perhaps in our happy state we felt no need to reflect on our coming together. As survivors of unhappy families, we must have been relieved and constantly delighted to find ourselves always happy. It would have seemed unnatural, surely, to live together for three years and never mention that we were English teachers or that we loved literature. But a far more basic fact about ourselves (or at least about me), emotional and sexual identity, went unmentioned.

I wish I could end this story on a good lesbian feminist note—perhaps this can't be a *real* coming out story without a good lesbian feminist conclusion. Such as: Peg and Mary discover that they are lesbians, rejoice in the discovery, drive off into the setting sun in the little blue VW, certain to grow more deeply attached to each other, thanks to their raised consciousnesses, and to continue their relationship many years. Before the discovery and the rejoicing, unfortunately, we separated, without pain, partly because we could not get jobs in the same town and partly because we were ready for a change. But I'm afraid that we separated not really knowing that a female couple could be together indefinitely, or even that we had in fact been a couple. We experienced something for which we had no room in our imaginations—an alternative to marriage, a way of living ideally suited to us.

Between

Elizabeth Graver

For Juda

It is hard to tell among so many bodies—and some of them in skirts—but I think I am the only woman in the bar. Dancing there, close up to the go-go boys on their boxes, the men gleaming like seals, eyes only for each other. It used to be I was a stiff, small dancer, one leg forward, one leg back— jerk, jerk, a tight nod of the head, a bird bobbing for seed. How do I know? I could see my limbs lit red with awkwardness. Now I do not see myself, too small among the bodies, and mine the wrong kind.

I dance myself outside myself. No one looks.

Why does Paolo bring me to the bar? I'm not sure. Sometimes I think it is because he loves me. Other times I think it is because I am a fashion accessory, like the dashshunds or Chihuahuas the other men parade down Commercial Street. I do, in some ways, fit the part, small and lean, almost like a boy, now that we have cut my hair. "Time for a new you," said Paolo this morning on the beach, snip snip on each long strand, and then the ceremonial flinging of my locks into the sea. Sheared I was, cropped close. Paolo held my tiny, light skull between his hands and told me where my hair would go: wrapped around the *Titanic*, swallowed by sharks, part of the great blue.

"I'm ugly now," I said, though I could not see myself on the beach. "No one will ever want me."

"You're adorable, you could be the cutest little dyke."

I shook my weightless head.

"OK, then, just enough boy in you to excite the boys."

"You think?"

He snipped at stray hairs on my neck. "Of course. I could almost have a conversion experience over you."

"Right."

"No, I mean it, with angels and the works. A hundred naked cherubs."

I tried to smile. "By the time you get through with them, I'll be past menopause."

Paolo brushed off my neck with his towel, backed up and surveyed his work. "Exquisite," he said, turning me around. "I get dinner for this. Let's go home."

When we got back, I saw in the mirror how smooth I had become, my neck longer, my eyes somehow darker than before. And in the shower I was a boy, almost, my hands smoothing away the lines of breast, the hip curves. In the soap dish was a nub of lemon soap, a present Tim had given me before he left. What would he think now, I wondered. Would he want me more, like this, or less?

Paolo and I are in many ways the perfect couple. In the winter, when the town is almost empty, we play at being married, at "Honey, you forgot the coupons," or "No more heavy cream, you need to watch your cholesterol." The locals love us, for we are gentle and playful with each other and look a pair, both of us dark and smallish. "A deal for you," they'll say at a garage sale, "since you're just starting out." It has been five years now since we met through a roommate ad in the paper, and still we cook and clean together, to Bonnie Raitt played loud. At eleven-thirty on nights when both of us are home, we watch "Love Connection" and lament the cruelty of dating, and over the long, bitter winters, we read aloud to each other, mostly from children's books. This winter Tim took turns reading too, from *Alice in Wonderland*. One night tucked between them on the couch, the three of us wrapped in a quilt, I realized that for the first time since I was a tiny child, I knew what the term "well-being" meant.

Sometimes I think Paolo brings me dancing for protection; it has been over a year since he has had a lover, though he is pretty as can be, and even at thirty-eight he is taken for a boy. We have our signals all worked out—the head scratch, the biting of the lip, the yawn. And then, on the way home, his regrets—how this one was all over him, how that one asked him for a walk on the beach. "Why not?" I coax. He has a thousand answers: too old, too young, too queeny, not smart enough, too trendy, never leaving, leaving the next day. All around us men are dying. "It's OK," I tell him, "if you're careful." But under my words I am afraid for him, and even further down, some-place fierce and selfish in my gut, I want him just for me.

We live two lives here. Summers we dance till late at night, then stop at Spiritus for an ice-cream shake. The nursery school where I teach closes for two months, and I spend my days sleeping, reading or making jam. Summer is Paolo's time, men everywhere, and I cook dinner for his friends, lie with them on the jetty, take boat rides with them when Paolo waits tables. They are fond of me; "fond" is the right word, not like Paolo, who loves me. These are men from the city—doctors, lawyers, and models who come down for the weekend. When I sun on the end of their sailboats, they spray water on me and heap careless compliments on my breasts.

Winter is my time. There are fewer men around, but they *see* me as I walk down the street, and I live the life of a fishing village girl, a date here, a date there, and then, when something goes a little bit right, a nice tousled, salty man in my bed, and then—careful, careful, each step could be the last—maybe another night and maybe I find out what he likes to read and who he voted for, and Paolo says, "This one sounds good" or "A man who hates his mother is bad news."

Tim he approved of from the start. "Notice his chest," said Paolo, "when he comes out of the shower and the hair curls in those little blond tendrils. Plus he's totally in love with you; he picked up your fingernail clippings and *played* with them. He probably saved them to light a candle to."

And Tim, like me, a teacher, tall and bulky and a man, but playful when he rolled down hills with his second graders and did the floppy scarecrow dance in their production of *The Wizard of Oz*.

In the beginning it was fine between the three of us—almost, for a while, perfect. Sometimes I would go to Tim's, a few streets away, and eat dinner with him and his two roommates. More often he came to our place, and somehow the three of us fit into the narrow galley kitchen, where we cooked fish stews and chowders, apple and cheese omelettes. When I told my friend Emily how we were together, she said it sounded great, the best way not to scare Tim off.

"Break him in gradually," she said, and I pictured Tim tossing his hair like a mane, stomping his hoof. "You'll be moving in together before he realizes what's happened."

But the thing was, three was a number that pleased me. I loved being in the middle, the frosting inside the cookie, the door hinge, the go-between. I loved feeling *surrounded*, like a kid between her parents: one, two, and—swing—aloft over the curb. I loved the safety of our threesome, but also the shiver: between Tim and Paolo, maybe even between Paolo and me—nothing strong enough to act upon, but enough to put a gentle buzz of static in the air. With each of my two men I discussed the other, late at night in bed with Tim— "He thinks you're beautiful"—or at dinner alone with Paolo—"The longest time he's been with anyone in a year." And for a time, they liked it too, Paolo happy to have a man dripping in his shower, Tim pleased, I think, to be admired by the both of us, titillated, almost, to be safely with me and yet tousle Paolo's hair goodnight before we went to bed.

And in bed—this perhaps the strangest part—the way we played was not a play of two, but three, although Paolo never came inside the room. It began one night when I made my voice gravelly low and told Tim I liked his chest hair. I was joking, but he kept coming back to it: "My long-haired hippie boy," he called me. "My little sailor." Maybe, I told him, you want to sleep with men, with Paolo, but he said no, he was only fooling around, it was me he wanted. Yet I, too, could feel Paolo's presence through the wall, lying there sad, stiff, and alone, trying not to hear our sounds. And if it hadn't been a move into the outrageous (for Paolo and I were, in our way, the most domestic, conventional of people, with our canisters which said Sugar, Flour, Tea, correctly filled), I would have opened the door and asked him in, if he would come. Then Tim could be in the middle, the boy we both desired. It was too terrible, a house buzzing with sex and loneliness at the same time.

It was my mother who began to worry first.

"You'll never get really involved in a romantic relationship," she said, "as long as you live with Paolo."

"What are you talking about?" I said. "I have a boyfriend. Paolo doesn't keep me on a leash."

"I know you have a boyfriend—this boyfriend, that boyfriend. What about marriage? Children? You're already thirty and if I've understood you right, you want children and a full life."

What she meant was, you must work hard to guarantee yourself a better life than your mother's. Already she was unhappy about the fact that I had done so well in college and was now working for low wages in a nursery school. "It's just for now," I told her—and myself—at first, but the truth was I loved reading aloud to a ring of sleepy four-year-olds, watching them plunge their fists into tubs of finger paint, seeing how they came into my classroom as stunned toddlers and left as resolute children. Whole families had passed through my classroom in the seven years I had been there.

A good job was one way to a better life in my mother's eyes; the other was a man. First, she thought, I had to transform my boyfriend into a husband. Then (this the trickier part), I had to make sure he did not die on me the way her husband, the way my father did—leaving her alone with me, a girl of six who got too many nosebleeds and would not be good company for many years.

I know, I know, I wanted to say to her. Like you, I feel the world as a fragile, teetering place, your fears all tangled through my veins. But don't you think there are other ways around this? My mother raised orchids, coaxed miracles from plants which have no roots and live in pots filled with stones. Last year she drove from Utica, New York, to Oxford, Mississippi, with her friends Miriam and Charlotte and slept under the open sky. What, I wanted to ask her, is a full life?

"I've got plenty of time," I told her instead. I did not tell her how, when I pictured my children, they sometimes had black hair and brown eyes, slender ankles, Paolo's clever hands. Paolo and I had discussed it, even, but always as an if—if I wasn't with someone when I reached the eleventh hour on my ticking clock.

Then it was Tim who began to worry.

"Listen," he said after we had been together for eight months and both had a spring vacation coming up. "What do you think about spending a week away somewhere, just us?"

"Sure," I said, "I'd like that." But when we began to plan a trip to northern Vermont, I couldn't bear the thought of Paolo home by himself.

"He'll be fine," said Tim. "He's a grown man. He lived for years without you."

No, I thought, no, you don't know him, how fragile he is under all his joking. But as we drove to a cabin in the mountains, I began to wonder who, really, I was protecting. How would we cook, just the two of us? How would we sit at dinner, across from each other or side by side? And when we went to bed, what would we do without that feeling of closing the door away from someone else, of being alone or not?

In fact I did sleep, did cook and eat and make love and feel my life begin to take a slightly new shape, like a bubble blown from a child's wand that gets caught by a sideways wind. From the cabin you could see a birch grove on one side, a brook out in front, not another house in sight.

"Someday," said Tim one morning as we walked through the woods, "I'm going to build a place like this, out here somewhere. All by hand—you can help if you want."

It was a voice he used to talk about things he planned to do, which usually involved either wandering the earth or building things. Soon after we'd met, he had pulled out a wooden crate filled with brochures and articles on World Teach, mountain gardens, homesteading, and trekking. At the time I had been half-charmed by his enthusiasm and half-worried by the fact that the one constant theme in the box seemed to be *not here, not you*. Lately he had begun to include me a little more, but his plans still made me nervous for their

far-flungness. I pictured the two of us in a country where we were
the only ones to speak each other's language, or perched on a moun-
taintop where the only light for miles was our own.

"It can't be too much fun out here in winter," I said.

He shrugged. "You just stock up on wood and get a car with four-
wheel drive. It'd be great."

"You wouldn't miss the sea?"

"The Cape is becoming a zoo," he said. "Look at all these mountains. It's like no one even knows they're here."

"I'd go crazy."

"How do you know?"

How did I know? Maybe it would be peaceful; perhaps I would
learn to live more comfortably under the vast arch of sky. But I
doubted it. "I just know."

Each night I called Paolo. Each night he told me he missed me
and filled me in on pieces of our life: the dryer had broken, a mouse
had gotten into the pantry, my mother had called and sounded
thrilled to learn I was away with Tim. The first few times I dialed
the phone, I don't think I even noticed that Tim left the room, or sat
humming tunelessly, picking at the lint on his sweater. On the third
day when I hung up, though, he let out a sigh so loud I could not
miss it.

"What?" I asked from the couch.

"How's your husband?" Tim was crouched by the fireplace peeling
the bark off a log.

"What?"

"Your husband. Is he managing all alone in that great big house?
Has he found out about us?"

"Come here," I said, but he only hunched closer to the log. I went
over to him, leaned up against him, and kissed the back of his neck.

"Cut it out," he said, shaking me off. "I'm trying to talk to you."

"Jesus." I went back to the couch. "Look, I don't know what you're
reacting to so strongly. I never thought you seemed jealous and anyway there's no need to be—"

"I'm not jealous," Tim said.

"Then what?"

"I'm not jealous, I just—you don't worry about me being lonely, you
don't call me up to talk about the dryer—"

"We don't share a dryer, do you want to share a dryer?"

"Don't be an idiot."

"I'm sorry," I said. "If I don't worry about you being lonely it's because you have me."

But in my stomach I could feel fear beginning to stretch and un-
ravel. He would leave me, said a voice in there; I had known it all

along, from the day I saw his box of travel plans. And then another voice: But who can blame him, he's right, he should be jealous. You don't want to move to a far-off place where nobody breathes on the other side of the wall and the only way to Paolo is through a stretch of telephone wire.

"You do know," said Tim, "that he'd ditch you in a second if he found the right person."

In his voice I heard a hardness I had never heard before.

"You don't even know him," I said.

"Almost a year and I don't even know him? I've done everything but fuck the guy."

"In your dreams."

In my own voice I heard that same hardness. This, I wanted to say, this is what I'm afraid of—how easily, with these men I made love with, I came to be a snarling animal, claws flexed, baring all my teeth. This was nothing, compared to where we might end up. I had been there before—had made the long, cruel lists detailing another person's faults; kept secret count of gifts received, money spent; smashed pottery like a character in a TV movie.

With Paolo, too, I fought sometimes, but it wasn't like this, maybe because we couldn't *break up* (in my mind I saw a stick being cracked in two). I didn't know the smell of Paolo's hair, the feel of his spine, the slippery smooth wall of the inside of his mouth. With Tim—with every man I had ever slept with—I came so close to letting myself be turned inside out. Now I could feel an emptiness in my sternum, my pelvis, everywhere bones came together and formed a space.

"Come here, please?" I said again, and this time he did, though he sat turned away from me, and I wrapped myself around his back and spoke close to his ear.

"It's partly," I tried to explain, "it's maybe really screwed up, but it's partly because I *want* us to work out that I need to have Paolo. Otherwise I get too scared, like I'm putting too much weight on a bearing wall or something—"

Tim squirmed. "I'm glad you have such faith in us."

"It's not us, it's the whole thing, expecting that much of one person, it doesn't work, it shouldn't have to work. I mean, look around. But also—" I pictured Paolo stirring soup, tying the tomato plants to stakes with strips of his old shirts, curled before the TV. "Also I do love him, not like I love you, but he's my best friend. I thought you really liked him too."

"Of course I like him. Do I want to marry him? I'm not sure."

I pushed the words out of my mouth. "And me?"

He turned around and looked at me. "I'm not sure. Really I have no idea, but it seems pretty hard to figure out anything the way things are. I want—" He trailed off.

"What?"

"I want to travel again, I told you that before, and maybe end up someplace like this, or someplace else, where there's room to think. The Cape is hardly the most amazing place on earth, you know."

"I like to travel," I said, but my words came out weak. The truth was I loved to sit at home and watch how the dunes shifted, the shoreline changed shape, the summer people came and went and still I stayed.

"Maybe the real problem is you want to marry your roommate," said Tim.

"Stop."

"I don't think you'd leave him."

"It's not him, I'm settled, I have a whole life there."

"What if I decide to go to India?"

"I don't know." I pictured him with a walking stick, trekking somewhere. A place where there's room to think, he had said, as if thinking couldn't happen in a room. "Would you invite me?"

"Maybe. But not Paolo."

"Paolo hates to travel. He always get sick." I turned away from Tim; outside the birches were shining in the dark. "Do you think we'll be OK?"

"I guess we should just go slowly," he said, "and wait and see."

I nodded, but as we lay in bed that night I could feel how guarded we had both become. It always happened after eight or nine months, the same time it took to make a baby. Suddenly it was almost a year you'd been together; everything tightened, crystallized. Before I started living with Paolo, I was the one who kept dragging my reluctant boyfriends to look at apartments. My mother, who now told me to want more, used to caution me: "Push too hard, Annie, and they'll run away."

I remembered the Pushmi-Pullyu beast from the Dr. Dolittle story Paolo and I had read aloud two winters before. If I was the one pushing, probably Tim would pull away. And if neither of us pushed or pulled? I wanted to see something lovely, cantering across the sand, but instead I saw a waterlogged, dead beast sinking down into the waves.

What happened instead was the world crashed in, Tim's father in Denver diagnosed with liver cancer. Tim got a month's leave from work and I drove him to the airport and gave him a long, tight hug good-bye.

"I don't know how to handle this," he said just before he got onto the plane. "I honestly have no idea."

"I know. But you will, you'll be OK, I know you will. Call me when you get there, do you promise?"

He nodded. "Listen—"

"What?"

"I don't know. If, I mean if I really flip out or something, do you think you might come out there, I'd help you pay for it—"

My mother crouched in the garden sobbing at night because she thought I could not hear her from my bedroom, but I could hear her, could see her bent shape as I knelt on my bed and bit into the chalky paint of the windowsill. The day of the funeral, she told me later, I brought out crackers into the living room where the aunts, the uncles, my mother sat; I passed around oyster crackers and patted backs, said don't worry, it'll be OK.

"Of course, just let me know," I said to Tim, but I was not thinking the right things. At least you'll know who he was, I was thinking. At least you'll have someone to remember.

After he got to Denver we talked on the phone every few days. "I miss you," I told him, and I did miss him, but I told him so extra, as if the word itself could save a space for us on his return. He did not ask me to come out there, and I did not offer. Sometimes when we were finished, he asked to speak to Paolo. Once, hearing in my silence some kind of hesitation, he said, "What? He's my friend, I can't talk to my friend?"

"Of course," I said and tried not to listen in or ask Paolo for a report after he hung up.

When I got the letter from Tim it was already July, and I thought, seeing my name on the envelope in his tiny, neat print, that it would tell me his father had died. The letter was short: "Annie, I've realized you're not someone I feel like I can depend on in times like this and so I think we should call things off. I'm too wiped out to explain any better. I'm sorry. Love, Tim."

"What does he mean?" I said to Paolo. "Did he want me to come out there? I said I would—he didn't bring it up again. I should have just gone. He's right, he can't depend on me."

I started crying, the slack sobs of a child.

"He's just going through a hellish time," said Paolo. "He'll be back, he just needs time to figure out his own stuff. Shhh—Stop." He sat me down on the porch steps, rubbed my back. "Don't cry, goose, it's OK. Come inside, we'll cook. Don't cry. The neighbors will think we're getting a divorce."

That night I called Tim. His voice sounded far away and blurry, the voice of my mother when I was six and she came back from the hospital at night, paid the baby-sitter, looked down at me from a great distance, and said, "Hi, Annie, how was school?"

"Hey," said Tim. "How's everything going out there?"

"All right. I mean, not so great, really. I got your letter."

"Yeah—"

"I said I'd come out," I blurted. "I want you to be able to depend on me."

"In the airport, you mean, before I left."

"Yes."

There was a long silence.

"Please talk to me," I said.

"You might have offered again, you could—"

"I will come out. I am offering. I'm sorry, I was waiting for you to ask. I'll come there as soon as you want."

"Look," he said. "It's not just this. I think it would have ended sooner or later anyway, I've thought that for a while."

"Since when?"

"I don't know. Our trip, maybe. Before that, even. I should have talked to you more about it, I just—it just seemed like it had to end."

"Why?"

"I don't know," he said. "A lot of things. I'm not even sure when I'll be back there, or for how long. Look, the hospital might call, I can't tie up the phone. Someday we'll talk about this, I just can't right now. I've really got to go."

"I'm sorry," I said. "You have enough to deal with. Will you call me, if you need someone to talk to?"

"OK," said Tim. But we both knew he would not.

August came. Each morning I woke thinking Alone. Thinking it, but not the way I would have before I met Paolo. The thought felt more like a habit now, a reflex I didn't quite believe. I missed Tim, his hands on my back, his voice in my ear, but I did not feel like a stick snapped in two. Maybe my mother was right. Maybe I was cushioning myself too much; perhaps I needed to live on the thin, sharp edge of desperation in order to find and keep a man. I wrote letters to Tim trying to mend things, read them to Paolo, tore them up. I could not write about lovers' spats to a man whose father was dying.

This morning Paolo said it was time to cut my hair.

"Shorter," I told him when the first clump fell. "Keep going, still shorter."

Paolo snipped and looked and snipped. After dinner he came into my room and pulled out a purple silk shirt from my closet.

"This," he said and grabbed some earrings from my dresser. "And these. And your black jeans."

"No." I burrowed down in my bed.

"Get up," he said. "Get dressed."

Now they make a circle around me, the only woman in the place; they form a ring and clap and have me dance there in the middle. They are not watching so much as protecting me—I can feel it—the way the male whales form a ring around the nursing mothers and circle while they feed their calves. I do not know how they can tell I need that just now. These are men who have been forced to grow good at sensing rawness, at dancing around loss, or maybe Paolo told them about Tim. I know I must look beautiful, that I have found some sort of grace, and for a moment I pretend that with my short hair I am a boy, and they all want me, each and every one of them. But when I start to feel desire in that crowd, my limps grow stiff and unfriendly, and a few seconds later the circle breaks apart.

When I look for Paolo to go home, I cannot find him.

"Have you seen Paolo?" I ask first this one, then that one, leaning up to their ears, close to their sweat. Finally I start home alone, make my way through the crowds on Commercial Street and then turn down our side street where everything, all at once, is from a different world: the rose hips, shingles, crushed shells, the rusty bikes and creaking gates, not even an echo of music, just the sound of sea and wind.

"Paolo, Paolo?" I sing inside my head, trying to pronounce it the way his mother, born in Italy, does, his mother who wants him to marry so badly that she brought a ring for me when she visited last fall.

"No, no," I tried to explain one morning when I got up early and found her sitting on the porch. "It's not like that. We're just good friends."

"He's a good boy," she said. "I don't care what anyone says."

I gave her back the ring and she tried to slip it onto her own finger, above her wedding ring, but it would not fit.

"Just take it," she said. "Maybe he'll change his mind."

I told her I couldn't, I had a boyfriend already.

"But you live with Paolo. Will you marry this other one? Has he given you a ring?"

I shook my head.

"Just take it," she said, "I have no use for it," and out of awkwardness or maybe something worse, I did take it, and never told Paolo. It is a pretty ring, a tiny diamond chip on a band of braided gold, and though I do not wear it and rarely look at it, it lies in a box inside my drawer.

In the morning when I wake up he is still not there, and by the time he comes home in the evening I have rehearsed what I will say so many times that I am not surprised when it comes out right.

"You met someone," I say. "That's great! That's so great, let me guess, the guy in the yellow shirt, the gorgeous one with the beard, I could see him checking you out all night, and then you disappeared. Tell me everything—"

He throws himself down on the sofa. "What am I doing, Annie? I'm too old for this, what am I doing?" He stretches out his legs, looks down at himself fondly, like someone who has just been tumbling in love. "He's just a kid, he's in his early twenties."

"What happened?"

"He—you know, we just kind of hit it off. I don't even know what happened, you know how petrified I am of all this stuff, we just started talking, it took forever for something to happen, I'm like a goddamn virgin starting all over again—"

"And?"

I know he will not tell me, can feel how a space is opening between us. *I told you everything*, I want to say, but I know it is not quite true, remember how when Tim and I used to close the door at night, Paolo was shut outside of a liquid, salty dark that could not fit inside words.

"He's sweet," Paolo says. "He *is* pretty gorgeous, isn't he? He has a terrible name, Harry, I've got to come up with something else to call him. He's even local, he works in Hyannis, and I guess—I think he likes me, the poor man doesn't know what he's getting into. God, I'm beat." He looks up at me. "Are you OK? Your hair looks great."

I nod. He sits up and glances at his watch. "I'm meeting him at ten at the bar. I've got to go rest for a couple minutes and them jump in the shower. You want to lie down?"

We do this sometimes, lie down together in his room with its gauzy white curtains, white sheets, blue speckled floor. It started when we only had one fan, but it was nice to nap together, to hear another person breathing, watch the curtains billow out, and even when we got another fan, we kept doing it. I tried to explain it once to Emily—how it wasn't sexual, how I didn't want to have sex with him but just liked to lie there. How safe it felt. But she kept saying how cute Paolo was, how could I keep my hands off him? He's not into women, I said, and anyhow, once we did it, it wouldn't feel safe anymore.

"That's OK," I tell him now.

Instead I go down into the basement to do my laundry. It is damp there, the place lit by one dim bulb, but after I put in the load, I drag over an old chair and sit beside the machine for a while with my hand on its belly, feeling its pulse. In my laundry are two shirts that used to be Tim's, one that was Paolo's, a camisole my mother gave me when it shrank. I try to picture which clothes have been mine from the beginning, the ones I bought and have been the only one to wear. The underwear, certainly, but I cannot remember what else is in there, now that it is all sloshing together in the tub.

I am startled by Paolo's voice calling, "Annie? Annie?"

I stand and lean up the stairs. "Down here. I'm doing laundry."

"I'm going to the bar," he calls down. "Do you want to come?"

"Do you want me to?"

"Of course. If you want."

"I might, but not right now. Maybe I'll show up later."

"All right, I'll see you."

I run up the stairs. "Paolo?"

He turns, bright and scrubbed in a turquoise shirt, on his way out the door.

"Huh?"

"Have fun. I hope it works out. He sounds nice." I must look dazed, blinking in the light.

"Yeah," he says. "It'll probably fall apart, he's probably fucked up, I'm probably fucked up." He puts out his hands, palms up. "I'm not any good at this."

"Sure you are," I say. "You'll be great."

And I do want him to be great, do want him to have someone to soothe the places I'll never be able to reach, at the same time that I can already imagine how sweetly he will include me for a while, how we will all three do things together until Harry gets too frustrated, how nicely Paolo will ask me to move out. Or maybe Harry will last two days, or two months; it almost doesn't matter, because eventually someone will come along, if not for Paolo, then for me.

I want to sit him down, then, before he leaves for the bar, and ask him if he thinks three is impossible, if it always comes down to two, or one. I want to ask him if he will marry me in a certain way, or just never stop cooking dinners with me or lying down for naps before the fan.

But this is not the sort of question you ask your friends, not the sort of promise you exact without a contract and a ring. I think of my mother, alone at my age with a skinny little girl who was me, of Paolo's mother, whose husband drank himself to death. I think of Tim's father who is dying like my father has died and all fathers will, and of Tim who is across the country and cannot depend on me.

And then I go down to put my laundry in the dryer. As I sat by the washing machine, I sit now by the dryer and feel my clothes tumble, arms tangling with legs, all of it pressed close around the circle of the sides. Later I will go dancing at the bar. First I will wait for my clothes to come out, and they will be warm and clean, and I will fold them, piece by piece, one by one.

"First Love"

R. A. Sasaki

It was William Chin who started the rumor. He had been crossing California Street on a Saturday afternoon in December when he was almost struck down by two people on a Suzuki motorcycle. As if it weren't enough to feel the brush of death on the sleeve of his blue parka, a split second before the demon passed, he had looked up and caught sight of two faces he never would have expected to see on the same motorcycle—one of which he wouldn't have expected to see on a motorcycle at all. No one would have imagined these two faces exchanging words, or thought of them in the same thought even; yet there they were, together not only in physical space, but in their expressions of fiendish abandon as they whizzed by him. He was so shaken, first by his nearness to death, then by seeing an F.O.B. hood like Hideyuki "George" Sakamoto in the company of a nice girl like Joanne Terasaki, that it was a full five minutes before he realized, still standing in amazement on the corner of California and Fourth, that Joanne had been driving.

When William Chin's story got around, there was a general sense of outrage among the senior class of Andrew Jackson High—the boys, because an upstart newcomer like George Sakamoto had done what they were too shy to do (that is, he had gotten Joanne to like him), and the girls, because George Sakamoto was definitely cool and Joanne Terasaki, as Marsha Aquino objected with utter contempt, "doesn't even like to dance." Joanne's friends remained loyal and insisted that Jo would come to her senses by graduation. George's motorcycle cronies were less generous. "Duke's fuckin' crazy," was their cryptic consensus. Opinions differed as to which of the two lovers had

142

completely lost their minds; however, it was unanimously held that the pairing was unsuitable.

And indeed, the two were from different worlds.

Hideyuki Sakamoto ("George" was his American name) was Japanese, a conviction that eight years, or half his life, in the States had failed to shake. He had transferred into Jackson High's senior class that year from wherever it was that F.O.B.s (immigrants fresh off the boat) transferred from; and though perhaps in his case the "fresh" no longer applied, the fact that he had come off the boat at one time or another was unmistakable. It lingered—rather, persisted—in his speech, which was ungrammatical and heavily accented, and punctuated by a mixture of exclamations commonly used on Kyushu Island and in the Fillmore District.

An F.O.B. at Jackson High could follow one of two routes: he could be quietly good at science or mathematics, or he could be a juvenile delinquent. Both options condemned him to invisibility. George hated math. His sympathies tended much more toward the latter option; however, he was not satisfied to be relegated to that category either. One thing was certain, and that was that George wanted no part of invisibility. As soon as his part-time job at Nakamura Hardware in Japantown afforded him the opportunity, he went out and acquired a second-hand Suzuki chopper (most hoods dreamed of owning a Harley, but George was Japanese and proud of it). He acquired threads which, when worn on his tall, wiry frame, had the effect—whether from admiration, derision, or sheer astonishment—of turning all heads, male and female alike. He had, in a short span of time, established a reputation as a "swinger." So when William Chin's story got around about George Sakamoto letting Joanne Terasaki drive his bike, the unanimous reaction among the girls who thought of themselves as swingers was voiced by Marsha Aquino: "God dog, what a waste."

Joanne Terasaki, or "Jo," as she preferred to be called, was, in popular opinion, a "brain." Although her parents were living in Japantown when she was born, soon afterwards her grandparents had died and the family moved out to "the Avenues." Jo was a product of the middle-class, ethnically mixed Richmond District. She had an air of breeding that came from three generations of city living, one college-educated parent, and a simple belief in the illusion so carefully nurtured by her parents' generation, who had been through the war, that she was absolutely Mainstream. No one, however, would have thought of her in conjunction with the word "swing," unless it was the playground variety. Indeed, there was a childlike quality about her, a kind of functional stupidity that was surprising in a girl so intelligent in other respects. She moved slowly, as if her mind were always elsewhere, a habit that boys found mysterious and alluring at first, then exasperating. Teachers found it exasperating as well, even slightly insulting, as she earned As in their classes almost as an afterthought. Her attention was like a dim but powerful beacon, slowing sweeping out to sea for—what? Occasionally it would light briefly on the world at hand, and Jo would be quick, sharp, formidable. Then it would turn out to far-away places again. Perhaps she was unable to reconcile the world around her, the world of Jackson High, with the fictional worlds where her love of reading took her. In her mind, she was Scarlett O'Hara, Lizzy Bennet, Ari Ben Canaan. Who would not be disori-ented to find oneself at one moment fleeing the Yankees through a burning Atlanta, and the next moment struggling across the finish line in girls' P.E.? Tart repartee with Mr. Darcy was far more satis-fying than the tongue-tied and painful exchanges with boys that oc-curred in real life. Rebuffed boys thought Jo a snob, a heartless bitch. The world of Andrew Jackson High was beneath her, that was it—a passing annoyance to be endured until she went out into the wider world and entered her true element. It must be on this wider world, this future glory, that her vision was so inexorably fixed.

Or perhaps it was fixed on a point just across San Francisco Bay, on the imposing campanile of the Berkeley campus of the University of California. She had always known she would go there, ever since, as a child, she had often gone to her mother's dresser and surrepti-tiously opened the top drawer to take out the fuzzy little golden bear bearing the inscription in blue letters, "CAL." It was one of the few "heirlooms" that her mother had salvaged from the wartime reloca-tion. She had taken it with her to internment camp in the Utah desert, an ineffectual but treasured symbol of a shattered life. The government could take away her rights, her father's business, her home, but they could never take away the fact that she was U.C. Berkeley, Class of '39. Jo would have that, too. People often said of Jo that she was a girl who was going places; and they didn't mean on the back (or front) of George Sakamoto's bike.

Only love or drama could bring together two people cast in such disparate roles. When auditions began for the play that was tradi-tionally put on by the senior class before graduation, Jo, tired of be-ing typecast as a brain, tried out for the part most alien to her im-age—that of the brazen hussy who flings herself at the hero in vain. For a brief moment she stood before her fellow classmates and sang her way out of the cramped cage that their imaginations had fash-ioned for her. The moment was indeed brief. Marsha Aquino got the part.

"You have to admit, Jo," said William Chin apologetically, "Marsha's a natural." And Jo agreed, somewhat maliciously, that Marsha was.

George, for his part, went for the lead. It was unheard of for a hood (and an F.O.B., at that) to aspire to the stage, much less the leading part. So thoroughly did George's aspect contradict conventional expectations of what a male lead should be, that the effect was quite comic. His good-natured lack of inhibition so charmed his audience that they almost overlooked the fact that his lines had been unintelligible. At the last moment, a voice of reason prevailed, and George was relegated to a nonspeaking part as one of six princes in a dream ballet, choreographed by Jo's friend Ava.

And so the two worlds converged.

"Grace," Ava was saying. "And—flair." She was putting the dream princes and princesses through their paces. "This is a ballet."

The dancers shuffled about self-consciously. After hours of work the princes and princesses, trained exclusively in soul, were managing to approximate a cross between a square dance and a track-and-field event.

"You've got to put more energy into it, or something," Jo, who was a princess, observed critically as a sheepish William Chin and Ed Bakowsky leaped halfheartedly across the floor.

"Like this, man!" George yelled suddenly, covering the stage in three athletic leaps. He landed crookedly on one knee, arms flung wide, whooping in exhilaration. There was an embarrassed silence.

"Yeah," Jo said. "Like that."

"Who is that?" she asked Ava after the rehearsal.

"I don't know," Ava said, "but what a body."

"That's George Sakamoto," said Marsha Aquino, who knew about everyone. "He's bad."

Jo, unfamiliar with the current slang, took her literally.

"Well, he seems all right to me. If it wasn't for him, our dream ballet would look more like 'The Funeral March.' Is he new?"

"He transferred from St. Francis," Marsha said. "That's where all the F.O.B.s go."

Jo had always had a vague awareness of Japanese people as being unattractively shy and rather hideously proper. Nothing could have been further from this image than George. Jo and her friends, most of whom were of Asian descent, were stunned by him, as a group of domesticated elephants born and bred in a zoo might have been upon meeting their wild African counterpart for the first time. George was a revelation to Jo, who, on the subject of ethnic identity, had always numbered among the ranks of the sublimely oblivious.

George, meanwhile, was already laying his strategy. He was not called "*Sukebe* Sakamoto" by his friends for nothing.

"This chick is the door-hanger type," he told his friend Doug. "You gotta move real slow."

"Yeah," Doug said. "Too slow for you."

"You watch, sucker."

He called her one weekend and invited her and Ava to go bowling with him and Doug. Jo was struck dumb on the telephone.

"Ha-ro, is Jo there?"

"This is Jo."

"Hey, man. This is George."

"Who?"

"George, man. Sakamoto."

"Oh." Then she added shyly, "Hi."

The idea of bowling was revolting, but Jo could bowl for love.

She told her mother that she had a date. Her mother mentally filed through her list of acquaintances for a Sakamoto.

"Is that the Sakamoto that owns the cleaner on Fillmore?"

"I don't think so," Jo said.

"Well, if Ava's going, I guess it's all right."

When George came to pick her up, Jo introduced him to her father, who was sitting in the living room watching television.

"Ha-ro," George said, cutting a neat bow to her startled father.

"Was that guy Japanese?" her father asked later when she returned.

"Yeah," Jo said, chuckling.

There was an unspoken law of evolution which dictated that in the gradual march toward Americanization, one did not deliberately regress by associating with F.O.B.s. Jo's mother, who was second generation, had endured much criticism from her peers for "throwing away a college education" and marrying Jo's father, who had graduated from high school in Japan. Even Jo's father, while certainly not an advocate of this law, assumed that most people felt this way. George, therefore, was a shock.

On their second date, Jo and George went to see Peter O'Toole in a musical. From then on, they decided to dispense with the formalities, a decision owing only in part to the fact that the musical had been wretched. The main reason was that they were in love.

They would drive out to the beach, or to the San Bruno hills, and sit for hours, talking. In the protective shell of George's mother's car they found a world where they were not limited by labels. They could be complex, vulnerable. He told her about his boyhood in Kyushu, about the sounds that a Japanese house makes in the night. He had been afraid of ghosts. His mother had always told him ghost stories. She would make her eyes go round and utter strange sounds: "*Ka-ra . . . ko-ro . . . ka-ra . . . ko-ro . . .*"—the sound made by the wooden sandals of an approaching ghost. Japanese ghosts were different from American ghosts, he said. They didn't have feet.

"If they don't have feet," Jo asked curiously, "how could they wear sandals?"

George was dumbfounded. The contradiction had never occurred to him.

They went for motorcycle rides along the roads that wound through the Presidio, at the edge of cliffs overlooking the Golden Gate. Then, chilled by the brisk winter fog, they would stop at his house in Japantown for a cup of green tea.

He lived in an old Victorian flat on the border between Japantown and the Fillmore, with his mother and grandmother and cat. His mother worked, so it was his grandmother who came from the kitchen to greet them. (But this was later. At first, George made sure that no one would be home when they went. He wanted to keep Jo a secret until he was sure of her.)

The Victorian kitchen, the green tea, all reminded Jo of her grandparents' place, which had stood just a few blocks away from George's house before it was torn down. Jo had a vague memory of her grandmother cooking fish in the kitchen. She couldn't remember her grandfather at all. The war had broken his spirit, taken his business, forced him to do day work in white people's homes, and he had died when Jo was two. After that, Jo's family moved out of Japantown, and she had not thought about the past until George's house reminded her. It was so unexpected that the swinger, the hood, the F.O.B. George Sakamoto should awaken such memories.

But they eventually had to leave the protective spaces that sheltered their love. Then the still George of the parked car and Victorian kitchen, the "real" George, Jo wanted to believe, evolved, became the flamboyant George, in constant motion, driven to maintain an illusion that would elude the cages of other people's limited imaginations.

He took her to dances Jo had never known existed. Jo had been only to school dances, where everyone stood around too embarrassed to dance. The dances that George took her to were dark, crowded. Almost everyone was Asian. Jo knew no one. Where did all these people come from? They were the invisible ones at school, the F.O.B.s. They *dressed* (unlike Jo and her crowd, who tended toward corduroy jeans). And they danced.

George was in his element here. In his skintight striped slacks flared at the calf, black crepe shirt open to the navel, billowing sleeves and satiny white silk scarf, he shimmered like a mirage in the strobe lights that cut the darkness. Then, chameleonlike, he would appear in jeans and a white T-shirt, stocking the shelves of

Nakamura Hardware. At school, George shunned the striped shirts
and windbreaker jackets that his peers donned like a uniform. He
wore turtleneck sweaters under corduroy blazers, starched shirts in
deep colors with cuff links. When he rode his bike, he was again
transformed, a wild knight in black leather.

"The dudes I ride with," George confided to Jo in the car, "see me
working in the store, and they say, 'Hey, what is this, man? You
square a-sup'm?' Then the guys in the store, they can't believe I hang
out with those suckers on bikes. 'Hey George,' they say, 'you one crazy
son-of-a-bitch.' In school, man, these straight suckers can't believe it
when I do good on a test. I mean, I ain't no hot shit at English, but I
ain't no dumb sucker neither. 'Hey George,' they say, 'you tryin' to get
into college a-sup'm?' 'Hey, why not, man?' I say. They can't take it if
you just a little bit different, you know? All them dudes is like that—
'cept you."

Jo was touched, and tried to be the woman of George's dreams. It
was a formidable endeavor. Nancy Sinatra was the woman of
George's dreams. For Christmas Jo got a pair of knee-high black
boots. She wore her corduroy jeans tighter in the crotch.

"Hey, George," Doug said. "How's it goin' with Slow Jo?"

"None of your fuckin' business, man," George snapped.

"Oh-oh. Looks bad."

On New Year's Eve Jo discovered French kissing and thought it
was "weird." She got used to it, though.

"You tell that guy," her father thundered, "that if he's gonna bring
that motorcycle, he doesn't have to come around here anymore!"

"Jesus Christ!" Jo wailed, stomping out of the room. "I can't wait
to get out of here!"

Then they graduated, and Jo moved to Berkeley in the spring.

The scene changed from the narrow corridors of Andrew Jackson
High to the wide steps and manicured lawns of the university.
George was attending a junior college in the city. He came over on
weekends.

"Like good ice cream," he said. "I want to put you in the freezer so
you don't melt."

"What are you talking about?"

They were sitting outside Jo's dormitory in George's car. Jo's room-
mate was a blonde from Colusa who had screamed the first time
George walked into the room with Jo. ("Hey, what's with that chick?"
George had later complained.)

"I want to save you," George said.

"From what? Jo asked.

He tried another analogy. "It's like this guy got this fancy shirt, see? He wants to wear it when he goes out, man. He don't want to wear it every day, get it dirty. He wears an old T-shirt when he works under the car—get grease on it, no problem. It don't matter. You're like the good shirt, man."

"So who's the old T-shirt?" Jo asked, suddenly catching on.

"Hey, nobody, man. Nobody special. You're special. I want to save you."

"I don't see it that way," Jo said. "When you love someone, you want to be with them and you don't mind the grease."

"Hey, outasight, man."

So he brought her to his room.

George's room was next to the kitchen. It was actually the dining room converted into a young man's bedroom. It had the tall, narrow Victorian doors and windows, and a sliding door to the living room, which was blocked by bookshelves and a stereo. The glass-doored china cabinet, which should have housed Imari bowl, held tapes of soul music, motorcycle chains, Japanese comic books, and Brut. In Jo's grandparents' house there had been a black shrine honoring dead ancestors in the corner of the dining room. The same corner in George's room was decorated by a life-sized poster of a voluptuous young woman wearing skintight leather pants and an equally skintight (but bulging) leather jacket, unzipped to the waist.

George's mother and grandmother were delighted by Jo. In their eyes she was a "nice Japanese girl," something they never thought they would see, at least in conjunction with George. George had had a string of girlfriends before Jo, which had dashed their hopes. Jo was beyond their wildest expectations. It didn't seem to matter that this "nice Japanese girl" didn't understand any Japanese; George's grandmother spoke to her anyway, and gave her the benefit of the doubt when she smiled blankly and looked to George for a translation. They were so enthusiastic that George was embarrassed, and tried to sneak Jo in and out to spare her their effusions.

They would go to his room and turn up the stereo and make love to the lush, throbbing beat of soul. At first Jo was mortified, conscious of what her parents would say, knowing that "good girls" were supposed to "wait." But in the darkness of George's room, all of that seemed very far away.

So her first experiences of love in a darkened room filled with the ghosts of missing Japanese heirlooms; in the spaces between the soul numbers with which they tried to dispel those ghostlike shadows, sounds filtered in from the neighboring kitchen: samurai music from the Japanese program on television, the ancient voice of his grandmother calling to the cat, the eternal shuffle of slippers across the kitchen floor. When his mother was home and began to worry about what they were doing in his room, he installed a lock, and when she began pounding on the door, insisting that it was getting late and that George really should take Jo home, George would call out gruffly, "Or-righ! Or-righ!"

But there was that other world, Jo's weekday world, a world of classical buildings, bookstores, coffee shops, and tear gas (for the United States had bombed Cambodia).

Jo flitted like a ghost between the two worlds so tenuously linked by a thin span of steel suspended over San Francisco Bay. She wanted to be still, and at home, but where? On quiet weekday mornings, reading in an empty courtyard with the stillness, the early morning sun, the language of Dickens, she felt her world full of promise and dreams. Then the sun rose high, people came out, and Jo and her world disappeared in a cloak of invisibility, like a ghost.

"Her English is so good," Ava's roommate remarked to Ava. "Where did she learn it?"

"From my parents," Jo said. "In school, from friends. Pretty much the same way most San Franciscans learn it, I guess."

Ava's roommate was from the East Coast, and had never had a conversation with an "Oriental" before.

"She just doesn't know any better," Ava apologized later.

"Well where has that chick been all her life?" Jo fumed.

Then she would long for George, and he would come on the weekend to take her away. Locked together on George's bike, hurtling back and forth between two worlds, they found a place where they could be still and at peace.

George tried to be the man of her dreams. They went on hikes now instead of soul dances. He would appear in jeans and a work shirt, and he usually had an armload of books. He was learning to type, and took great pains over his essays for Remedial English.

But they began to feel the strain. It began to bother George that Jo made twenty-five cents an hour more at her part-time job in the student dining room than he did at the hardware store. He had been working longer. He needed the money. Jo, on the other hand, never seemed to buy anything. Just books. Although her parents could afford to send her to college, her high-school record had won her a scholarship for the first year. She lived in a dream world. She had it so easy.

He asked to borrow fifty dollars, he had to fix his car, and she lent it to him immediately. But he resented it, resented his need, resented her for having the money, for parting with it so easily. Everything, so easily. And he tortured her.

"Hey, is something wrong, man?" George asked suddenly, accusing, over the phone.

"Wrong?" Jo was surprised. "What do you mean?"

"You sound funny."

"What do you mean, funny?"

"You sound real cold, man," George said. His voice was flat, dull.

"There's nothing wrong!" Jo protested, putting extra emphasis in her voice to convince him, then hating herself for doing so. "I'm fine."

"You sound real far away," George went on, listlessly.

"Hey, is something bothering *you*?"

"No," George said. "You just sound funny to me. Real cold, like you don't care." He wanted her to be sympathetic, remorseful.

And at first she was—repentant, almost hysterical. Then she became impatient. Finally, she lapsed into indifference.

"I have the day off tomorrow," George said over the phone. "Can I come?"

Jo hesitated.

"I have to go to classes," she warned.

"That's okay," he said. "I'll come with you."

There was another long pause. "Well . . . we'll see," she said.

As soon as she saw him the next day, her fears were confirmed. He had gone all out. He wore a silky purple shirt open halfway to his navel, and skintight slacks that left nothing to the imagination. There was something pathetic and vulnerable about the line of his leg so thoroughly revealed by them. As they approached the campus, George pulled out a pair of dark shades and put them on.

He was like a character walking into the wrong play. He glowed defiantly among the faded jeans and work shirts of the Berkeley campus.

Jo's first class was Renaissance Literature.

"If you want to do something else," she said, "I can meet you after class."

"That's okay, man," George said happily. "I want to see what they teaching you."

"It's gonna be real boring," she said.

"That's okay," he said. "I have my psych book."

"If you're going to study," Jo said carefully, "maybe you should go to the library."

"Hey," George said, "you tryin' to get rid of me?"

"No," Jo lied.

"Then let's go."

They entered the room. It was a seminar of about ten people, sitting in a circle. They joined the circle, but after a few minutes of discussion about *Lycidas*, George opened his psychology textbook and began to read.

Jo was mortified. The woman sitting on the other side of George was looking curiously, out of the corner of her eye, at the diagram of the human brain in George's book.

"Would you care to read the next stanza aloud?" the lecturer asked suddenly. "You—the gentleman with the dark glasses."

There was a horrible moment as all eyes turned to George, bent over his psychology textbook. He squirmed and sank down into his seat, as if trying to become invisible.

"I think he's just visiting," the woman next to George volunteered. "I'll read."

Afterwards, Jo was brutal. Why had he come to the class if he was going to be so rude? Why hadn't he sat off in the corner, if he was going to study? Or better yet, gone to the library as she had suggested? Didn't he know how inappropriate his behavior was? Didn't he care if they thought that Japanese people were boors? Didn't he know? Didn't he care?

No, he didn't know. He was oblivious. It was the source of his confidence, and that was what she had loved him for.

And so the curtain fell on their little drama, after a predictable denouement—agreeing that they would date others, then a tearful good-bye one dark night in his car, parked outside her apartment. Jo had always thought it somewhat disturbing when characters who had been left dead on the set in the last act, commanding considerable emotion by their demise, should suddenly spring to life not a minute later, smiling and bowing, and looking as unaffected by tragedy as it is possible to look. She therefore hoped she would not run into George, who would most certainly be smiling and bowing and oblivious to tragedy. She needn't have worried. Their paths had never been likely to cross.

Jo was making plans to study in New York when she heard through the grapevine that George was planning a trip to Europe. He went that summer, and when he returned, he brought her parents a gift. Jo's parents, who had had enough complaints about George when Jo was seeing him, were touched, and when Christmas came around Jo's mother, in true Japanese fashion, prepared a gift for George to return his kindness. Jo, of course, was expected to deliver it.

She had had no contact with him since they had broken up. His family was still living in Japantown, but the old Victorian was soon going to be torn down for urban renewal, and they were planning to move out to the Avenues, the Richmond District where Jo's parents lived.

As Jo's dad drove her to George's house, Jo hoped he wouldn't be home, hoped she could just leave the gift with his mother. She was thankful that she was with her father, who had a habit of gunning the engine as he sat waiting in the car for deliveries to be made, and was therefore the ideal person with whom to make a quick getaway.

George's grandmother opened the door. When she saw who it was, her face changed and she cried out with pleasure. Jo was completely unprepared for the look of happiness and hope on her face.

"Jo-chan!" George's grandmother cried; then, half-turning, she called out Jo's name twice more, as if summoning the household to her arrival.

Jo was stunned.

"This is for George," she said, thrusting the gift at George's grand-mother, almost throwing it at her in her haste. "Merry Christmas."

She turned and fled down those stairs for the last time, away from the doomed Victorian and the old Japanese woman who stood in the doorway still, calling her name.

PART 4
THE FAMILY LIFE CYCLE

THE FAMILY LIFE CYCLE

In the United States, the traditional family is thought to consist of a mother, father, and children. In recent years, scholars have recognized additional types of family structures. With rising divorce rates and teen pregnancies, the single-parent family has become increasingly common. Additionally, the number of blended families has risen as remarriage after death or divorce brings children from partners' previous marriages together under one roof. Couples, who by choice or circumstance, do not have children, form another type of family while intergenerational or extended families also exist.

The construction and experience of family are affected by culture, race, and gender. For example, regarding the family social network, some cultures, such as Asian American and Latino/a cultures, value intergenerational ties, while others, such as Irish American and African American, promote age-similar ties where siblings and friends are accorded more importance (Johnson, 1995). Cultures also have different expectations for women's roles in the family, the role of the older generation in the extended family, and the balance between personal independence and family interdependence (Johnson, 1995). Class also has an impact on the family experience. For example, working class Irish Americans' lives are more closely tied to the Catholic church and neighborhood, while middle-class Irish Americans "remain close to the church, but they advocate a reformed church that favors abortion and other liberal issues" (Johnson, 1995, p. 320).

The introduction of a child into a household means the lifelong job of parenting has begun. It also marks the beginning of the life cycle of a family, however defined. Most of us become parents at some point in our lives and experience different stages of family life as our children grow from infants to adolescents, are launched into adulthood and begin their own families. Normally, during the family life cycle

157

we will experience our children's marriages, the death of our parents, and becoming a grandparent.

These normative events are times of family transition but it is the non-normative events, or crises that can especially test a family. The death of a child causes particular stress because children are expected to outlive their parents. All the care and energy used to raise the child is sometimes considered futile, particularly when the death occurs in young adulthood (Hocker, 1988). The parents have not only invested materially, but may think of the daughter or son as an extension and in the child's death, the parents lose part of themselves (Hocker, 1988).

These feelings of loss are all part of the grieving process which may consist of phases or stages such as shock, anger and guilt, sadness (which may include searching, yearning, or withdrawal), and finally acceptance (Blank, 1998). Cultures may express bereavement in a variety of ways and may utilize different ways to cope with loss.

In *The Management of Grief,* Mrs. Bhave is an Indian Canadian woman whose husband and sons are killed in a plane crash over Ireland. Her cultural upbringing has left her with regrets. She says, "'I never once told him that I loved him,' I say. I was too much the well-brought-up woman. I was so well brought up I never felt comfortable calling my husband by his first name." The only child of a wealthy Indian family, she journeys to India to bury her husband and sons. She and her family travel throughout India for six months where "astrologers and palmists seek [her] out and for a fee offer [her] cosmic consolations." Mrs. Bhave wryly observes that arrangements in India are always made for widowers to marry again. She says, "They must marry; it is the duty of a man to look after a wife." She adds, "No one here thinks of arranging a husband for an unlucky widow." While in a temple, she sees a vision of her husband who tells her, "You must finish alone what we started together."

After returning to Canada, Mrs. Bhave bridges the cultural gap between Canadians and Indians when she accompanies a social worker to an Indian Canadian couple's home whose sons have died. The social worker is mystified as to why the couple won't sign papers allowing a trustee, instead of their dead sons, to pay the bills. Mrs. Bhave notes that this Indian family believes that signing the papers means giving up hope that the sons will return.

Families are also called upon to help a member accept impending death. Such is the case in *This Place.* David, a gay, Native American comes home to die after becoming ill with AIDS. His medicine-man grandfather, Joseph, helps David review and accept his life and guides him toward a peaceful death using song and examples from nature. Before David dies he reports to Joseph, " I saw my grandmother, my father. They touched me." Joseph answers, " You found your parts, your pieces. . . . The sun is real bright today. It's a good day to go."

Older family members can serve the vital function of passing on family history to the younger generation in the form of stories. In *The Storyteller,* Jose spends a day alone with his ailing Filipino grand-mother, Lola Silang. Jose remembers her from his childhood in the Philippines as "the earthly villain, the heartless crone who despised my father and caused my mother grief." During this visit, Lola Silang provides an oral family history for Jose and helps him appre-ciate his Filipino heritage and himself. He recognizes his grand-mother's strength and sees her in a new light.

Marriage is also a facet of the family life cycle. For some cultures, it is a family affair where arranged marriage is a common practice. Arranged marriage occurred primarily in the middle and upper classes in Japan prior to 1868 (Blood, 1967). This system was ex-tended to the lower classes during the reform period of the Meiji era in the late 1800s (Blood, 1967). Set in the late 1800s, *1895 The Hon-eymoon Hotel* shows Sono and Chika emigrating from Japan to Hawaii to meet their prospective husbands. Sono's uncle had arranged the match between Sono and Yamamoto-san and when Sono sees Yamamoto-san appears older than she anticipated, Sono is disappointed and says, "But Yamamoto-san was known to her uncle. Shouldn't he have prevented such an awkward match, knowing the man's true age?" Yet, she is "obliged to Uncle . . . for his support through the difficult years."

Sono comes from a poor family and recognizes that Yamamoto-san will provide for her economic needs. Sono comes to terms with her situation. The author writes, "Sono reminded herself, why not rest with this choice? In the matter of how to feel about things, she would remain in charge. Then it was settled; there was no problem." The couples sit down together and wish themselves good luck.

Marriage is also the subject of Michael Dorris's *Groom Service.* In this Native American tale, the mothers of the prospective couple arrange the courtship ritual. Bernard, the future husband, must im-press Marie, his future wife, and her female relatives by waiting in front of his prospective in-laws' house with the choicest pieces of meat from his daily hunting expeditions. Blanche, his future mother-in-law, picks from his daily offerings and finally invites him into the house to share a meal with her family. He is accepted into the fam-ily and at story's end he and Marie are expecting their first child.

In summary, many different types of families exist. The structure of the family, whether it is traditional, a single parent family or an extended family, also intersects with family life cycle events to create different experiences. For many, the family life cycle includes expected events such as the birth, growth, and launching of children into the world. Cultures handle different family life cycle events such as marriage, the death of a child and passing down family stories in different ways. Ultimately, our family is the first place we learn about our cultural heritage.

The Management of Grief

Bharati Mukherjee

A woman I don't know is boiling tea the Indian way in my kitchen. There are a lot of women I don't know in my kitchen, whispering, and moving tactfully. They open doors, rummage through the pantry, and try not to ask me where things are kept. They remind me of when my sons were small, on Mother's Day or when Vikram and I were tired, and they would make big, sloppy omelets. I would lie in bed pretending I didn't hear them.

Dr. Sharma, the treasurer of the Indo-Canada Society, pulls me into the hallway. He wants to know if I am worried about money. His wife, who has just come up from the basement with a tray of empty cups and glasses, scolds him. "Don't bother Mrs. Bhave with mundane details." She looks so monstrously pregnant her baby must be days overdue. I tell her she shouldn't be carrying heavy things. "Shaila," she says, smiling, "this is the fifth." Then she grabs a teenager by his shirttails. He slips his Walkman off his head. He has to be one of her four children, they have the same domed and dented foreheads. "What's the official word now?" she demands. The boy slips the headphones back on. "They're acting evasive, Ma. They're saying it could be an accident or a terrorist bomb."

All morning, the boys have been muttering, Sikh Bomb, Sikh Bomb. The men, not using the word, bow their heads in agreement. Mrs. Sharma touches her forehead at such a word. At least they've stopped talking about space debris and Russian lasers.

Two radios are going in the dining room. They are tuned to different stations. Someone must have brought the radios down from my boys' bedrooms. I haven't gone into their rooms since Kusum came

161

running across the front lawn in her bathrobe. She looked so funny, I was laughing when I opened the door.

The big TV in the den is being whizzed through American networks and cable channels.

"Damn!" some man swears bitterly. "How can these preachers carry on like nothing's happened?" I want to tell him we're not that important. You look at the audience, and at the preacher in his blue robe with his beautiful white hair, the potted palm trees under a blue sky, and you know they care about nothing.

The phone rings and rings. Dr. Sharma's taken charge. "We're with her," he keeps saying. "Yes, yes, the doctor has given calming pills. Yes, yes, pills are having necessary effect." I wonder if pills alone explain this calm. Not peace, just a deadening quiet. I was always controlled, but never repressed. Sound can reach me, but my body is tensed, ready to scream. I hear their voices all around me. I hear my boys and Vikram cry, "Mommy, Shaila!" and their screams insulate me, like headphones.

The woman boiling water tells her story again and again. "I got the news first. My cousin called from Halifax before six A.M., can you imagine? He'd gotten up for prayers and his son was studying for medical exams and he heard on a rock channel that something had happened to a plane. They said first it had disappeared from the radar, like a giant eraser just reached out. His father called me, so I said to him, what do you mean, 'something bad'? You mean a high-jacking? And he said, *behn*, there is no confirmation of anything yet, but check with your neighbors because a lot of them must be on that plane. So I called poor Kusum straightaway. I knew Kusum's husband and daughter were booked to go yesterday."

Kusum lives across the street from me. She and Satish had moved in less than a month ago. They said they needed a bigger place. All these people, the Sharmas and friends from the Indo-Canada Society had been there for the housewarming. Satish and Kusum made home-made tandoori on their big gas grill and even the white neighbors piled their plates high with that luridly red, charred, juicy chicken. Their younger daughter had danced, and even our boys had broken away from the Stanley Cup telecast to put in a reluctant appearance. Everyone took pictures for their albums and for the community newspapers—another of our families had made it big in Toronto—and now I wonder how many of those happy faces are gone. "Why does God give us so much if all along He intends to take it away?" Kusum asks me.

I nod. We sit on carpeted stairs, holding hands like children. "I never once told him that I loved him," I say. I was too much the well brought up woman. I was so well brought up I never felt comfortable calling my husband by his first name.

"It's all right," Kusum says. "He knew. My husband knew. They felt it. Modern young girls have to say it because what they feel is fake."

Kusum's daughter, Pam, runs in with an overnight case. Pam's in her McDonald's uniform. "Mummy! You have to get dressed!" Panic makes her cranky. "A reporter's on his way here."

"Why?"

"You want to talk to him in your bathrobe?" She starts to brush her mother's long hair. She's the daughter who's always in trouble. She dates Canadian boys and hangs out in the mall, shopping for tight sweaters. The younger one, the goody-goody one according to Pam, the one with a voice so sweet that when she sang *bhajans* for Ethiopian relief even a frugal man like my husband wrote out a hundred dollar check, *she* was on that plane. *She* was going to spend July and August with grandparents because Pam wouldn't go. Pam said she'd rather waitress at McDonald's. "If it's a choice between Bombay and Wonderland, I'm picking Wonderland," she'd said.

"Leave me alone," Kusum yells. "You know what I want to do? If I didn't have to look after you now, I'd hang myself."

Pam's young face goes blotchy with pain. "Thanks," she says, "don't let me stop you."

"Hush," pregnant Mrs. Sharma scolds Pam. "Leave your mother alone. Mr. Sharma will tackle the reporters and fill out the forms. He'll say what has to be said."

Pam stands her ground. "You think I don't know what Mummy's thinking? *Why her*? that's what. That's sick! Mummy wishes my little sister were alive and I were dead."

Kusum's hand in mine is trembly hot. We continue to sit on the stairs.

She calls before she arrives, wondering if there's anything I need. Her name is Judith Templeton and she's an appointee of the provincial government. "Multiculturalism?" I ask, and she says, "partially," but that her mandate is bigger. "I've been told you knew many of the people on the flight," she says. "Perhaps if you'd agree to help us reach the others . . .?"

She gives me time at least to put on tea water and pick up the mess in the front room. I have a few *samosas* from Kusum's house-warming that I could fry up, but then I think, why prolong this visit?

Judith Templeton is much younger than she sounded. She wears a blue suit with a white blouse and a polka dot tie. Her blond hair is cut short, her only jewelry is pearl drop earrings. Her briefcase is new and expensive looking, a gleaming cordovan leather. She sits with it across her lap. When she looks out the front windows onto the street, her contact lenses seem to float in front of her light blue eyes.

"What sort of help do you want from me?" I ask. She has refused the tea, out of politeness, but I insist, along with some slightly stale biscuits.

"I have no experience," she admits. "That is, I have an MSW and I've worked in liaison with accident victims, but I mean I have no experience with a tragedy of this scale—"

"Who could?" I ask.

"—and with the complications of culture, language, and customs. Someone mentioned that Mrs. Bhave is a pillar—because you've taken it more calmly."

At this, perhaps, I frown, for she reaches forward, almost to take my hand. "I hope you understand my meaning, Mrs. Bhave. There are hundreds of people in Metro directly affected, like you, and some of them speak no English. There are some widows who've never handled money or gone on a bus, and there are old parents who still haven't eaten or gone outside their bedrooms. Some houses and apartments have been looted. Some wives are still hysterical. Some husbands are in shock and profound depression. We want to help, but our hands are tied in so many ways. We have to distribute money to some people, and there are legal documents—these things can be done. We have interpreters, but we don't always have the human touch, or maybe the right human touch. We don't want to make mistakes, Mrs. Bhave, and that's why we'd like to ask you to help us."

"More mistakes, you mean," I say.

"Police matters are not in my hands," she answers.

"Nothing I can do will make any difference," I say. "We must all grieve in our own way."

"But you are coping very well. All the people said, Mrs. Bhave is the strongest person of all. Perhaps if the others could see you, talk with you, it would help them."

"By the standards of the people you call hysterical, I am behaving very oddly and very badly, Miss Templeton." I want to say to her, *I wish I could scream, starve, walk into Lake Ontario, jump from a bridge.* "They would not see me as a model. I do not see myself as a model."

I am a freak. No one who has ever known me would think of me reacting this way. This terrible calm will not go away.

She asks me if she may call again, after I get back from a long trip that we all must make. "Of course," I say. "Feel free to call, anytime."

Four days later, I find Kusum squatting on a rock overlooking a bay in Ireland. It isn't a big rock, but it juts sharply out over water.

This is as close as we'll ever get to them. June breezes balloon out her sari and unpin her knee-length hair. She has the bewildered look of a sea creature whom the tides have stranded.

It's been one hundred hours since Kusum came stumbling and screaming across my lawn. Waiting around the hospital, we've heard many stories. The police, the diplomats, they tell us things thinking that we're strong, that knowledge is helpful to the grieving, and maybe it is. Some, I know, prefer ignorance, or their own versions. The plane broke into two, they say. Unconsciousness was instantaneous. No one suffered. My boys must have just finished their breakfasts. They loved eating on planes, they loved the smallness of plates, knives, and forks. Last year they saved the airline salt and pepper shakers. Half an hour more and they would have made it to Heathrow.

Kusum says that we can't escape our fate. She says that all those people—our husbands, my boys, her girl with the nightingale voice, all those Hindus, Christians, Sikhs, Muslims, Parsis, and atheists on that plane—were fated to die together off this beautiful bay. She learned this from a swami in Toronto.

I have my Valium.

Six of us "relatives"—two widows and four widowers—choose to spend the day today by the waters instead of sitting in a hospital room and scanning photographs of the dead. That's what they call us now: relatives. I've looked through twenty-seven photos in two days. They're very kind to us, the Irish are very understanding. Sometimes understanding means freeing a tourist bus for this trip to the bay, so we can pretend to spy our loved ones through the glassiness of waves or in sun-speckled cloud shapes.

I could die here, too, and be content.

"What is that, out there?" She's standing and flapping her hands and for a moment I see a head shape bobbing in the waves. She's standing in the water, I, on the boulder. The tide is low, and a round, black, head-sized rock has just risen from the waves. She returns, her sari end dripping and ruined and her face is a twisted remnant of hope, the way mine was a hundred hours ago, still laughing but inwardly knowing that nothing but the ultimate tragedy could bring two women together at six o'clock on a Sunday morning. I watch her face sag into blankness.

"That water felt warm, Shaila," she says at length.

"You can't," I say. "We have to wait for our turn to come."

I haven't eaten in four days, haven't brushed my teeth.

"I know," she says. "I tell myself I have no right to grieve. They are in a better place than we are. My swami says I should be thrilled for them. My swami says depression is a sign of our selfishness."

Maybe I'm selfish. Selfishly I break away from Kusum and run, sandals slapping against stones, to the water's edge. What if my boys aren't lying pinned under the debris? What if they aren't stuck a mile below that innocent blue chop? What if, given the strong currents. . . .

Now I've ruined my sari, one of my best. Kusum has joined me, knee-deep in water that feels to me like a swimming pool. I could settle in the water, and my husband would take my hand and the boys would slap water in my face just to see me scream.

"Do you remember what good swimmers my boys were, Kusum?"

"I saw the medals," she says.

One of the widowers, Dr. Ranganathan from Montreal, walks out to us, carrying his shoes in one hand. He's an electrical engineer. Someone at the hotel mentioned his work is famous around the world, something about the place where physics and electricity come together. He has lost a huge family, something indescribable. "With some luck," Dr. Ranganathan suggests to me, "a good swimmer could make it safely to some island. It is quite possible that there may be many, many microscopic islets scattered around."

"You're not just saying that?" I tell Dr. Ranganathan about Vinod, my elder son. Last year he took diving as well.

"It's a parent's duty to hope," he says. "It is foolish to rule out possibilities that have not been tested. I myself have not surrendered hope."

Kusum is sobbing once again. "Dear lady," he says, laying his free hand on her arm, and she calms down.

"Vinod is how old?" he asks me. He's very careful, as we all are. *Is*, not was.

"Fourteen. Yesterday he was fourteen. His father and uncle were going to take him down to the Taj and give him a big birthday party. I couldn't go with them because I couldn't get two weeks off from my stupid job in June." I process bills for a travel agent. June is a big travel month.

Dr. Ranganathan whips the pockets of his suit jacket inside out. Squashed roses, in darkening shades of pink, float on the water. He tore the roses off creepers in somebody's garden. He didn't ask anyone if he could pick the roses, but now there's been an article about it in the local papers. When you see an Indian person, it says, please give him or her flowers.

"A strong youth of fourteen," he says, "can very likely pull to safety a younger one."

My sons, though four years apart, were very close. Vinod wouldn't let Mithun down. *Electrical engineering*, I think, foolishly perhaps: this man knows important secrets of the universe, things closed to me. Relief spins me lightheaded. No wonder my boys' photographs haven't turned up in the gallery of photos of the recovered dead. "Such pretty roses," I say.

"My wife loved pink roses. Every Friday I had to bring a bunch home. I used to say, why? After twenty odd years of marriage you're still needing proof positive of my love?" He has identified his wife and three of his children. Then others from Montreal, the lucky ones, intact families with no survivors. He chuckles as he wades back to shore. Then he swings around to ask me a question. "Mrs. Bhave, you are wanting to throw in some roses for your loved ones? I have two big ones left."

But I have other things to float: Vinod's pocket calculator; a half-painted model B-52 for my Mithun. They'd want them on their island. And for my husband? For him I let fall into the calm, glassy waters a poem I wrote in the hospital yesterday. Finally he'll know my feelings for him.

"Don't tumble, the rocks are slippery," Dr. Ranganathan cautions. He holds out a hand for me to grab.

That it's time to get back on the bus, time to rush back to our waiting posts on hospital benches.

Kusum is one of the lucky ones. The lucky ones flew here, identified in multiplicate their loved ones, then will fly to India with the bodies for proper ceremonies. Satish is one of the few males who surfaced. The photos of faces we saw on the walls in an office at Heathrow and here in the hospital are mostly of women. Women have more body fat, a nun said to me matter-of-factly. They float better.

Today I was stopped by a young sailor on the street. He had loaded bodies, he'd gone into the water when—he checks my face for signs of strength—when the sharks were first spotted. I don't blush, and he breaks down. "It's all right," I say. "Thank you." I had heard about the sharks from Dr. Ranganathan. In his orderly mind, science brings understanding, it holds no terror. It is the shark's duty. For every deer there is a hunter, for every fish a fisherman.

The Irish are not shy; they rush to me and give me hugs and some are crying. I cannot imagine reactions like that on the streets of Toronto. Just strangers, and I am touched. Some carry flowers with them and give them to any Indian they see.

After lunch, a policeman I have gotten to know quite well catches hold of me. He says he thinks he has a match for Vinod. I explain what a good swimmer Vinod is.

"You want me with you when you look at photos?" Dr. Ranganathan walks ahead of me into the picture gallery. In these matters, he is a scientist, and I am grateful. It is a new perspective. "They have performed miracles," he says. "We are indebted to them."

The first day or two the policemen showed us relatives only one picture at a time; now they're in a hurry, they're eager to lay out the possibles, and even the probables.

The face on the photo is of a boy much like Vinod; the same intelligent eyes, the same thick brows dipping into a V. But this boy's features, even his cheeks, are puffier, wider, mushier.

"No." My gaze is pulled by other pictures. There are five other boys who look like Vinod.

The nun assigned to console me rubs the first picture with a fingertip. "When they've been in the water for a while, love, they look a little heavier." The bones under the skin are broken, they said on the first day—try to adjust your memories. It's important.

"It's not him. I'm his mother. I'd know."

"I know this one!" Dr. Ranganathan cries out suddenly from the back of the gallery. "And this one!" I think he senses that I don't want to find my boys. "They are the Kutty brothers. They were also from Montreal." I don't mean to be crying. On the contrary, I am ecstatic. My suitcase in the hotel is packed heavy with dry clothes for my boys.

The policeman starts to cry. "I am so sorry, I am so sorry, ma'am. I really thought we had a match."

With the nun ahead of us and the policeman behind, we, the unlucky ones without our children's bodies, file out of the makeshift gallery.

From Ireland most of us go on to India. Kusum and I take the same direct flight to Bombay, so I can help her clear customs quickly. But we have to argue with a man in uniform. He has large boils on his face. The boils swell and glow with sweat as we argue with him. He wants Kusum to wait in line and he refuses to take authority because his boss is on a tea break. But Kusum won't let her coffins out of sight, and I shan't desert her though I know that my parents, elderly and diabetic, must be waiting in a stuffy car in a scorching lot.

"You bastard!" I scream at the man with the popping boils. Other passengers press closer. "You think we're smuggling contraband in those coffins!"

Once upon a time we were well brought up women; we were dutiful wives who kept our heads veiled, our voices shy and sweet.

In India, I become, once again, an only child of rich, ailing parents. Old friends of the family come to pay their respects. Some are Sikh, and inwardly, involuntarily, I cringe. My parents are progressive people; they do not blame communities for a few individuals.

In Canada it is a different story now.

"Stay longer," my mother pleads. "Canada is a cold place. Why would you want to be all by yourself?" I stay.

Three months pass. Then another.

"Vikram wouldn't have wanted you to give up things!" they protest. They call my husband by the name he was born with. In Toronto he'd changed to Vik so the men he worked with at his office would find his name as easy as Rod or Chris. "You know, the dead aren't cut off from us!"

My grandmother, the spoiled daughter of a rich *zamindar*, shaved her head with rusty razor blades when she was widowed at sixteen. My grandfather died of childhood diabetes when he was nineteen, and she saw herself as the harbinger of bad luck. My mother grew up without parents, raised indifferently by an uncle, while her true mother slept in a hut behind the main estate house and took her food with the servants. She grew up a rationalist. My parents abhor mindless mortification.

The zamindar's daughter kept stubborn faith in Vedic rituals; my parents rebelled. I am trapped between two modes of knowledge. At thirty-six, I am too old to start over and too young to give up. Like my husband's spirit, I flutter between worlds.

Courting aphasia, we travel. We travel with our phalanx of servants and poor relatives. To hill stations and to beach resorts. We play contract bridge in dusty gymkhana clubs. We ride stubby ponies up crumbly mountain trails. At tea dances, we let ourselves be twirled twice round the ballroom. We hit the holy spots we hadn't made time for before. In Varanasi, Kalighat, Rishikesh, Hardwar, astrologers and palmists seek me out and for a fee offer me cosmic consolations.

Already the widowers among us are being shown new bride candidates. They cannot resist the call of custom, the authority of their parents and older brothers. They must marry; it is the duty of a man to look after a wife. The new wives will be young widows with children, destitute but of good family. They will make loving wives, but the men will shun them. I've had calls from the men over crackling Indian telephone lines. "Save me," they say, these substantial, educated, successful men of forty. "My parents are arranging a marriage for me." In a month they will have buried one family and returned to Canada with a new bride and partial family.

I am comparatively lucky. No one here thinks of arranging a husband for an unlucky widow.

Then, on the third day of the sixth month into this odyssey, in an abandoned temple in a tiny Himalayan village, as I make my offering of flowers and sweetmeats to the god of a tribe of animists, my husband descends to me. He is squatting next to a scrawny *sadhu* in moth-eaten robes. Vikram wears the vanilla suit he wore the last time I hugged him. The *sadhu* tosses petals on a butter-red flame, reciting Sanskrit mantras and sweeps his face of flies. My husband takes my hand in his.

You're beautiful, he starts. Then, *What are you doing here?*

Shall I stay? I ask. He only smiles, but already the image is fading. *You must finish alone what we started together.* No seaweed wreathes his mouth. He speaks too fast just as he used to when we were an envied family in our pink split-level. He is gone.

In the windowless altar room, smoky with joss sticks and clarified butter lamps, a sweaty hand gropes for my blouse. I do not shriek. The *sadhu* arranges his robe. The lamps hiss and sputter out.

When we come out of the temple, my mother says, "Did you feel something weird in there?"

My mother has no patience with ghosts, prophetic dreams, holy men, and cults.

"No," I lie. "Nothing."

But she knows that she's lost me. She knows that in days I shall be leaving.

Kusum's put her house up for sale. She wants to live in an ashram in Hardwar. Moving to Hardwar was her swami's idea. Her swami runs two ashrams, the one in Hardwar and another here in Toronto.

"Don't run away," I tell her.

"I'm not running away," she says. "I'm pursuing inner peace. You think you or that Ranganathan fellow are better off?"

Pam's left for California. She wants to do some modelling, she says. She says when she comes into her share of the insurance money she'll open a yoga-cum-aerobics studio in Hollywood. She sends me postcards so naughty I daren't leave them on the coffee table. Her mother has withdrawn from her and the world.

The rest of us don't lose touch, that's the point. Talk is all we have, says Ranganathan, who has also resisted his relatives and returned to Montreal and to his job, alone. He says, whom better to talk with than other relatives? We've been melted down and recast as a new tribe.

He calls me twice a week from Montreal. Every Wednesday night and every Saturday afternoon. He is changing jobs, going to Ottawa. But Ottawa is over a hundred miles away, and he is forced to drive two hundred and twenty miles a day. He can't bring himself to sell his house. The house is a temple, he says; the king-sized bed in the master bedroom is a shrine. He sleeps on a folding cot. A devotee.

There are still some hysterical relatives. Judith Templeton's list of those needing help and those who've "accepted" is in nearly perfect balance. Acceptance means you speak of your family in the past tense and you make active plans for moving ahead with your life. There are courses at Seneca and Ryerson we could be taking. Her gleaming leather briefcase is full of college catalogues and lists of cultural societies that need our help. She has done impressive work, I tell her.

"In the textbooks on grief management," she replies—I am her confidante, I realize, one of the few whose grief has not sprung bizarre obsessions—"there are stages to pass through: rejection, depression, acceptance, reconstruction." She has compiled a chart and finds that six months after the tragedy, none of us still reject reality, but only a handful are reconstructing. "Depressed Acceptance" is the plateau we've reached. Remarriage is a major step in reconstruction (though she's a little surprised, even shocked, over *how* quickly some of the men have taken on new families). Selling one's house and changing jobs and cities is healthy.

How do I tell Judith Templeton that my family surrounds me, and that like creatures in epics, they've changed shapes? She sees me as calm and accepting but worries that I have no job, no career. My closest friends are worse off than I. I cannot tell her my days, even my nights, are thrilling.

She asks me to help with families she can't reach at all. An elderly couple in Agincourt whose sons were killed just weeks after they had brought their parents over from a village in Punjab. From their names, I know they are Sikh. Judith Templeton and a translator have visited them twice with offers of money for air fare to Ireland, with bank forms, power-of-attorney forms, but they have refused to sign, or to leave their tiny apartment. Their sons' money is frozen in the bank. Their sons' investment apartments have been trashed by tenants, the furnishings sold off. The parents fear that anything they sign or any money they receive will end the company's or the country's obligations to them. They fear they are selling their sons for two airline tickets to a place they've never seen.

The high-rise apartment is a tower of Indians and West Indians, with a sprinkling of Orientals. The nearest bus stop kiosk is lined with women in saris. Boys practice cricket in the parking lot. Inside the building, even I wince a bit from the ferocity of onion fumes, the distinctive and immediate Indianness of frying *ghee*, but Judith Templeton maintains a steady flow of information. These poor old people are in imminent danger of losing their place and all their services.

I say to her, "They are Sikh. They will not open up to a Hindu woman." And what I want to add is, as much as I try not to, I stiffen now at the sight of beards and turbans. I remember a time when we all trusted each other in this new country, it was only the new country we worried about.

The two rooms are dark and stuffy. The lights are off, and an oil lamp sputters on the coffee table. The bent old lady has let us in, and her husband is wrapping a white turban over his oiled, hip-length hair. She immediately goes to the kitchen, and I hear the most familiar sound of an Indian home, tap water hitting and filling a teapot.

They have not paid their utility bills, out of fear and the inability to write a check. The telephone is gone; electricity and gas and water are soon to follow. They have told Judith their sons will provide. They are good boys, and they have always earned and looked after their parents.

We converse a bit in Hindi. They do not ask about the crash and I wonder if I should bring it up. If they think I am here merely as a translator, then they may feel insulted. There are thousands of Punjabi-speakers, Sikhs, in Toronto to do a better job. And so I say to the old lady, "I too have lost my sons, and my husband, in the crash."

Her eyes immediately fill with tears. The man mutters a few words which sound like a blessing. "God provides and God takes away," he says.

I want to say, but only men destroy and give back nothing. "My boys and my husband are not coming back," I say. "We have to understand that."

Now the old woman responds. "But who is to say? Man alone does not decide these things." To this her husband adds his agreement.

Judith asks about the bank papers, the release forms. With a stroke of the pen, they will have a provincial trustee to pay their bills, invest their money, send them a monthly pension.

"Do you know this woman?" I ask them.

The man raises his hand from the table, turns it over and seems to regard each finger separately before he answers. "This young lady is always coming here, we make tea for her and she leaves papers for us to sign." His eyes scan a pile of papers in the corner of the room. "Soon we will be out of tea, then will she go away?"

The old lady adds, "I have asked my neighbors and no one else gets *angrezi* visitors. What have we done?"

"It's her job," I try to explain. "The government is worried. Soon you will have no place to stay, no lights, no gas, no water."

"Government will get its money. Tell her not to worry, we are honorable people."

I try to explain the government wishes to give money, not take. He raises his hand. "Let them take," he says. "We are accustomed to that. That is no problem."

"We are strong people," says the wife. "Tell her that."

"Who needs all this machinery?" demands the husband. "It is unhealthy, the bright lights, the cold air on a hot day, the cold food, the four gas rings. God will provide, not government."

"When our boys return," the mother says. Her husband sucks his teeth. "Enough talk," he says.

Judith breaks in. "Have you convinced them?" The snaps on her cordovan briefcase go off like firecrackers in that quiet apartment. She lays the sheaf of legal papers on the coffee table. "If they can't write their names, an X will do—I've told them that."

Now the old lady has shuffled to the kitchen and soon emerges with a pot of tea and two cups. "I think my bladder will go first on a job like this," Judith says to me, smiling. "If only there was some way of reaching them. Please thank her for the tea. Tell her she's very kind."

I nod in Judith's direction and tell them in Hindi, "She thanks you for the tea. She thinks you are being very hospitable but she doesn't have the slightest idea what it means."

I want to say, humor her. I want to say, my boys and my husband are with me too, more than ever. I look in the old man's eyes and I can read his stubborn, peasant's message: *I have protected this woman as best I can. She is the only person I have left. Give to me or take from me what you will, but I will not sign for it. I will not pretend that I accept.*

In the car, Judith says, "You see what I'm up against? I'm sure they're lovely people, but their stubbornness and ignorance are driving me crazy. They think signing a paper is signing their sons' death warrants, don't they?"

I am looking out the window. I want to say, *In our culture, it is a parent's duty to hope.*

"Now Shaila, this next woman is a real mess. She cries day and night, and she refuses all medical help. We may have to—"

"—Let me out at the subway," I say.

"I beg your pardon?" I can feel those blue eyes staring at me.

It would not be like her to disobey. She merely disapproves, and slows at a corner to let me out. Her voice is plaintive. "Is there anything I said? Anything I did?"

I could answer her suddenly in a dozen ways, but I choose not to. "Shaila? Let's talk about it," I hear, then slam the door.

A wife and mother begins her new life in a new country, and that life is cut short. Yet her husband tells her: Complete what we have started. We, who stayed out of politics and came halfway around the world to avoid religious and political feuding have been the first in the New World to die from it. I no longer know what we started, nor how to complete it. I write letters to the editors of local papers and to members of Parliament. Now at least they admit it was a bomb. One MP answers back, with sympathy, but with a challenge. You want to make a difference? Work on a campaign. Work on mine. Politicize the Indian voter.

My husband's old lawyer helps me set up a trust. Vikram was a saver and a careful investor. He had saved the boys' boarding school and college fees. I sell the pink house at four times what we paid for it and take a small apartment downtown. I am looking for a charity to support.

We are deep in the Toronto winter, gray skies, icy pavements. I stay indoors, watching television. I have tried to assess my situation, how best to live my life, to complete what we began so many years ago. Kusum has written me from Hardwar that her life is now serene. She has seen Satish and has heard her daughter sing again. Kusum was on a pilgrimage, passing through a village when she heard a young girl's voice, singing one of her daughter's favorite *bhajans*. She followed the music through the squalor of a Himalayan village, to a hut where a young girl, an exact replica of her daughter, was fanning coals under the kitchen fire. When she appeared, the girl cried out, "Ma!" and ran away. What did I think of that?

I think I can only envy her.

Pam didn't make it to California, but writes me from Vancouver. She works in a department store, giving make-up hints to Indian and Oriental girls. Dr. Ranganathan has given up his commute, given up his house and job, and accepted an academic position in Texas where no one knows his story and he has vowed not to tell it. He calls me now once a week.

I wait, I listen, and I pray, but Vikram has not returned to me. The voices and the shapes and the nights filled with visions ended abruptly several weeks ago.

I take it as a sign.

One rare, beautiful, sunny day last week, returning from a small errand on Yonge Street, I was walking through the park from the subway to my apartment. I live equidistant from the Ontario Houses of Parliament and the university of Toronto. The day was not cold, but something in the bare trees caught my attention. I looked up from the gravel, into the branches and the clear blue sky beyond. I thought I heard the rustling of larger forms, and I waited a moment for voices. Nothing.

"What?" I asked.

Then as I stood in the path looking north to Queen's Park and west to the university, I heard the voices of my family one last time. *Your time has come*, they said. *Go, be brave.*

I do not know where this voyage I have begun will end. I do not know which direction I will take. I dropped the package on a park bench and started walking.

This Place

Beth Brant

"Mother, I am gay. I have AIDS." The telephone call that it almost killed him to make.

The silence. Then, "Come home to us."

David came home because he was dying. He expected to see his place of birth in a new way, as if he were a photographer capturing scenes through diverse lenses. *Scene one: through a living man's eyes. Scene Two: through a dying man's eyes.* But the beauty remembered was the beauty that still existed. Nothing had changed in ten years. The water of the Bay just as blue and smooth. The white pines just as tall and green. The dirt roads as brown and rutted as the day he had left. His mother as small and beautiful, her dark hair with even more grey streaks running through the braid she wrapped around her head.

Had nothing changed but him?

He had left this place and gone to the city to look for other men like himself. He found them. He found a new life, a different life. He found so much. Even the virus that now ate at him. David came home and was afraid of death.

David could feel the virus changing his body, making marks on his insides. Outside, too, his body was marked: by the tumors growing on his face and the paleness of his skin. He worried that the virus was somehow taking away his color, bleaching the melanin that turned him polished copper in the summer and left him light terra cotta in winter. He could feel the virus at war with the melanin and he could not check the battle.He couldn't hold this virus in his fist and squeeze the death out of it. He could only wait and look in the mirror to see the casualty of this war. David was afraid.

176

"Mother, am I turning white?"

"No, my baby son. You are dark and beautiful. Your hair is black and shiny as ever. Your eyes are tired, but still as brown and strong as the day you left this place."

He knew she lied to him. Mothers lie about their children's pain. *It will go away*, they say. *I'll make it better*, they say. *Oh, Mother, make it better, make it go away. I'm afraid of death.*

He felt the virus eating his hair. It fell out in clumps as he combed it. His forehead got broader and receded further. The blackness of the strands had dulled to some nondescript color. His braid was thin and lifeless, not as it used to be, snapping like a whip across his back, or gliding down his back like a snake.

David's sister brought her children to see him. They crawled on his lap and kissed him. He was afraid for them. Afraid the virus would reach out of his body and grab these babies and eat at them until they, too, disappeared in its grip. The virus put a fear in him—a fear that he could wipe out his people by breathing, by talking, by living. David saw, in his dreams, the virus eating away at this place until it was gone.

His dreams were also about a place called death. Death seemed to be a gaping hole in the world where David looked and there was nothing. He would wake from these dreams sweating, his limbs filled with pain. He had lived his life so well, so hard, clutching it to him like food, swallowing and being nourished. He wanted to greet death like that, opening his arms to it, laughing and embracing that other world. But he was afraid.

"Mother, I am afraid of death."

"Joseph is coming to visit."

On a day when David was seated in his chair before the window, looking out at the way the bright sun had turned everything in the yard golden, he heard the pickup truck making its way down the dirt road to the house. He also heard a voice singing. David laughed out loud. The song being sung was "All My Exes Live in Texas," and he knew that Joseph was on his way to him.

The truck came to a screeching, convulsive stop. David's mother went out to greet the man who jumped from the truck laughing, "Where's the patient?" As David watched, Joseph extracted a brown paper bag and an orange-striped cat from the truck. "Meet my friend, the Prophet. You can call her Prophet." David's mother reached for the cat who nudged at her breast and looked into her face. Joseph kissed Grace on the cheek. Prophet licked Grace's face. David wondered at the fact that Joseph looked the same as he had when David was a child. Dressed in faded jeans and a flannel shirt, Joseph's face was lean and unlined. His nose was sharp and slightly curved at the end, like a bird's beak. His eyes were black and round, reminding David again of a bird, perhaps a kestrel or a falcon. Joseph wore long, beaded earrings that draped across the front of his shirt. His hair, black and coarse, was tied back with a leather string. His fingers were covered with silver-and-garnet-studded rings, his hands delicate but used. Joseph looked at the young man in the window and lifted his hand in a greeting. Then he smiled and his face took on the unfinished look of a child. David waved back, feeling excitement— the way he used to feel before going to a party.

"This ain't goin' to be like any party you ever went to," Joseph remarked as he stepped through the doorway. "Here, have a Prophet," and he lifted the orange cat from Grace's arms onto David's lap.

Prophet looked intently at David's face, then kneaded his lap and settled herself on it, where she purred. David stroked the orange fur and scratched the cat's head. She burrowed deeper in his lap. "I would get up to greet you, but I think Prophet's got something else in mind."

Joseph laughed. "We wouldn't want to disturb her highness. David, we have not seen each other in many years." He bent down to kiss the young man on his forehead. "You don't look so good." Joseph eyed him critically.

"Thanks. But you look the same as ever."

"You in a lot of pain," Joseph said in a statement, not a question.

"Yeah, a lot of pain. I take about fifty pills a day. They don't seem to make that much of a difference." David continued to stroke Prophet.

"You think I can cure you?"

"No."

"Good, because I can't. All of us are afraid of death, though. We don't know what to expect, what to take with us." He looked in his paper sack. "Maybe I got the right things here."

Grace went into the kitchen, and Joseph pulled up a chair and sat beside David. Looking at Prophet asleep on David's lap, Joseph remarked, "Cats is smart. This one had a brother looked just like her. I called him Tecumseh. One morning I woke up and he was gone. I asked the Prophet if she knew where her brother went. She looked at me and blinked, then turned her head away like I'd said somethin' rude. I went outside to look for Tecumseh and I found him, layin' dead under a rose bush. It was a good year for the roses, they was bloomin' to beat the band. He had chosen the red roses to die under. That was a good choice, don't you think? I buried him under that red rose bush. The old man knew what *he* wanted, but he had to let me know, me not bein' as smart as a cat. Prophet came out and sat on the grave. She sat there for three days and nights. Cats are different from us. We worry about fittin' things to our own purpose. Cats don't worry

about them things. They live, they die. They get buried under a red
rose bush. Smart, huh?"

"You got any spare rose bushes? Only make mine flaming pink!"
David laughed, then began coughing, blood spattering the kleenex
he held to his mouth.

The Prophet jumped from David's lap and sat on the floor, her back
to him.

"Now I've done it," David gasped. "Come back. Here kitty, kitty,
kitty."

The Prophet turned and gave him a look of contempt, her back
twitching, her tail moving back and forth on the floor.

"Huh," Joseph said. "She ain't comin' back for a while. Don't like
the name Kitty."

Grace came in to announce dinner. David grabbed his cane and
shuffled to the table. He sat down, gasping for breath. "Takes longer
every time. I think I'm losing feeling in my right leg, but what the
hell, I'd crawl to the table for Mother's beef stew." He half-heartedly
lifted the spoon to his mouth. "My appetite's still pretty good, isn't it,
Mother?"

Grace smiled at her son. "The day your appetite goes is the day I
go."

She had made fresh bread to eat with the stew and set dishes of
pickles and cheese on the table. Joseph rubbed his hands together in
glee. "This looks good!" They ate, talking local gossip, the Prophet sitting daintily beside Joseph's chair. David's hands shook as he barely
fed himself, spilling stew on his blue shirt. Grace fussed and tied a
napkin around his neck. David smiled, "Next, she'll be feeding me or
giving me a bottle." He winked at his mother and blew a kiss across
the table to her. She caught it and put it on her cheek.

Joseph watched while he fed bits of meat to Prophet. He looked in
his sack and pulled out a dish covered in wax paper. "I made these
this mornin'. Butter tarts. The flakiest crust you'll find anywhere.
You gotta use lard, none of that shortenin'. Lard is what makes a
crust that'll melt in your mouth. It's my gift to you, David."

As David bit into the sweetness of the tart, he looked at Joseph,
his earrings swinging against his shoulders, his hands making pat-
terns in the air as he described the making of the tarts, and David
thought, *He acts like a queen.* He looked harder at Joseph, thinking,
if you put him in a city, in a gay bar, the old nelly would fit right in.
David laughed out loud.

Grace looked startled, but Joseph grinned and nodded his head.
"Catchin' on, my young friend?"

As he helped clear the table, David smiled with his new knowledge.
Collapsing into his reclining chair, David swallowed his medicine and

laid his head back, closing his eyes. He could hear the murmurs between Joseph and Grace, his mother always a living, vivid presence
in his life—his reason for hanging on so long to life. "I love you,
Mother," he whispered. He opened his eyes to the dry touch of
Joseph's fingers on his face. His mother was bringing out the moccasins he had made from rabbit hide and had beaded the nights they
sat and watched TV. She presented them to Joseph. He unlaced his
red hightops and slipped the beautiful moccasins on his feet. He put
his feet out in front of him in admiration. He got up and walked in
them. He jumped and clicked his heels together. "Thank you, Grace.
You haven't lost your touch, have you? Now it's time for you to go.
Don't come back till the mornin'."

Grace gathered her things together and stood looking at David.
Her face shifted with emotions: sorrow, pride, fear, love. She kissed
her son and hugged Joseph. They watched her leave.

Joseph turned and asked David, "You tryin' to be brave for your
mom? Let me tell you somethin' about mothers. They know everything. She feels what you're goin' through. Can't hide it, even though
you try."

"No! I don't want her to know how bad it gets. I can see it in her
face, she gets crazy not knowing what to do for me. But this is the
real crazy part, I don't want to let go of her. That death . . . that place
. . . she won't be there."

The Prophet jumped on Joseph's lap and began washing herself.
"That's true. Her time isn't here yet. David, you have lived your life
in the way that was best for you. You think Grace didn't know why
you left here? Think she didn't know you was gay? You can't tell
someone like Grace not to go crazy when her son is dyin'. You can't
tell her how to mourn you. And you can't be draggin' her along with
you when you leave this place."

"I don't want to do that. I feel like a little kid when I was scared
of a nightmare. Mother would make it go away. Death is like that
nightmare. I gotta meet it on my own, but I'm scared."

"Yes, I know you are," and Joseph reached for David's hand.
David's bony fingers closed over Joseph's.

"When I lived in the city, I used to get so homesick for this place.
I'd picture the way it looked—the sky, the trees, my relatives. I'd
dream it all up in my mind, but I never thought I would come back. I
made my life in the city, thinking I couldn't come back here. My people don't want queers, faggots living among them. But now, some of
us are coming home to die. Where else would we go but back to our
homes, our families? What a joke, eh? They couldn't deal with my life,
now they gotta deal with my death. God, I think about the guys that
really can't go home. They have to die alone in some hospital, or even

on the street. There was a guy I knew, Ojibwe, and he died outside his apartment. I heard about it after it happened and I got in this rage! People just walking by him, probably thinking, oh here's another drunk Indian, just walking by him! And him, getting cold and no one would touch him." Tears were moving down David's face. He lifted his hand to wipe his face. "That's when I hated being an Indian. My own people, hateful to that guy. He was scared to go home. Probably thought they'd throw him out again, or stone him or something."

"Well, Indians got no immunity from hatefulness or stupidity, David. Maybe he had made his choice to die alone. Maybe he didn't have a home to go to."

David looked shocked. "No, that can't be true. I know what it's like. I grew up here, remember? It seemed like I had to make a choice, be gay or be an Indian. Some choice, eh? So I moved to the city." David sighed, then began to cough.

Joseph stroked Prophet, whose ears were twitching. "Even a city can't take the Indian part away. Even a virus can't do that, my young friend." He dipped into his sack and held out a piece of metal to David. "Look in this. What do you see?"

David held the piece of metal to his face. He saw a blurred image of himself, tumors covering his face. When he tilted the piece of tin, he saw himself laughing and dressed in his finest clothes, dancing in the bar in the city. He tilted it yet another way and saw himself dancing at a pow wow, his hair fanning out as he twirled and jumped. In another tilt, he saw himself as a child, sitting on Grandmother's lap.

"Which one is you?" Joseph asked.

"All of them."

"When the Prophet was a kitten," Joseph said, petting the now sleeping cat, "she used to keep me awake at night. She'd jump on my head just as I was dozin' off. I'd knock her away and turn over, but just when that sweet moment of sleep was callin' me, she'd jump on my head again. I thought maybe she was hungry and I'd get up to feed her. She'd eat, then start the whole routine all over again. She even got Tecumseh in the act. While she'd jump on my head, he'd get under the covers and bite my feet. I finally gave up and got out of bed and went outside and looked at the sky. About the fifth night of these carryin' ons, I *really* looked at the sky. I saw all the stars as if they was printed on the insides of my eyes. I saw the moon like she really was. And I started to pray to Sky Woman, blinkin' and shinin' up there. She answered me back, too, all because the cats was smarter than me. Nothin' hides in front of old Sky Woman. You might think *she's* hidin' when you can't see her, but she's there, checkin' everything out. People can't hide from her. And people can't hide from themselves."

"Is that what I've done?" David asked, his face sad. "I've always been proud of being Mohawk, of being from here. I *am* proud of being gay even though everywhere I turned, someone was telling me not to be either. In the city they didn't want me to be Native. In this place, they don't want me to be gay. It can drive you crazy! *Be this. Be that. Don't be this way.* So you get to be like an actor, changing roles and faces to please somebody out there who hates your guts for what you are." David laughed. "When I was diagnosed I thought, well, now I don't have to pretend anymore. It's all out in the open. I'm going to die, and why did I waste my time and tears worrying about all this other stuff? I got real active in AIDS work. I wanted to reach out to all the Indian gays I knew, form support groups, lean on each other. 'Cause the other guys just didn't understand us. I was a fireball for two years, real busy, but then I got too sick to do much of anything. My friends were good, but they couldn't take care of me anymore. I came home. Here I sit, Grandfather, waiting for death, but scared shitless."

Joseph began to hum and sing, "Crazy . . . I'm crazy for feelin' so lonely." He stuck is hand inside the sack and handed David a piece of paper.

> *We, as the original inhabitants of this country, and sovereigns of the soil, look upon ourselves as equally independent and free as any other nation or nations. This country was given to us by the Great Spirit above; we wish to enjoy it, and have our passage along the lake, within the line we have pointed out. The great exertions we have made, for this number of years, to accomplish a peace and have not been able to obtain it; our patience, as we have observed, is exhausted. We, therefore, throw ourselves under the protection of the Great Spirit above, who will order all things for the best. We have told you our patience is worn out, but that we wish for peace and whenever we hear that pleasing sound, we shall pay attention to it. Until then, you will pay attention to us.*

"My ancestor. Quite a man." David held the paper in his thin hands.

"Yes, he was. Diplomats, they called him and his sister. We call them warriors."

David read the words again. "Grandfather, I would like to be a warrior like this man. I would like to see death coming and run to meet it, not afraid, not hiding behind my mother."

"Who says you ain't a warrior? David, the bravest people I knew were the ones that lived and kept on livin'. Those two, Tyendinaga and Molly, they fought to keep us alive as a people. Looks to me like you're as fine a warrior as they was. David, you lived!"

The Prophet suddenly came awake and stretched to her full length. She sat up and washed her face. She blinked at David, her yellow eyes staring at him until he looked away. She jumped off Joseph's lap and settled herself in front of David's feet.

"Trust the Prophet to interrupt the proceedings. Let's go outside and sit on the porch." Joseph stood up and stretched his arms and shook his legs.

David reached for his cane, his body curved and stooped. Joseph got a blanket to wrap him in against the cool night air. David made his way toward the front door. Joseph went to the kitchen and brought out two mugs of coffee and the rest of the butter tarts. They settled on the porch steps.

"David, look at the moon. When she's a crescent like that, I think Sky Woman's smilin' at us. More than likely, laughin'. She has big jobs to do like pullin' in the tides, and we sit here yappin' about life and death."

"The moon is beautiful. Somehow, it never seemed to shine like that in the city." David began coughing again, his body shaking and throbbing.

Joseph held onto him until the shaking stopped. "David, you're just a rez boy, ain't you? Nothin' looks as good as here, eh? But I think so, too. One time, a long time ago, I thought about leavin' here."

"Why didn't you? It can't have been easy for you. Or were things different then? Maybe not so homophobic, not so much hatred?"

"Oh, things was bad. But not in that way. There was hatred, alright. The kind that makes people turn to the bottle or put a gun in their mouth and shoot." David winced, remembering his father's death. Joseph continued. "That kind of hatred, self-hatred. I stayed because I was supposed to. I fought it, but I had to stay. It was my job." He began a song. "*Your cheatin' heart will tell on you. You'll cry and cry, the way I do*. Sing with me, David." And they sang until the last words were finished and Joseph hugged David.

"I thought medicine men were supposed to chant and cast spells, not sing old Hank Williams' songs," David teased.

Joseph looked surprised. "Oh, some do. Some do. But how many medicine people you know, David?"

"Only you, Grandfather."

"Well then, there you go. What you see is what you get."

"When my father died, I remember being shut out from what was going on. I know they were all trying to protect me and Sister, but we were scared. One day he was there, the next day he wasn't. He wasn't the greatest dad, but he was ours! You were there, Grandfather. Why did he do it?"

Joseph took a deep breath and let it out. It lingered in the night air like a puff of smoke. "Because he didn't know any other way. Are you judgin' him, David? 'Cause if you are, you can forget it. Too many people made a judgment on your father all his life. He doesn't need yours to add to it." Joseph's face became angry, then softened as he took David's hand again. "Children get scared. We fail you because we fail ourselves. We think *you'll* get over it because you're younger and have fewer memories. Grownups are fools, David. Your father didn't know what else to do with his life, a life he thought was worthless. So he shot it away."

David wept. "I've thought about shooting mine away, like him. Like father, like son, isn't that what the people would say? So, I didn't, all because I don't want to be mentioned in the same breath with him. Pride, that's all that kept me going. And I couldn't do the same thing to my mother and sister that he did to us."

"You're a lot like your dad. Sweet, like he was. Oh yes," Joseph looked at David's disbelieving face, "a sweet man. When we was at residential school together, he's the one that took me under his wing. He fought the grownups and the other kids that ganged up on me. He was always my friend. He didn't fail me, ever. And I tried not to let him down, but I wasn't enough to keep that gun out of his hand. Nobody was enough, David. Not you, or your mom or your sister. Don't you judge him. He wouldn't have judged you." Joseph raised his face to the crescent moon and closed his eyes.

David felt a small piece of pain dislodge from inside him. It floated away in the night's darkness. "Thank you for telling me that, Grandfather. I always loved him."

Joseph smiled, his crooked teeth shining white in the moon's light. "Love is a funny thing, David. It stays constant, like her," he pointed to the crescent. "When you cut through all the crap, the need and greed part, you got the good, lastin' stuff. She knew that," and he pointed again to the moon. "She put herself up there to remind us of her love, not to admire her pretty shine. Of course, the pretty shine doesn't hurt, does it?" And they laughed together.

David said, "I met my pretty shine in the city. He will always be the love of my life, even though he doesn't feel that way about me. We're still friends. . . . God, the city was so different for me—I loved it! Excitement. All those gorgeous men. If I'd stayed here, I wouldn't have known the world was full of gay people. If I'd stayed here though, maybe I wouldn't have gotten AIDS." David pulled the blanket closer around him and shivered.

Joseph squeezed David's wasting fingers. "Do you regret any of it?"

"No. I've thought about that a lot. I only wish I could have stayed, but I thought I had to make the choice and don't know what would have happened if I hadn't left."

Joseph rustled in his sack. "Who can read the future? Well, maybe I can, but can you read the past as well? Here, take this."

David held out his hand. A dry snakeskin was deposited into his dry palm. The skin was faded but still showed orange-and-black markings.

"I saw this snake shed her skin. I was walking in the bush and heard a very small noise. I watched her wriggle out of her old life, just like she was removin' an overcoat. It took this snake a long time, but then, there she was in her new overcoat, her old skin just lyin' there waitin' for me to pick it up and give it to you."

"Thank you, Grandfather. It's beautiful." David touched the snakeskin and looked into Joseph's face. "I think it would be wonderful if we could shed ourselves like this and have a brand-new, beautiful skin to face the world. Or maybe, to face death."

"We do, David. A snake doesn't put on a new skin with different colors. She has the same one, just layers of it. She doesn't become a new snake, but older and wiser with each shedding. Humans shed. We don't pay attention to it, though. We get new chances all the time. A snake makes use of her chances; that's why she's a snake and we're not. We never know when we got a good thing goin'."

"That's true! Mother used to tell me I was lucky, I had it good compared to other little boys. She was right, of course." David giggled into his hand. "She is always right. Why is that, Grandfather?"

"Now you got me. That's something I'll never know either!"

They laughed, the sound filling the night air. Prophet scratched at the door to be let out. "The Prophet's afraid she's missin' out on something. Those butter tarts, maybe." Joseph got up to open the door.

The Prophet streaked out the open door and ran to the cluster of apple trees. She climbed one and sat on a branch. David could see the yellow glow of her eyes as she watched the men drink their coffee and bite into the tarts.

Joseph remarked between bites, "Prophet does it every time. I'd sit around all night talkin' if she didn't remind me why I was here."

David started to shake. "I'm afraid, Grandfather."

"Yes, I know, David. We'll go inside, and you can lay down while I make some special tea. I'm here with you, David. I won't leave you."

David clutched the snakeskin in his hand and struggled to his feet. He made his way into the house and to the couch where he started coughing and spitting up blood. Joseph cleaned David's face and wrapped the blanket tightly around his skinny body. He went to the kitchen, and David could hear him singing, "I fall to pieces . . . each time I see you again." David smiled, the voice reassuring to him.

"The Prophet's still in that apple tree, starin' at the house," said Joseph, as he brought a steaming mug of liquid to David.

David sipped the tea and made a face. "What is this stuff? It tastes like wet leaves!"

"It is wet leaves. Drink up. It's good for what ails you."

"Yeah, right," David smiled, "I notice you're not drinking any."

"Well, I'm not the sick one, am I?"

David drank the brew, watching Joseph walk around the room, picking up books and stacking them neatly, straightening a picture hanging on the wall, tidying a lamp table. "There's a dust rag in the broom closet. The rug could use a shake and the windows need a wash," David said teasingly.

"You're a regular Henny Youngman, ain't you?"

"Who?"

"All finished?" Joseph pointed to the mug. "If you want more, you can't have it. I only brought enough for one cup."

David pushed the mug toward Joseph. "Please, no more. I think I'll survive without it."

"Ah, survival. Let me tell you about that one," Joseph sat on the couch at David's feet.

David felt heavy in his body. He tried to lift his hand, but it was too much of an effort. He tried to speak, but his voice wouldn't move out of him. He looked at Joseph who was talking, but his voice was thin and far away. He saw the Prophet had come back into the house and was sitting on Joseph's lap. The Prophet stared at David with her yellow eyes and smiled at him. Was that a smile? What was that tea? Wet leaves . . . and David was falling was falling back into wet leaves and it was autumn the air smelled like winter he was a boy a boy who jumped up from wet leaves and ran he ran he was chasing something he felt so good so good this is what childhood is you run you laugh you open your mouth you feel the wind on your tongue the sun on your head the apple trees were giving up their gifts of fruit you picked an apple you feel you taste the juice running down your throat the apple made a loud crunch as you bit and the swallows in the tree were waiting for the core to be thrown down so they could share the fruit of the tree the geese were flying you ran you ran into the cornfield and scared the pheasant who was picking at the seed you laughed you laughed it was a perfect day you picked up a feather and put it in your pocket the day was perfect when you were a child you ran you laughed you played you were loved you loved you were a child it was good so good good to be a child in this place this place this place never changed this place this place.

David opened his eyes. The Prophet was washing her tail. Joseph held a turtle rattle in his left hand. He was talking . . . *and then the*

church people sent their missionaries here to teach us to be christian
but we . . .

David was falling he fell into the sound of the turtle's rattle he
fell into the turtle's mouth he shook his body shook and . . . *fought*
them . . . he fell into the sound of the rattle he was the rattle's sound
the music the music he was dancing dancing with the first man he
ever loved they were dancing holding holding the music the music
the turtle's music was in them through them in them . . . *killed us*
. . . he went home he went with the first man he ever loved the music was beating was beating their hearts the rattle the music they
fell onto the bed the music the music touched them the turtle
touched them the rattle touched them they touched they touched
the touching was music was music his body singing music his body
the rattle of the turtle the first man he loved . . . *we fought back . . .*
their bodies singing shaking joining joining everything was music
was music so good so good the first man he loved Thomas Thomas
. . . *they kept killing us off . . .* Tommy Tommy singing sighing joining . . . *but we . . .* singing our bodies singing Tommy David Tommy
Tommy . . . *survived. . . .*

David's eyes opened. The room was dark. The Prophet was staring, smiling, her eyes brilliant yellow. Joseph was staring also, his
eyes sending out shafts of brilliance, laser beams into his soul.

"Grandfather."

Joseph held up the rattle and sang a song with no words, a song
in a high, quivering voice. Joseph's face changed shape. He became
a cat. The Prophet sat smiling, her teeth white in the dark room.
Joseph sang and became a wolf, lemon-yellow eyes steady on David.
Joseph sang and he became a snake hissing his song, he eyes sending out shards of light. Joseph sang and shook the turtle. He sang.

"Grandfather."

David was falling he fell into the song of the cat the song of the
wolf the song of the snake the song of the turtle he fell he fell into the
turtle's mouth the turtle's song he was shaking was shaking his
grandmother was singing was singing a song a song in Indian his
grandmother was singing singing he was singing with Grandmother
he was sitting on Grandma's lap her lap she was holding him close
so close . . . *our people survived . . .* she sang his mother sang his sister sang his father sang he sang he was singing in Indian Indian the
voices the songs in Indian . . . *the sicknesses came . . .* singing singing
his grandmother holding him his mother his father singing . . .
measles, smallpox . . . Grandmother talking singing in Indian the
language the song of Indian the people the song Grandma's hair
brushing against his face as she whispered and told him he . . . *AIDS*
. . . was an Indian Mohawk singing songs Mohawk the voices

Kanienka 'ha'ka the song the song of this place this Indian place this place.

The rattle was silent. The Prophet was sitting in a hump, the fur around her neck electric, like an orange ruff. Joseph sat, his laser eyes bright in the face of an old, old man. He spoke, his voice not audible, the words not recognizable, and David heard.

"They took parts of us and cut them up and threw them to the winds. They made lies we would believe. We look for the parts to put ourselves back together. To put the earth back together. It is broken. We look for truth to put us all together again. There is a piece here. A part there. We scavenge and collect. Some pieces are lost. We will find them. Some parts are found, and we do not see them yet. We gather the pieces and bring them together. *We* bring them together. *We* make the truth about ourselves. *We* make the truth."

David was falling was falling he fell he fell into the sound of the ancient voice the ancient words he was falling into the sounds of screaming screaming in his face dirty Indian faggot fucking faggot the voices screaming you dirty Indian you the sound of fists of fists the sound of hate the sound of hate you dirty Indian you dirty faggot the sound of hate the sound of blood the taste of blood in his mouth the taste the hate the hate . . . *we collect the parts that have been damaged* . . . the hate the pain as they raped him you dirty Indian faggot the hate the blood the rape the sound of rape . . . *we hunt for the pieces* . . . the hate the pain the fear the dirty Indian faggot . . . *we gather it all together* . . . you filthy Indian scum you dirty you dirty you dirty . . . *we are resisters, warriors* . . . you dirty Indian you dirty faggot the rape the sound of you dirty filthy . . . *we do not believe the lies they* . . . the taste the taste the taste of hate in his mouth.

David cried out. Joseph stroked his thinning hair, the turtle held over his body. "They hurt us in so many ways. The least of what they did was to kill us. They turned us into missing parts. Until we find those missing parts we kill ourselves with shame, with fear, with hate. All those parts just waitin' to be gathered together to make us. Us. A whole people. The biggest missing piece is love, David. *Love!*"

The Prophet leapt in the air and hissed. She leapt again and knocked the turtle rattle back into Joseph's lap.

"The Prophet says we are not finished. Who am *I* to argue with *her?*"

David tugged at the man's arm. "Joseph. Grandfather. I am so thirsty, so thirsty."

David was falling was falling into the shake of the rattle he fell he fell into the turtle's mouth he fell he was flying he flew he was inside the turtle the turtle shook he fell into voices voices asking him are you ready his heart his heart was beating are you ready his heart grew larger his heart was beating his heart the turtle asked him are you ready his grandmother held out her hand and touched him are you ready are you ready his grandmother touched his heart are you ready his father touched his heart are you ready the people held out their hands are you ready he reached for their hands his heart was beating inside the turtle a drum a drum are you ready Turtle touched his heart are you ready he fell he put out his arms he held out his arms I am ready they touched him I am ready I am ready I am ready.

David opened his eyes. The taste of tears was in his mouth. "I saw it." Prophet jumped delicately on David's chest and licked the salt tears from his face. She sat back on her haunches and watched David speak. "I saw my grandmother, my father. They touched me." He began coughing again, retching blood.

Joseph held a towel to David's mouth and touched the young man's face. "You found your parts, your pieces." Digging into his sack, he pulled out a white feather. "This is from a whistling swan. They stop here in the spring before goin' on to Alaska. The thing about them—they never know what they'll find when they get there. They just know they got to get there. When our bodies are no longer here, *we* are still here." He stood up, his joints creaking and snapping. "Your mother is comin'. The sun is real bright today. It's a good day to go." He scooped Prophet up from David's lap and draped her across his shoulder.

"Thank you, Grandfather," David whispered, his breath coming in ragged bursts.

David heard him go out the front door. He couldn't see, but he heard Joseph talking to the Prophet. He heard the truck door slam and the engine start its rattling and wheezing. David moved his hands on the blanket to find the tin, the snakeskin, his ancestor's words, the feather. He touched them and felt Joseph's presence. The sound of his mother's car made him struggle to sit up. He heard the door open and the footsteps of his mother coming into the room. He felt her standing by him, her cool fingers touching his face and hands.

He opened his mouth to say good-bye.

The Storyteller

Jason Laus Baluyut

It was the summer of my eighteenth birthday. My parents and I had flown into California from Michigan to visit relatives and catch up on old times, or so my mother said—although I had been witness to enough of her strained conversations with my father, enough of her frustrated long-distance arguments with the folks in L.A., enough of the lines of tension that defined her movements as she packed our suitcases for the trip, to know that this was anything but an innocent family vacation. This was, more than anything, a business trip, regarding the same subject which had kept the members of my mother's family feuding for years: who would assume responsibility for my mother's mother, who would feed her, who would wash her and move her as her limbs daily lost their strength, who would describe for her the world she could no longer see with her own eyes; and finally, whenever she died, who would hold the title to the land she owned in Manila which—so legend had it—had once belonged to the first *encomenderos* who arrived, with their soldiers and their Jesuit priests, at the virgin shores of the country.

I had grown up in the shadow of my mother's arguments with her brothers. I had played and laughed and gotten into fistfights and fallen in love in Manila's noisy and dust-choked streets as Mama made phone calls in the shadows of the ancestral house, wrote letters to Uncle Teodoro and Uncle Emmanuel who in my youth had already made new lives for themselves in the States, held meetings with her remaining three brothers in the old family dining rooms that had grown damp and dusty with neglect and was invaded by a perennial chill. Always, when I came in at dusk scratched and filthy from play or weary from school, I would pass by the dining room on

190

my way upstairs to the family bedroom and catch a glimpse of Mama sitting there, alone or with her arguing brothers, her brows knitted together and her mouth compressed in a tight line that tried to keep in the tension that rose from her throat and brimmed in her eyes. I had never allowed myself to dwell on it. But at night, as I drifted to sleep between the silent forms of my parents, I connected Mama's restless stirring with the coughing and the sing-song babbling that came from the room below, and my thoughts turned to the old woman there who was slowly fading from the world. My *Lola* Silang is dying and Mama is sad, I thought, because no one wants to save her.

A decade later still no one did. My mother's family had dispersed, scattered like seeds into destiny's various corners: Uncle Fidel married the grand-daughter of a *gobernador* and moved away to one of the country's far provinces; Uncle Teodoro wrote from the States and told us how the latest earthquake had all but devastated his restaurant business; Uncle Manny announced from Berkeley that he had graduated from his medical studies; and Uncle Ignacio lay peacefully under the grass of Loyola Memorial Park, dead four years from a stray bullet in the revolution. That was the last straw for Mama; she swore at Ignacio's funeral that her son would never be raised in a place so thick with shotgun politics, and the same wave of panic and political upheaval that had claimed my uncle's life swept my parents and me to the United States, to Michigan, where we settled down with the blessings of the Department of Immigration and tried as best we could to stitch the patches of our lives back together. And through all the cataclysms, the marriages and deaths and revolutions that tore my mother's family apart, Lola Silang remained in the darkness of the ancestral house in Manila, singing her hymns softly to herself, her eyes dimmed by a descending cloak of shadows, her mind unravelling into a chaos of memories and dreams.

Only Uncle Eduardo stayed with her now, and when Mama found out how her youngest brother had surrounded the old mansion with German shepherds and kept Lola Silang confined in her room like a prisoner with the barest provisions, she flew into a rage. She began anew her correspondence with her brothers, denouncing Eduardo for his lack of love and respect for an old woman, for his base greed for property and his devil's patience as he waited for her to die. And it was devil's patience indeed, said Mama, for he had been waiting quietly for years—ever since the shadows began to encroach upon Lola Silang's eyes and the quivering sickness first touched her nerves, when he decided to approach her with a cool smile on his lips and tell her fervently that her favorite son was going to do her proud, was going to ignite a Charismatic movement among the heathen of this backwards country, was going to build churches upon the rocks and

in the valleys all dedicated to the God she loved. Lola Silang believed
him in her religious delirium, Mama recalled aloud whenever she
could get me to listen; she believed him, hung a halo of praise around
him whenever his name came into her head, and in a muddled ecstasy signed her name to any sheet of paper that Eduardo pushed in
front of her.

"God knows how hard I've had to fight that bastard brother of
mine," Mama would tell me in the quiet hours of the night as she
sipped her *kape*, her mouth drawn into that tight line of pain. "God
knows how long and how hard. You should be thankful your cousin
Lita's a practicing lawyer in Manila and that she'd do these things
for free, or we'd be up to our necks in debt before you've even started
your life . . ." And she would lapse into the foreign tongue of lawyers,
trying to explain to me the world of affidavits and contracts and litigation and how much she'd gone through in her battles with Eduardo in the arena of the courts, while I sat nodding next to her and
noticed only the bitter shape of her mouth, the eyebrows furrowed
like scars over old pain. The legal skirmishes alone couldn't possibly
have caused such deep sadness, I thought. I remembered then those
distant nights in the ancestral house, when my grandmother and my
three uncles and my parents and I occasionally sat down to a communal dinner in the chill of that dusty room, when Lola Silang offered smiling words to Fidel and Ignacio and heaped upon Eduardo
all the benedictions worthy of a servant of the Lord, and I thought I
understood. She never turned her face in Mama's direction, never acknowledged Mama's kind attentions, never spoke a word to her except in resentment or accusation—you, who are always trying to
turn me against my Eduardo, you, who married that good-for-
nothing *impakto* from the projects, you, who would have done great
things for the Lord had you been a son, you, my useless, useless
daughter. As Mama sipped her *kape* and talked of litigation I saw
scorned love inside her downturned eyes, like an eternal tear that
survived a journey across the sea and the hardships of a harsh northern land, to well up within her once more in hours of anger and re-
membrance.

And now the cause of her pain was here. On the summer of my
eighteenth birthday Uncle Eduardo called from Manila and told
Mama that their mother had fallen extremely ill, that she could no
longer speak nor walk, that she refused to have herself moved from
place to place and simply lay stiffly and stubbornly in bed, letting the
teaspoons of baby food which the hired help fed her trickle out of her
mouth and down her cheeks. He'd talked to all the doctors, exhausted all his resources, he said, and didn't know what else to do;
so he'd bought two one-way tickets to California and was sending

Uncle Fidel to take Lola Silang there, where he knew that Uncle Manny—now a certified doctor, after all—would give her the proper attention. "*Ang walanghiya*," Mama cursed Eduardo as she put down the receiver. "All those years treating her like a prisoner, like a dog from the streets, and now he wonders why she's so sick, doesn't even have the guts to face up to what he's done. Now he's sending Del to dump her here, like garbage, just like garbage, and he's expecting us to fix all his mistakes."

I watched her from the next room, listened quietly to her anger. She didn't mention that with Lola Silang and the surviving brothers gathered together a thousand miles away, Eduardo could easily snatch up the rights to the ancestral property the moment the old woman died, but I knew that Mama couldn't escape that realization. That was part of the fabric of her pain—the tension between love and strategy, the difficulty of treating Lola Silang as a pawn in a war for property and at the same time as a mother, to be cherished purely and simply, on the heart's unconditional terms. Mama gave voice to none of this, although her body sagged in a curve of weariness; but she straightened herself up, lips firmly together, told Papa to ask for vacation leave from the office the next day, and dialed the airport to make the earliest possible reservations for Los Angeles. While she waited on hold, the receiver cradled against her cheek, she saw me standing in the doorway and knew that I'd heard everything. But she smiled anyway, putting on a face to revive the dying cheer that still lingered from my birthday celebration a few days back, thinking perhaps that I deserved a life untainted by her sorrow. "Pack your bags, Pepe," she said. "We're going to see relatives and say hello to Uncle Emmanuel, you haven't seen him in a long time. And Lola Silang will be there too, I bet she'll be really glad to see you."

Uncle Manny stood at the entrance to his compact house, his giant, thick-boned frame barely contained in the doorway, and greeted us with outspread arms. "*Oy*, Alma, Federico!" he beamed, and in the brilliance of that smile there could be nothing wrong in the world. Papa laughed and waved hello. Mama simply smiled and said nothing. She touched her younger brother's arm to acknowledge him while her restless eyes looked beyond him into the house, as if trying to seek out her mother's presence. "Long time no see, *ha*?" Uncle Manny continued. "And who's this? *Diyos ko*, who is this fine young man? Not Pepito, is it, not my little Peping? My God, Pepe, how you've grown!"

I found myself crushed, without warning, against the hard warmth of his barrel chest, his arms squeezing all air and self-conscious aloofness out of me. "For you, Uncle Manny," I said when

I had regained my breath, "just for you I'll let myself be called Pepe.
All my friends call me Johnny."

"*Johnny?*" he boomed, his eyes wide with laughing disbelief. "Not
even Jose Lorenzo, your given name? My God, that's worse than what
these *Amerikanos* have done to me, shortening my name to Manny.
What have you done to this boy, Alma? Only here four years, and already he's speaking with the perfect G.I. Joe accent. Took me sixteen
years to wash that Filipino thickness off my tongue, and I still don't
speak as good as he does. That's a real risk at work, you know, being
misunderstood by the patients, and someday God knows when they're
going to take pills when I just ask them to grab pillows."

I laughed along with my parents as Uncle Manny showed us in,
but I felt a twinge of discomfort at the joke. He had drawn a line between my roots and the roots of the people I found around me, and
it was a division I had not yet discovered how to deal with, a quivering high wire that I toed everyday, hoping not to fall. It had been
a tremendous ordeal when I first arrived in Michigan, practically a
child unschooled in the ways of the country, enduring the slow passage of the weeks and months and seasons as I bore the secret stares
of strangers, heard their laughter at my accent and my ignorance,
struggled with textbooks that chronicled the history they knew so
well, and glimpsed the reflection in the locker-room mirrors that
told me I had dull black hair and too-dark skin and narrow, luster-
less eyes. It had taken me four years to abandon my ethnic luggage
at the station of my alienation and loneliness—four years to exchange the warmth of a brotherly embrace for the cool aloofness of
a limp handshake or a distant nod, to master the strangers' catch-
words and speak with ease of their loves and lusts and griefs, to finally come into a circle of acceptance whose cocky smiles and ap-
proving eyes banished the self-loathing like bonfires against the
darkness and allowed me to forget, at least in waking hours, that I
was a shipwrecked alien from another world named Jose Lorenzo
Guzman.

But four years are not enough to wipe out a lifetime of memories
deeper than blood. In the middle of the night I would wake from
dreams of childhood joys and fears, of feasts of *balot* and *lechon* and
pancitmalabon and the unforgotten bliss of the belly, of running
through the uncut cemetery grass under the gray November sky of
All Soul's Day, of playing *patintero* with grimy, dust-cloaked play-
mates in the noisy neighborhood streets, of people waving blood-red
banners and marching en masse from their homes to form a barri-
cade of bitter and hopeful faces against the rumbling of distant
tanks; and as these images faded from my head I would find my solitude and confusion present in the darkness of my room, undimin-

ished, crouched in a corner like a beast of shadows and watching me with silent, questioning eyes. In those naked hours I knew that the high-wire act had never ended—that it continued still, suspending me above a chasm between two worlds as I nervously thrust out my arms and tried to learn how to fly.

Uncle Manny's voice was low and his tense eyes belied the cheer in his broad smile. "Mother's in the kitchen with Del and Dodi," he told my parents. "Eduardo hasn't called since the day he told me he'd bought the tickets. I've tried calling him but no one ever answers. And Mother, she's . . . well, I don't know just how bad it is, I haven't diagnosed her formally yet, but it doesn't look good. She still has spells of, well, clearheadedness, as clear as she'll ever get in her condition. But *Diyos ko*, sister, how bad she's gotten, it really breaks your heart . . ."

Papa put his hands on Mama's shoulders, as if to absorb some of the tightness there. "Why don't we all just go in together and say hello and see how she is," he said, "and then Del and Dodi can just join us and talk about old times." Uncle Manny nodded and led us into the kitchen, where Uncle Fidel and Uncle Teodoro stood up to greet us with embraces and with the how-have-you-beens that accompany reunions.

Lola Silang sat motionless in her battered wheelchair, her eyelids crumpled shut, blind to the midday light that poured in from the windows thrown open to the California summer. "She's been like that ever since she got here," Uncle Del said quietly as Mama knelt down beside her and looked at her wilted face, a faded map of lines and creases that charted the territory of her ancient pain. "Once, here, she spoke," he continued. "It was in the middle of the night, and she was giving an oration to an invisible audience of women, telling them they were all her sisters and that she had gathered them there to call them to arms, to help their men fight off Magellan and his *conquistadores*." He shook his head. "And once, on the plane, she called me and I said I'm here, Ma, and she said she was so sorry that I'd died in the womb, that she'd tried so hard to bring me out alive." Uncle Manny smiled broadly at this and murmured, "She still knows she loves her kids, at least that's something," but his eyes remained sad. "Aside from that," Uncle Del continued, "nothing. She's been sitting there like a stone, and God knows if the sunshine and the short trips in the car are doing her any good." Mama stayed on her knees and took her mother's limp hand in hers, whispering, "Mother, it's me, Mother, it's Alma," as if she were gently calling her back from a wilderness.

I stood by the doorway to the kitchen and regarded my grandmother from a distance, invaded by unwanted memories. Lola Silang

was part of the fabric of my pain as well: the old woman was a cor-
nerstone in the house of my childhood, an embarrassing mark upon
my life that I had tried to come to terms with or disguise or erase like
an unwanted tattoo, a scar in a secret place. I could not remember
feeling anything positive at all towards Lola Silang, anything that
would offset the shadow she had cast upon my youth. My earliest
memory of her was an odor, the sickening too-sweet stench of the un-
capped perfume bottles and medicine vials that lined the shelves and
cupboards of her room. It oozed out from underneath her door and
assaulted my nostrils as I passed by on my way to or from the streets.
When she still had full use of her limbs she would appear silhouet-
ted in the rectangle of the doorway and beckon me towards her in a
voice made unearthly by the echoes of the house—the voice of the
wrinkled ghost with the heavy cloying smell, the phantom who
lurked in my childhood nightmares. As I grew older Lola Silang shed
her ghostly garb and became for me the earthy villain, the heartless
crone who despised my father and caused my mother grief, the
source of Mama's frustrated correspondence and nightly arguments
with her brothers—threads in the tapestry of anger that formed the
backdrop of my days. Finally, as night took her eyes and her mind,
even this illusion of villainy dissolved and I saw clearly the emaci-
ated limbs, the shrunken frame, the deep furrows in the face of an
old woman whom Mama often had me wash and feed like a helpless
infant and whose delirious silence acknowledged no help. She became a ghost once more, removed from this world, lost in a realm of
shadows that she imagined to be real. More than anything, she was
for me an annoying inconvenience, an unthinking cancer that ate at
my mother's soul, a feeble creature made small and useless by her
age.

    And now she looked smaller still. I stood across the room and
stared at her, wondering, as I often did secretly, if it would not have
been better for Lola Silang to collapse without noise or fanfare into
a heap upon the earth, to release her daughter from her misery and
grant her warring children peace.

    "O, pictures na, pictures anyone! It's mandatory, I insist! A group
picture of Mrs. Priscilla Sanchez and what's left of her kids, courtesy
of my brilliant nephew, said Uncle Manny, tossing me the camera
with a wink. "Some shots can take away from this family, like the one
that took Ignacio," he added in one of his ceaseless attempts at wit,
"but other shots hopefully can preserve it."

    I doubted that silently, as Uncle Manny wheeled Lola Silang into
his sunlit garden and marshaled everyone into position, Papa and
Uncle Del and Uncle Dodi and himself flanking my grandmother like
soldiers, Mama kneeling beside her as if still begging for her with-

held love. I doubted that as I peered into the viewfinder and saw
their smiles pretending to unity while their eyes betrayed their dis-
cord, their unconnected solitudes. "Say cheese," I said as I clicked the
shutter open, and in my mind I saw other scenes from other photographs, gray and faded portraits that I'd once come upon as I was
idly going through my parents' shoeboxes filled with memories. In
those photos Lola Silang sat in the courtyard of the ancestral house,
her husband standing beside her and her children at her knees,
Teodoro and Ignacio and Fidel and Alma and Emmanuel and Eduardo all suppressing their forbidden laughter and standing in awkward, formal poses that barely contained their youth; and at the center of her family Lola Silang smiled with quiet dignity and conscious
grace, held her head high and looked out of the portraits as if to tell
their audience *this* was a family, *this* was tradition, *this* was joy. As
I took their picture in the garden, I wondered what they had lost, and
what had been lost to me.

They left shortly after that, Papa and Mama and her brothers, to
have lunch at one of Uncle Dodi's restaurants and see a bit of the
town and discuss the perennial question of Lola Silang. "Take care
of your grandmother for us, Pepe, we won't be long," Uncle Manny
had said before leaving. "Give her lots of sunshine and air and water, if she'll take it, and talk to her, sometimes it does her some good
and makes her open up. Like a plant in bloom." I laughed, and asked
him if that was his professional opinion; he chuckled and shook his
head, but looked at me with those eyes, incongruous to his smile,
which said that perhaps sunshine and water and conversation were
the last hope she had. They piled into Uncle Dodi's van, then, already
murmuring among themselves about Eduardo and lawsuits and
land. The sound of the motor died away, eventually and a hush fell
upon the garden, broken only by the chirping of a sparrow or my
quiet sips of water or the faint hiss of Lola Silang's breathing as she
sat in her wheelchair, with me on a stool beside her, in the middle of
a square of green space that glowed with summer. "It's really beautiful out here," I said to Lola Silang, to no one in particular.

My grandmother stirred. "Mmm, beautiful," she murmured,
mildly startling me. Then, as if she could discern shapes within the
shadows that caged her, she furrowed her brows and slightly moved
her head from side to side. "*Sino 'yan?* Who's there, *ha?* Why don't
you show yourself?"

I patted her hand in reassurance. "Relax, Lola. It's just me, I'm
keeping you company for a while." I listened to myself as I spoke.
Without meaning to, I had slipped into the heavily-accented English
that I'd used in the past to speak to elders as a sign of deference. I'd

always felt that my native Tagalog was too intimate, rolled off the tongue too quickly and with too much of a sense of conspiracy; G.I. Joe English, on the other hand, was hard and rude on my elders' ears, a staccato gibberish that for them evoked memories of imperialism and deceit. So I'd decided to compromise, long ago, with the stumbling Filipino *Ing-leesh* that conveyed my respect to the older folks and endeared me to their hearts. As I found myself compromising now, after all these years of wearing only proper English on my tongue, calling out to my grandmother as my mother had before me: "It's me, Lola, it's me, your *apo*, it's Pepe."

Her voice seemed smaller too, as if it had atrophied with her long silence. "Ay, Pepe, Pepe, is it really you, my child? Come here into my room, come here where I can see you, sit down here beside me so we can talk."

"Your room? Ah," I said, understanding. She had turned me back into an eight-year-old, transported us back to the room in the ancestral house where the shadows stood brooding in the corners and the fumes of mingled medicines choked the stagnant air. I decided not to tell her where she was. The past was her last refuge, and I had no wish to be cruel. "Okay, I'm here, Lola. I'm right here."

"Can you still recite it, my little Pepito? Can you recite it for me?"

I had no idea what she meant until, softly, she began to hum. And then I remembered: Lola had summoned me many times to her room, sat me down on her lap as I squirmed in restlessness and secret terror, lifted the Bible from her dresser with reverent hands, and, turning now to this chapter and now to that, taught me passages, psalms, hymns. One psalm, the twenty-third, she recited over and over with such emphasis and such fervor that despite my terror at the wrinkled ghost the words embedded themselves in my memory; and then she sat back, humming the melody to the *Ama Namin* that early churchgoers sang on Sunday, and listened to me struggle to repeat the psalm to her.

She was humming the *Ama Namin* now, a melancholy air that wove itself into the silence of the garden, and almost against my wishes the words came to mind, came to my lips. "The Lord is my shepherd; I shall not want. He maketh me to lie down in green pastures; he leadeth me beside the still waters. He restoreth my soul; he leadeth me in the paths of righteousness for his name's sake. Yea, though I walk in the valley of the shadow of death I shall fear no evil . . ."

I faltered, searching for the words, and stopped. Lola Silang stopped humming as well, and burst into a laughter that surprised me with its vitality. "Poor Pepito," she gasped, "still trapped as always in the valley of the shadow of death."

I smiled, half-heartedly, thinking of the tightrope that stretched over my personal abyss, and a quiet gloom overcame me. "Ah, Lola, who knows? Maybe you're right. If you only knew how true that is, maybe you wouldn't be laughing so much."

"Ay, Pepito," she said, "you're too small to be thinking about such big things."

She disconcerted me. For most of my years I had known her face to wear no expression save bitterness, save anger, save a haughty, frowning pride. Then, as she descended into her shadows, I grew accustomed to the stoic mask that hardened on her features, the jaw thrust stubbornly forward in defiance of the efforts of bewildered doctors, the eyes screwed shut against the sight of her crumbling family, the quarrels of her errant children. But in the garden illuminated by the softening light of afternoon, I had seen her laugh; and now, as she sensed my self-pity, her worn and wrinkled features bore a compassion I had never seen before, startling in its newness. "You're too small for such big thoughts," she was saying. "You let God take care of you, Pepito, like he takes care of the smallest of his creatures. And after God, your family. Your family will always protect you."

"Family." I scowled, involuntarily, and wondered if she could sense it; and I almost told her point-blank, you don't like my family, Lola, you despise your own daughter and the man she married. I swallowed the words before they could be uttered. Whatever reasons she had for denying her love to Mama seemed beside the point now; she was old, and would take her petrified loves and hatreds to her grave. "Tell me about my family, Lola," I said instead.

"Your family," she replied, cackling at her own private joke, "is a flock of chickens running around in the backyard when the master is gone." She wheezed, trying to catch her breath, as laughter shook her. "Ay, Pepito! When your *Lolo* Enchong comes home from *sabong*, he will tie all those chickens' heads together and teach them how to behave. He will bring order to his house, and he will sing praise to the Lord on Sundays. Oh, you should hear your Lolo Enchong sing, Pepito! His voice is like thunder, ringing from the mountains, ringing in the high heavens. His voice is like the voice of God himself, as God was once heard speaking in the wilderness. *Ay*, Pepito, when your Lolo Enchong comes home, then you will hear the thunder in his voice and see the fire in his eyes, and then he will tell you about your family . . ."

I sat, listening, dumbfounded. Lola Silang rambled on, describing Lolo Enchong for me, the grandfather who never lived to see my birth—bringing to life his vigorous hands, his fat man's laugh, his mane of silver hair, his booming baritone which drowned out the rest of the choir and rocked the walls of the church, the curt *pok-pok* of his cane on the wooden floors of the ancestral house, the monstrous snores that rattled the bedroom at night, the fiery, flashing eyes that ran in both sides of the Sanchez family and diminished with the generations. And from her disjointed phrases and fragmented recollections, I pieced together stories. How Lolo Enchong drank ten cups of *kape* at six o'clock every morning before he was awake, how he drained a bottle of gin every night at eleven before he could fall asleep, how he'd once smashed Ignacio across the cheek when he discovered him doing the same. How he'd ordered, on a Valentine's Day, a truckload of roses for Lola and a bouquet of *sampaguita* flowers for Mama, all costing a small fortune that put him in debt for a year despite his considerable wealth. How he'd once carried a sick Teodoro six miles to the hospital on foot, in the driving rain, when his car broke down after the first four miles. How he'd seized a student making noise at the back of his class and thrown him bodily out the window, ensuring perfect behavior from his class for the remainder of the year. How he'd celebrated for weeks, with wine and song, with his neighbors and his students and his colleagues, when he was declared the champion *sabongero* of the town, his fighting cocks standing bloody but undefeated in the sandy arena. How he had done all this and so much more, as Lola Silang fed me on her memories, until I could no longer help but believe in the powerful existence of Don Lorenzo Sanchez.

I had asked about my family. She gave me stories of the family I never knew, the generations that had long since faded from all memory but hers; and she spoke of them in the present tense, as though they were still alive, with an immediacy and an informality that implied that the dead were not dead, that they had simply gone to market for the day and would return by nightfall to chat with Lola in her world of shadows. Lolo Enchong first, and then the others—her brothers and sisters, her mother and father, her uncles and cousins and aunts who grew larger as they receded further into legend. Maximilio, who fought with the guerrillas in the Filipino-American war, and Teofilo, who betrayed him to the puppet government. Eulalia, driven mad by her husband's affairs, who roamed the streets at night moaning and tearing at her hair and finally returned home and set her children on fire. Ramon, the poet, who wrote for his lover songs so beautiful that men cried when they heard them, and sang them to warm their souls in the darkest hours of the night. Lucia, whose grave was decorated with ten thousand flowers, one for each of the souls she'd saved with her medical arts when the bubonic plague hit the town. Benjamin—*ang relihiyoso*, Lola called him—who rose to become the highest Catholic bishop in the country and whose illegitimate children scattered across the land, gazing at the world with their fierce, flashing eyes. Rebeca, *ang rebelde*, who trained a secret battalion of women in the mountains during the Spanish-American war and led them to slaughter a thousand troops, without the aid of the foreigners, before the final destruction of the Spanish fleet.

The waning light turned my grandmother's hair a softly-glowing silver as she talked on into the afternoon, as animated as her stiff and feeble limbs allowed her to be, gesturing with her gnarled and trembling fingers and tracing portraits of the dead in the hushed garden air. That day, as I watched her and touched the vivid surface of her memories, I saw Lola Silang as I had never seen her before. She wasn't simply a victim, I thought, a limp and sightless rag doll tossed about in the battle for her soul and for her land. She was a survivor, a story-teller, who held her history together even as it tore her apart. These stories, I realized, were what she'd guarded all this time in her silence, a treasurehouse of secret memory that sustained her through the long years of darkness.

"Listen to me now," she was saying, "listen to me, Pepito. I will tell you now about my grandfather, that brave, wonderful man, are you listening, *ha*, Pepito? Because when he comes home from the war, when he defeats those bastard *Amerikanos*, those devil troops, he will take you and me and my mother and my grandmother into his big, strong arms and we will dance to his beautiful music on top of the bird-hill, higher than the treetops, Pepito, higher than the clouds."

She went on, her rambling voice a trembling enchantment, and from the images she wove I deciphered the last and the oldest of her stories—how in the last wounded days of the Spanish-American war a tall, nameless stranger with blue eyes fierce as lightning arrived at her grandmother's town. He was a demon, some said; others said that he was a messenger from God, an ivory-skinned archangel come to save the souls of the town; others, less given to superstition, guessed from gossip and from the news telegrams from the capital that he was a legendary Spanish general, defeated but still terrifying in his raging pride, driven from his fortifications in Manila and retreating slowly to the sea. His troops had abandoned him along the way, and now, alone, he made his way resolutely from town to town, heading towards the port where his ship waited to take him home. Spies watched him nervously to make sure he was not about to organize an attack against the capital, and they tracked his progress across the provinces by the birds that fell out of the sky—for the fearsome power of his eyes was such that as he strode, his head held high, his withering gaze killed the birds in mid-flight and made them decay into dust and bone as they spiraled to the earth. He did not get

any further than my great-great-grandmother's town, however, because when he heard Andalusia Santamaria sing, when he saw her
move with the pure grace that took men's hearts away, when he saw
her tangled midnight curls and her dark eyes which were unafraid
to look into his own, he knelt before her and declared his love with a
feverish passion that lasted for years as he stayed in that town, as
his lightning gaze continued to cause birds to rain from the sky, as
he spent his remaining time with Andalusia in the highest ecstasy a
lover could possibly know until sickness took him and he died, un-
wedded, in her arms. She buried him at the entrance to the town, on
the hill of bird bones that had grown constantly during the years of
their bliss, the same hill on which they had danced every night to
faint strains of music that wafted in on the wind, whispering their
love to each other under the blue eye of the moon.

"You must remember, Pepito," Lola Silang said, "you must remember to ask your great-great-*lolo* to take you to the hill, to take
you dancing there up high where you can see the rest of the land, yes,
where you can see the mountain of roses over there, see what your
Lolo Enchong gave me once, and there, Eulalia's house on fire, *ay,
kawawa*, poor girl, and there, Ignacio's grave and my Eduardo's wonderful churches. There, do you see, do you see," she said as she trailed
off into silence. In the stillness of the garden her stories shimmered
in the fading light.

"*Hoy*! What are you doing?" she shouted suddenly, sinking further
into her delirium. "What are you doing, Pepito, *bataka*? Don't stand
there, you'll fall! *Diyos ko*, come back from the edge, be careful!"

"I'm here, Lola, I'm right here, I'm not going anywhere," I said,
grasping her hands to calm her down as I looked, startled, into her
face. Her unseeing eyes were open for the first time, dark pools
coated with white mist, shifting and roving about as if they followed
the contours of her landscape of shadows. I wondered what she saw
as I held her, whispered to her, stroked her withered arms. "Don't
fall, don't fall," she murmured as the afternoon deepened, as the first
star winked open in the sky.

By evening Papa and Mama and her brothers were back, and Uncle Manny apologized to me for the long wait. They'd returned in
sullen silence, and the frowns they wore told me that they'd fallen
into one of their arguments, painful, guilt-laden, and unresolved, as
always. We ate dinner, and Uncle Manny helped Lola Silang into bed
before seeing us to the door. Uncle Del and my parents and I rode
back with Uncle Dodi to his house, where we would stay for the remainder of our trip.

I asked Mama that evening if she would enumerate for me all of her relations whom she could remember; she smiled, glad to be asked something that took her mind off her pain, and rattled names off the top of her head as I jotted them down on sheets of paper. Later, as my parents slept in the next room, I put the sheets together, drawing lines from brother to sister, from mother to son, until I had constructed an elaborate family tree that glittered with names and the promise of history. Mama was not good at telling stories. The names of most of her kin were just names to her, with no tales lurking beneath the sound of the words—just dates of births and deaths, at most, and documents of who was married to whom. But I filled in the hollow names with my grandmother's stories, gave the dead their flesh and bones again to hover above me and confess their secret lives in the silence of the room, felt the penciled web of relationships tremble and come alive and include me in its vibrant unity.

Two weeks later, when we had returned to Michigan, when the breathless voice of Uncle Manny at the other end of the line told my tearful mother that Lola Silang had died quietly in the night, I took out the folded sheets and gazed at the names once more, tracing with my finger the lines of relationships in which so much of my grandmother's memory was contained. All the time, I realized, I had been judging my life by measuring the distance I could put between her and myself, denying her blindness and her prayers and her stories and her hymns as I lost myself in a cacophony of foreign tongues, a chaos of strangers, trying to forget my name. Listening to my mother weep, I wondered if she would forget her name as well, if she and her warring brothers would drift silently apart and break the last threads that kept their family from oblivion, if somehow Lola Silang were the core that held the web of names together, without which the names would snuff themselves out, leaving wisps of smoke in the air.

That night I dreamed of my great-great-grandmother's town. I walked upon a landscape of bones, and wherever my foot fell the carcasses stirred and sprang to life—ravens and crows and nightingales, robins and sparrows and eagles and hawks, launching themselves into the air, one by one, until the sky was crowded with wings.

1895 The Honeymoon Hotel

Marie M. Hara

Surely it was disappointment. A simple matter of being disappointed, certainly. That was the problem. It was clear and not unexpected by any means. Rearranging her kimono properly around her legs, she sat on a western-style chair near a window which looked out across the street to a bustling park. Vendors sold food and newspapers. People in all manner of dress crossed the grass and the dirt road. She noticed Hawaiian women in long, loose dresses. In the distance spread the bare brown and green hills which she had seen from the deck of the ship; from here the mountaintops appeared to be misty in the mid-morning sunlight. Today as they traveled along the harbor in the open wagon, she had taken in the busy-ness of this town called Honolulu. Wagons, it seemed, hauled goods everywhere in an entertaining fashion. She had wanted to say, "It's not much like country living, is it?" Still she couldn't allow herself to comment so forwardly to Yamamotosan. She kept her observations private. She missed being able to talk to Chika.

Except for Chika-san, the other women, her fellow travelers, had all been called for. Chika alone had been left to wait for her new husband. Was her fate to be preferred? Maybe Chika would have to return to Japan if she had been forgotten.

The Immigration Station was a formidable building with intricate wooden decorations all over its multi-leveled roofs and windows. It could be mistaken for a temple, except that it was hardly Japanese in feeling. After the long ship voyage every detail of life on shore took her eager interest. Life here was such a novelty, just as people promised it would be. To think of it, within a season's time she had seen both the city of Hiroshima and now, Honolulu. Remarkable. And here there were no seasons. Curious. She had thought about the persistent heat while they passed long hours in quarantine.

They had to wait endlessly. Sectioned off separately for more medical questions, then lined up all together, and finally seated in a row on a polished bench, each of the women clung to the arm of a shipboard friend. Chika and she sat tensely that way for two hours of fretful anticipation.

Her name was called. When Yamamoto-san stepped out of the group of men to claim her as his wife, Sono saw his face from the vantage of her lowered head through half-closed eyes. She had to compose herself. He looked too old! The photograph she kept in her kimono depicted a smooth-shaven young man. The Yamamoto person who stood at the desk appeared to be at least forty years old and bearded heavily. Sono felt her lower lip quiver and Chika's reassuring clutch growing tighter on her now tingling arm.

So that was how he had managed to trick the family. Certainly people had forewarned them in Hiroshima that the Hawaii men were desperate in their desire to establish families. But Yamamoto-san was known to her uncle. Shouldn't he have prevented such an awkward match, knowing the man's true age? Sono was so obliged to Uncle, indeed, everyone was, for his support through the difficult years. But not to have guided her, when he must have known the true circumstances, his elderly friend's trickery. Yamamoto-san looked even older than her uncle when he moved about so cautiously, talking to the foreigners.

Her mind raced through scattered images, connecting her confusion with memories of her seated family, noisily discussing Sono's marriage, and her life faraway in Hawaii. Unconcerned by the bustle of activity around the bench, she brooded in turmoil. It was Chika who timed the little push forward when the stranger turned to face her.

Sono managed, somehow, to bow and maintain a calm demeanor, while she mentally totalled his positive attributes. He did seem to be clean, prosperous and kindly. He was polite. He smiled. Truly as hard as leaving with him was saying goodbye to Chika when all the papers had been signed, all the questions answered, and all the officials signaled them outward.

For some reason the man called Miura Seinosuke, who was Chika's husband, was not present. There must have been a delay in his traveling from another island. Without her having to ask, Yamamoto-san promised to check on Chika's situation tomorrow. She looked very unhappy, but she smiled graciously as she bid them farewell, the humiliated Chika, a lonely kimono-clad figure left waiting on the long beach. The other girls hurried off or looked away, not wanting to injure her further with their obvious pity.

When Sono walked out of the building, following Yamamoto-san to the wagon, she had no idea where they would be going. The horse-drawn vehicle, more an open air cart, carried a number of the couples past the waterfront to a three-story brick and wood building. She could not read the English name on the sign in front of the hotel. She had stayed in an inn only once before and this could not be the same. Once in, she noticed with relief that the clerks and maids were Japanese. A tiny lobby with large chairs and sofas quickly filled up with a dozen couples and the women's large willow trunks and cloth bundles. She saw that the other girls, like herself, seemed self-conscious and subdued. Only Kono-san and her sister, Kumi-san, continued to whisper and chatter as usual. Very rudely they discussed someone whose face, it seemed, took on the appearance of "a dog when it laughs out loud." In the silence around them, smiles materialized on the faces of silent listeners. Sono did not appreciate the joke; for all she knew, they were discussing one of their own husbands.

When the manager of the hotel appeared in the main doorway, however, it became obvious that he was the one. Beaming at the company, his lip curled upward in a cock-eyed manner. No one looked more like a smiling dog, Sono considered, than this slightly balding man. Suppose he had been Yamamoto-san. Sono inhaled deeply. There was a new mood of jocularity in the room; the group grew noisy.

Slowly they were being taken upstairs to their rooms. While Yamamoto-san talked with the manager at the desk, Sono gently adjusted the obi around her waist and pressed her perspiring face with a handkerchief which she had tucked away in her sleeve. A slowly growing numbness seemed to spread into her shoulders, causing her to sit up straighter and compose her features into a stern expressionlessness.

Looking surreptitiously at the other couples, she noted with fleeting envy that Tome-san was matched with a vigorous farmer. Sleepy-eyed Tome was no beauty, even as Sono assumed she herself was ordinary in looks. On ship the other women found themselves in idle agreement that Chika was the most attractive, a "born beauty." What an unlucky fate she had found in this place.

In an instant Yamamoto was leading Sono up to the little room over the street. He seemed to prance eagerly up the flights of steps.

"Leave the luggage," he counseled. "They will bring it up later."

But all of her possessions were in the *kori*. What would she have to change into, if delivery were delayed? What if someone was a thief? Frowning, Sono said nothing.

In silence they sat on the zabuton pillows set out on the grass-mat flooring. No table, no tea service, nothing but a tall chair, a lamp and a small window which drew a hazy light into the opposite end of the room, gave the space its details.

Presently her husband spoke, looking directly at her face with an appraising curiosity that embarrassed her. He asked questions about their families in Hiroshima, the crops, and the voyage across the Pacific. She answered each evenly.

"It is to be hoped, Sono-san, that you will be at home here in Hawaii." He cleared his throat and watched her face. Yamamoto-san seemed uneasy and did not continue. He must have practiced, it was such a formal tone.

She was not able to respond and kept her head lowered. She noticed his hands were sunburnt and calloused. Did this mean he was not truly a wealthy farmer? Or was it evidence of a hardworking man?

Directing his comments to her bowed head, he stared at her thick black hair, knotted expertly at the nape of her slender neck.

"Excuse me. While we are in Honolulu, I must go for a few hours' business and will return punctually within the afternoon. Please relax here. Is there anything you would like me to purchase in the shops?"

Sono shook her head. His voice filled her ears. She would have enjoyed walking around with him, but she felt empty and wearied by his strained attempt to communicate with her.

When she was sure that he was gone, she moved to the window to look out at the activity on the ground. She could see a stream leading down from the hills to the ocean. Glittering water. How she would have enjoyed following it up and up into the misty forest. No houses were built on the mountain slopes. One could get lost in the woodsy areas. They looked quite near. And yet, of course, there was no way of knowing for sure.

Standing, she pushed the edge of the thick drapery away. From the side of the open window frame she caught a glimpse of the town. The road crossed a small bridge over flat green river water and led the way past many small shops and saloons. In the distance she saw the roof tops of stone buildings. They had passed behind that area on their way along the docks. Sono backtracked through the memory of the past few hours and the time of quarantine until she reached the weeks aboard the ship. She saw herself standing at the deck of the S.S. Intrepid, looking at the distant shore of Oahu with the tight eagerness only someone seasick too long could muster.

At her side Chika calmly observed, "So we are here after all."

Sono replied, "If only our parents could know that we have arrived safely. All their prayers. They would be gratified."

"Then for our families' sake, we must write letters to send back
with the ship." Chika, so practical, comforted Sono, because she understood above all the loneliness as well as the obligation of leaving
the family circle. She had been the first friend Sono had made outside of village people. In long conversations they had promised to be
lifelong companions since they would be sure to see each other daily
on such a small island.

So many plans had to be reconsidered. The island. The husbands.
Their friendship. Everything changed as soon as they docked. What
would become of Chika-san now? She wondered when she would see
her friend again. For that matter, what would her own life be like
with this unexpected Yamamoto?

Resigning herself to the situation, Sono tasted her disappointment without self-pity. She had learned from her earliest years that
she was not going to be the child favored. That distinction went to
her eldest brother. Luck was not to be Sono's domain, and untested
expectations were always a mistake. She knew happiness to be a condition where simple needs were met. If there was enough food to eat,
enough clothing to wear, enough fuel for warmth and enough family
to gather around in enjoyment of a pleasant evening, that was
enough for her lot in life. She could be content with those ingredients. She was a poor farmer's daughter who had been schooled in sacrifice. She could hear the voices of the women in her clan reminding
her to be thankful that her widowed mother had one less mouth to
feed.

Now here was Yamamoto-san who was happy to take care of her
needs. She felt ashamed to have found him lacking. Sono knew a little about him. Everyone heard that he had been apprenticed as a car-
penter. They said he was a capable man, but he loved to drink and
had lost much of his parents' respect through his loose ways. City life
in Hiroshima had hardened him. As soon as a friend decided to leave
for California, Yamamoto took the chance of joining him to earn
enough to send his family his savings. A model son, the villagers declared. He had settled in Hawaii and money regularly arrived in the
village. Sono had been impressed by the tale. But in Hiroshima she
was impressed by the first three-story building she had ever seen.
She had been so impressed by the sight of the steamer that she trem-
bled as she crossed the gangplank. No wonder her mother prayed
continually for her well-being. "Is she praying now?" Sono wondered.
The marriage had been officially recorded. There was no turning
back. "Mother, pray for me now."

Two streaks of tears formed silver pathways on the face of the
young girl in the third floor window of the honeymoon hotel. She
made no sound in crying and after a while turned away, her atten-

tion taken by the arrival of the willow basket the maids had carried
up to the room.

The two aproned women, not much older than Sono, transferred a
look which referred to the crying girl. They were sorry for her, but
what could they say or do? Many of them suffered, the maids saw it
all the time.

As they left, politely bowing, they called out, "Thank you, Honorable Mrs. Housewife," as might ordinarily be said, but this time they
chorused their words in a childish teasing meant to bring laughter
up to every listener's lips. They repeated the absurd inflection and
emphasized the dignity of the word honorable with comic expressions. When they succeeded in making Sono giggle to hear their
strange manner of speech, the maids thumped each other on the
shoulder and disappeared down the corridor with boisterous laughter. Sono's surprise settled into restored spirits and she began to ex-
amine the clothes and goods in her basket as if she hadn't done so
dozens of times already. Each item represented the spirit of someone
dear to her, and their gifts anchored her with their presence.

When Yamamoto-san returned, he knocked cautiously before he
tried the door. Sono opened it carefully. To her surprise her husband
handed her a large bouquet of lilies, gingers and daisies, as well as
a package fashioned out of his handkerchief, tied up *furoshiki* style.

She rushed both to the window, propping the newspaper-wrapped
flowers against the chairback and opening the white muslin to find
two pinkish guavas, a tiny mottled banana and two small Kona oranges. Sono exclaimed, and Yamamoto beamed as if to say, this is just
the beginning, there will be more for you.

For the first time she spoke to him openly.

"Well, how nice of you to consider my feelings." She gazed shyly at
his eyes. He coughed. Confident now that she was appreciative of his
efforts and would be a responsive wife, he mumbled, "It's the least I
could do to welcome you to Hawaii." When her pale skin was flushed,
Sono seemed to convey a sweet delicacy beyond the proper wifely
qualities he imagined before.

Yamamoto would have enjoyed embracing her then and there as
was his husbandly right. Instead, hearing a great clattering noise
from the road below, he asked Sono if she had ever ridden in a mule-
tram.

In confusion Sono shook her head. "A mule-tram?"

He pointed out a curious open-sided conveyance passing directly
below them. It was dragged by a team of rattling collared mules.
Both laughed at the same time when they caught sight of a bare-
footed ragamuffin sneaking a ride on the rear of the crowded tram.
A small dog marked with a dark ring around one eye tried jumping

up several times to join the boy on the edge of the bouncing bumper. Finally he was caught in mid-leap by his master who smiled triumphantly, showing all of his teeth to the delighted onlookers.

"Things are different here, you see."

"Yes, people can be very merry." Her head dropped again as she studied the floor.

Realizing that she had not been entirely happy waiting for him, Yamamoto decided to take Sono out for a ride to a beach area called Waikiki, past the town of Honolulu.

"Let me show you what is here. You will be amused. The ride is fast and bumpy."

The couple boarded the tram at the turn-around point adjacent to the park across the street from their hotel. Yamamoto pointed out the beauty spots and major buildings along the way. They sat stiffly in their best clothes, holding on to the seats and surveying all the assorted activities of the heart of the capitol of the islands. Fifty-seven years later she would remind him about the miles of duck ponds and rice fields they passed before the end of the dusty road.

Through a small ironwood thicket which reminded her of certain Japanese seaside pines, they walked right next to the ever present ocean which surged and crackled at their bare feet. They carried their footwear and ate their fruit standing on the blazing beach. She became fascinated by the recurrent waves which washed fiercely against a half moon of rocky sand and stretched up to a grove of struggling coconut trees. She said, "This is not at all what I expected; it's so different."

He nodded curtly in acknowledgment without understanding her emotion. He said, "This very ocean touches our home shores. Someday we are sure to return. The gods willing, we won't be disappointed."

She turned her head and wiped away secret tears, because he was so totally convincing. He had been raised, after all, to be a chosen son. With her back to him she accepted his unwavering self confidence and never questioned his lack of worldly success in the more than half century allotted to their marriage.

From a distance the kimono-clad girl and the black-suited man seemed to be locked into a flirtatious battle of wills, a typical seaside lovers' tiff on a lazy afternoon, which resulted in his taking her hand to lead her back to the tram terminal. In truth they had merely decided to return home to their room.

All the way back, the words "we won't be disappointed" bounced through Sono's thoughts as the tram jostled them up and down from stop to stop.

Surely it was the best thing to do. Chika had accepted her fate. She could do no more. Since there was no way to be sure of anything at all at any time, Sono reminded herself, why not rest with this choice? In the matter of how to feel about things, she would remain in charge. Then it was settled; there was no problem.

The tram passed a field where a Chinese farmer guided an ox through a swampy rice paddy.

To Yamamoto-san she said, "It certainly isn't anything like the farming life we knew, is it?"

Surprised by her comment, he looked at Sono with attention to her observations. He began to tell her all the things he found unlikely or thought-provoking in the ten years since he had left home. Still in conversation when the tram pulled into the terminal, they didn't notice they had arrived home.

At dinner that evening by the doorway to the hotel's Japanese dining room, a bespectacled, portly Miura-san and his new bride Chika greeted Mr. and Mrs. Yamamoto with grateful formality. Startled, Sono grasped Chika's hand in joy.

"Chika-san!" Sono's voice tightened in escalating pleasure over the turn of events. Her friend stood surrounded by a surprising calm. As Sono studied Chika's delicate face, she thought she could see a deep relief that Miura had come to get her after all. At the table Sono decided not to say anything which might lead to further questions. They would have enough time later to discuss this day in detail, she felt certain of it.

Self-consciously dignified, Sono began to serve Yamamoto. Naturally Chika followed, and soon both women poured tea and served rice for the first time to their husbands. Acknowledging a good start and mirroring each other's pleasure, the Yamamotos and the Miuras ate their food with hearty appetites. They maintained a good-natured and respectful silence which graced their table as they ate the meal.

With sincerity the couples toasted each other, wishing themselves good luck. Others in the room looked in their direction and recognized them as fortunate.

Tomorrow they would leave for the port of Hilo and two outlying towns where they would begin the cane-growing work as family units. Tonight they would enjoy the honeymoon hotel.

A man and woman appeared at one of the third floor windows. For a moment they looked at the moonlight on the surface of the glittering river.

Groom Service

Michael Dorris

1

"She's a piece of pure quartz," Bernard's mother, Martha, said to Marie's mother, Blanche. "A one-in-a-million that you find after walking the beach for half your life with your eyes on the ground. If I had a child like that I would keep her in a safe place."

Blanche paused her blade midway down the side of the fish she was scaling. Her face betrayed no expression except exertion, and even in this intermission her teeth remained set, flexing her jaw. The trader steel reflected what little light filtered through the planks of the smokehouse, and the confined air still smelled green. Blanche had hewn the boards with a mallet and chisel in May, as soon as the ground firmed from the spring runoff, and it took a while before the scent of fire crowded that of drying wood. With her broad thumb she flicked a piece of fin off the carved knife handle, then continued her motion.

Martha waited. She had all the time it took.

"You don't know," said Blanche. She shook her head as if its secrets rolled like line-weights from side to side. She drew a heavy breath. "You can't imagine. You with such a boy."

Martha sat straighter, all ears, while her hands continued to explore, repairing the tears on the net that lay across her lap and hid her pants and boots. Her fingers moved automatically, finding holes, locating the ends of broken cord and twisting them into square knots. She kept her nails sharp and jagged, and when they weren't enough, she bowed her head and bit off any useless pieces. This was mindless work, the labor of ten thousand days, and could be done as easily in

212

the dark as in the light. It required no involvement. Her thoughts were elsewhere.

"You mean Bernard?" Her voice was wary. She had three sons and needed to be sure she knew the one Blanche had in mind.

"Ber-*nard*," Blanche nodded, giving the knife a last run, then inspecting the fish closely before tossing it into the large basket at her feet. The water slopped onto the floor and, from there, leaked to the shale ground inches below. Blanche arched her back and massaged her spine with her fist. With her other hand she reached for the cup of cooled tea that she had nursed for the past half-hour. Martha let the net rest and joined her.

"People talk about him, you know," Blanche said. "His looks, that goes without saying, but the other things too. The respect he pays the old folks. His singing. His calmness. His hunting skill. You must be proud."

Martha closed her eyes as if in great pain. "He is my punishment," she confessed, "but I don't know what I could have done so terrible as to deserve him. He stays out until morning. His hair is always tangled. I sometimes think that the game he brings home has died before he found it, the meat is so tough. You must have him confused with another boy. Or perhaps, with a girl like Marie, you find it hard to think ill of any child."

"Now you make fun of me," Blanche said. "It is well known that Marie has turned out badly. She is lazy and disrespectful, conceited and stubborn. I try my best to teach her, and so do my sisters and even my mother, but she folds her arms and stares at nothing. Hopeless. And she will never find a husband. A boy's mother would have to be desperate to send her son courting at my house."

"But not as desperate as the mother who could tolerate the thought of Bernard as a son-in-law," Martha said. "That would be true desperation. I will never be free of him. I will grow old with him at my side, and with no granddaughters or grandsons to comfort me."

"If only someone like your Bernard would find an interest in Marie," Blanche said as if she had not heard Martha. "If only some young man exactly like him would consent to live in my house, how I would welcome him. I would treat him as my own blood."

The two women met each other's gaze at last. Each held a cup to her lips, and after a few seconds, each drank. Each replaced her cup on the table between them. Each held her mouth firm. Blanche found her knife and reached for a new fish, cool and slippery as a stone over which much water has rushed. Martha shifted the net in her lap, moving a new section to the center. The smell of salt rose like steam as her hands went to work.

"I will speak to him," Martha said.

"And I to her," Blanche replied. "But I know her answer already. I have seen how she regards him."

"She will not be disappointed." Martha allowed one wave of pride to crest. "He's not so bad."

Blanche glanced up at Martha, then looked quickly back to her work. Bernard must be good indeed, she thought, if Martha could not better contain herself.

2

Bernard was drawing with charcoal on a piece of driftwood when his mother returned home. He was twenty-two, lean, and had large teeth. His eyes were dark beneath unusually thick brows, and his hands were long and broad. At the sound of Martha's step, he jumped to his feet and assumed the air of a person about to do something important. His fingers curved as if to hold a tool or a weapon and his eyes narrowed as if to see something far away. He was busy at nothing, his energy humming, ready for a focus. But for once she made no comment about his sloth. She did not despair at the time he wasted scratching on any smooth surface. She did not inspect his sketch and then toss it into the cooking fire. In fact, this afternoon she dealt with him rather mildly.

"Well, it's arranged," she announced. "I spent an endless morning with your future mother-in-law and before I left she had agreed to let you come to see Marie. Don't think it was easy."

Bernard's eyes followed his mother's movements as she crossed the floor and sat in exhaustion on the bed. She pushed off her boots, still caked with beach mud, and rubbed her feet together. She wore no socks.

"Marie?" he said at last. "She's too young. You should have asked me first."

Martha's glare clapped a hand over his mouth. In a moment, Bernard tried again.

"I know they're a good family. I know you want to do right for me. But you could . . . *we* could have discussed this. I mean, I think of her as a little girl, not a *wife*." The word, a stranger on Bernard's tongue, vibrated in the air.

"Stop whining." Martha lost patience. "Who do you 'think of' as a wife? *Doris?*"

Bernard blushed. He wasn't surprised that his mother knew about him and Doris, but it did not seem fair for her to mention it. Doris was a widow whose name brought nervous laughs to teenage boys and smiles of disapproval to everyone else. She was a woman almost twice Bernard's age with a missing front tooth and eyes that sparked in his memory, a woman who had summoned him for an errand six months ago and whom he now loved better than he would have thought possible. But it was true: he had never thought of Doris as a wife.

"You should see yourself," Martha said. "Keep that face and you won't have to worry about marrying anyone. But don't expect me to support you forever." She noticed the driftwood, still on the floor, and nudged it with her toe to get a better view. Bernard had outlined the mountain across the bay from the village, and tucked a large sun behind its peak. When he drew it he thought it was his best work, but now its lines looked smudged and shaky. Martha leaned forward to pick it up and turn it over, as if expecting another illustration on the back. Finding none, she held it out for Bernard to take.

"Give this to your Doris," she said. "It looks like her under the blanket where she spends her time."

Bernard didn't move, but he watched the wood until his mother let it fall to the floor. He was angry at the shame he felt. He was angry that he knew it was just a matter of time until he would have to call on Marie. He was angry that his mother was right: his mountain *did* look like Doris, turned on her side.

3

When Blanche went into the house and told Marie that their problems were over, that Bernard, the catch of the village, would be courting, she expected some reaction, but her daughter simply folded her arms and stared at the fire.

"Don't you hear me?" Blanche demanded. "Bernard. Coming to see you. Can't you be happy? Can't you say something?"

Marie, however, only rolled her eyes and drummed her fingers against the pine bench upon which she sat. She wore a close-knit woven cap that, in combination with her unfortunately weak chin, made her head resemble an acorn. She was fifteen, just out of her confinement, trained for adulthood to the limits of Blanche and her sister's patience, but still a sulking child. At length she drew up her knees, circled them with her arms, and watched her mother from the corner of her eye.

Blanche stood across the long room, talking to her older sister Bonnie. She was not hard to overhear.

"Does she say 'thank you'? Does she appreciate what it means to her, to all of us, to get that damn Martha to agree? Does she care that Bernard could have any girl, from any family?"

Bonnie shook her head sadly. Her surviving children had all been boys and had long since moved to the houses of their wives' families, so she had no experience with reluctant girls, unless, she thought, she counted her memories of Blanche. But that would not do to say, especially not in earshot of Marie, who sat with her head cocked in their direction. Blanche's daughter was the hope of the next generation, the one who had to bring in a husband and produce more daughters than her mother or aunt, if the family was to regain its position. For a moment Bonnie thought of suggesting to Blanche that they present that information to Marie directly, to drop the shadows and point out both her responsibility and her power, but then she rejected the idea. The girl was impressed enough with herself as it was. Instead, Bonnie sympathized with her sister and cast occasional looks at her niece in hopes of catching on Marie's face a secret, a streak of pleasure.

4

"What am I supposed to do?" Bernard asked the next time his uncle visited. Bernard had waited for a private moment, and it came when, just before sleep, Theodore had stepped outside to relieve himself. The trees around the village seemed closer at night, taller, like the sides of a box.

From the darkness came rattling sounds of strangulation that Bernard eventually identified as the older man's yawn. When it, and the noise of splashing water, had abated, Theodore spoke. It was clear that he understood Bernard's problem.

"You do whatever they tell you and you hope they're not as bad as they could be," Theodore said. "You don't complain. You don't assume anything. You stay out of the way, because you never know what they're going to find to dislike. You be what they want."

"It's not fair." Bernard leaned against the side of the house and searched the sky. Thin clouds, silver as wet spiderwebs, passed in the night wind.

"That's true, but there are other things in the world besides owning real estate. Your true home will remain here at your mother's, just as it has been for me, but you can't *live* here forever. You need independence, distance, the chance to be a man in a place where you were never a boy. Once you get yourself established, you'll understand what I mean. Your life is not all indoors. You'll hang around with your brothers-in-law, your uncles, your friends. Spend time at the men's house. Go to the sweat bath and gripe, or listen to the complaints of others and make jokes. In a year all your wife's family will

care about is whether or not you bring in your share. By then you'll
know what's what."

"But what if I don't get along with Marie?"

"*Do* get along with her. Get along with her mother. Get along with
her auntie. But on your own time do what you want. It's not a big
price to pay. It's a daughter-poor clan and the one they've picked out
for you is going to control everything someday: rich fishing sites, a
big house. Behave yourself now and you'll get your reward. It's not
like you're marrying a youngest sister with no prospects."

Which was, Bernard knew, what had happened to Theodore. No
wonder he was not more sympathetic.

"How do I tell Doris?" Bernard asked. This was something he had
struggled with for days.

"Doris! She could have told *you*. It's good news to her. She gets a
younger guy, fresh the way she likes them, and no hard feelings between you." Theodore laughed, and put an arm around Bernard's
shoulders. "Listen to some advice, from your great-uncle through me
to you," he said. "Groom service is the worst part, so make it as short
as possible. Convince her family you won't be a pain in the ass to live
with. Rule number one: appreciate everything they do. Compliment,
compliment, compliment."

"Did you do that?" Bernard asked. "Did my mother's husband do
that?"

"Do fish fry in hot grease? But don't take my word for it. Ask Pete.
He's your father."

"I'd be embarrassed," Bernard said. "He and I never talk about serious matters. He's not of the clan."

"A man's a man," Theodore said.

5

"This is what you do," Martha instructed.

It was not yet light and she had awakened Bernard from a sound
sleep. He blew into a cup of hot tea as he listened, let the darkness
hide the resentment in his face.

"You go hunting and you catch something *good*, I don't care what.
Something a little unusual. A beaver, maybe, or a goose. *Not* something small and easy. *Not* a squirrel. *Not* fish. You bring it home and
I'll help you clean it. You leave a portion for me as if that's what you
always do, to help provide for your family, but you take the best part
and you set yourself in front of Blanche's door. You only speak if
you're spoken to. You wait for *them* to ask *you*. And if they don't,
which they won't right away, you act unconcerned. You do this every

day until they invite you in, and then I'll tell you what to do next. This is your chance, so don't ruin it. Now move."

Bernard stepped out into the chill morning grayness, thought briefly of visiting Doris before he went hunting, but then abandoned the idea. He had heard through his mother's husband that Doris had made friends with a seventeen-year-old boy named James.

The dew from high grass had soaked through to Bernard's feet before he reached the edge of the woods. He realized his mother had forgotten to feed him breakfast, forgotten to make him a lunch. He heard a duck call from the lake and paused, but then continued on. He could hear his mother in his mind, and she said a duck wouldn't do.

6

"He's *there!*" Bonnie dropped the firewood she was carrying and rushed to Blanche's side.

Her sister was stirring a pot on the fire, as if what it contained were all that concerned her. "I have eyes," Blanche said. "Keep your voice down. He'll hear you."

"Did you see what he had?" Bonnie asked. "I got a glimpse of something flat and dark, but I didn't want him to catch me looking."

"I think it was a beaver tail. Would you believe, he had the nerve to hold it up to me and smile the first time I passed."

"No!"

"I thought he was better trained. It simply means he'll have to wait longer."

"Did Marie see him yet?"

"She won't go outside." Both sisters turned to the gloom in the rear of the room where Marie crouched, her head lowered over a stick game. Her long hair was loose and covered her shoulders like a shawl, her back to the doorway.

7

"Well, what happened?" Martha demanded when Bernard returned home late in the evening.

"Nothing happened," Bernard said, and threw himself down on his blankets. He raised an arm to cover his eyes, then turned to face the wall.

Martha spotted the sack her son had dropped on the floor and looked inside. The beaver tail and quarters were exactly as she had cleaned them that afternoon, and she took them out to add to the broth she had prepared.

"At least we'll eat well for a while," she said.

"I'm not hungry," Bernard replied, but his mother ignored him. "Tell me everything."

"There's nothing to tell. I walked over there, dressed like I was going to a feast, carrying that beaver. I trapped it clean, surprised it so completely, there wasn't even adrenaline in its flesh. I thought they'd taste it, invite me to supper, but they walked by me like I wasn't there, their noses in the air."

"Whose noses?" Martha wanted to know.

"The mother and the aunt."

"Not the girl?"

"I saw no girl. I heard no girl."

"Ah," said Martha. "So she's shy. Good."

"Why good?"

"Because then she won't bully you at first, stupid boy. I've seen what happens to the husbands of the bold ones."

The smell of stewing meat filled the room, warm, rich, brown. Martha's husband Pete came into the house at the scent, tipped his head in his son's direction, and asked, "Hard day?"

8

For a week, then two weeks, the same pattern was repeated. Only the animals changed: they ranged from a porcupine to a hind quarter of caribou, from a fat grouse on a bad day to a string of matched silver salmon on a good one. Once Bernard thought he saw a black bear dive into the brush at the side of a stream, but he was momentarily afraid to investigate, and later berated himself. With a bear skin, he thought too late, he would have been irresistible and his long afternoons and evenings at Blanche's closed door would have been over.

As a month passed, Bernard gave up hope. He lost the alertness he had once felt when Blanche or Bonnie or Marie, the most unsympathetic of them all, approached, and he soon tired of the commiseration that Blanche's and Bonnie's husbands cast in his direction as they went about their business. They could remember, their expressions said, what it was like to wait outside this house, but there was nothing they could do. A word from them might slow the process rather than speed it up, might do more damage than good. If boredom was patience, Bernard achieved patience. If learning to exist without expectation of fulfillment was maturity, Bernard matured. At first he used his time to remember Doris, to wonder what she was doing and to regret not doing it with her. Later he thought about hunting, how he could have succeeded the times he had failed, how the animals behaved, how they smelled and sounded. Finally he found himself thinking about Pete, his

father, in different ways than he ever had before. In Bernard's mind
Pete became more than just his mother's husband; he became another
man, an earlier version of Bernard, a fellow sufferer. It had not previously occurred to Bernard how hard it was to be forever a stranger in
the house where you lived, to be always a half-visitor. He wondered
how Pete stayed so cheerful, and wondered if his grandmother had
kept his father waiting long at the doorway before inviting him inside.
On an afternoon late in the second week, Bernard had a thought so profound, so unprecedented, that it straightened his back. What if, he
wondered, his grandmother had not let Pete in at all? What if Pete had
been judged inadequate? Where would that have left Bernard?

The next morning when he went hunting, Bernard returned to the
place where he had seen the bear, hid himself behind a log, and waited.

9

"Did you hear?" Pete asked Theodore as they walked the trail from
the sweat bath to their wives' houses.

"About Bernard's bear?"

"It must have weighed three hundred pounds. I didn't know
Bernard had it in him."

"Have you forgotten what sitting in front of a house will drive you
to? What did you catch to get inside Blanche's?"

"Nothing," Pete said. "It was me she couldn't resist."

"You forget," Theodore replied. "I was still a boy in that house. I
recall their words of you. Let me see . . . I seem to remember some
mention of the small size of certain of your parts."

"Poor brother-in-law," Pete said. "You still don't realize the lengths
to which they went to avoid hurting your feelings! And how *is* your
wife? How is the health of her many elder sisters? Is it true that they
become stronger and more robust with every year?"

10

On the second day of the fifth week, just as she passed through the
door, Blanche reached down her right hand and snagged one of the
bear claws that rested in the basket by Bernard's leg. So quick was
her movement, so apparently disconnected to the intent of her mind,
so complete her distraction, that Bernard had to look twice to make
sure it was gone. All the same, he felt a warm flush spread beneath
the skin of his neck, and a feeling of inordinate pride suffused him
so thoroughly that he had difficulty remaining still. He had been
found worthy, and now it was only a matter of time.

Every day, with more pause and deliberation, Blanche browsed through his offerings and always selected some choice token. Her expression betrayed no gratitude, yet Bernard was sure that occasionally she was pleasantly surprised. Afraid to unbalance their precarious arrangement, he sat still as a listening hare in her presence. He kept his eyes lowered and held his breath until she had departed, but remained ever watchful for any cue that his probation had progressed. At last it came.

"Bernard!" Blanche said one day. She stood in the doorway, her hands on her hips, her head cocked to the side in amazement. "Is that you crouching there so quietly? Please, come in and share our supper, poor as it is. What a pleasure to see you."

Bernard rose slowly, stiff in his joints and half-skeptical that this was some joke, some new test, but when he entered the house, Blanche's hospitality continued and was joined by that of Bonnie, who sat by the fire trimming her husband's hair with a squeaking scissors. "Sit, sit," she motioned to a bench near the door. "What a shy boy you are. Luckily we have some nice moose to feed you."

Indeed they did. Bernard recognized the remains of the foreleg he had offered yesterday. Bonnie passed him a plate with a small portion of tough gristle, gray and cooled. He knew what to say.

"This is wonderful," he exclaimed. "The best I've ever tasted. What cooks you are. But you are too generous. Let me put some back in the pot."

When they refused, politely and with many denials of his compliments, Bernard made a great show of eating. The act of digestion absorbed his total concentration. He rubbed his stomach and cast his eyes to the ceiling in delight. With great subtlety he periodically raised his hand to his mouth, as if to wipe some grease, and used that motion to conceal the small bits of undigestible food he removed from his cheeks and tucked secretly into his pockets.

When he finished, Bernard sat nervously, breathless with anxiety. From the corner of the room he detected a space so devoid of movement that it attracted his attention. He looked, then quickly looked away. Yet his eyes still registered the image of Marie, her hair oiled and braided, wearing a new dress and a necklace made of bear claws, sitting as composed and shaded as a perfect charcoal sketch.

11

"You know, Pete," Martha said as she lay by her husband's side under a robe, "watching Bernard lately brings back memories."

"To me too. Your mother was a terror."

"I notice you still whisper such words, even though she's more than four years gone."

Pete shifted his position and propped on an elbow. In the moonlight Martha's face was seamless and young. A beam like the hottest part of a coal danced off her dark eye. He ran his fingers along her cheek and she turned her head in comfort. "You look the same as then," he said.

Martha caught his hand and brought it to her mouth, let it feel the smile.

"I pestered her, you know, to let you in," she said.

"You didn't care."

"I didn't care the day you found the eagle feathers? I didn't care the day you came an hour later than always?"

"It was raining," Pete said. "The ground was soft and I kept sinking to my knees. I couldn't arrive at your door covered in mud."

"I thought you weren't coming. I confronted my mother and told her that her slowness had cost me . . ."

"Cost you what?" Pete asked, when Martha's silence persisted.

"Enough talk."

12

Marie watched the back of Bernard's head and admired the sleek sheen of his long hair, the play of muscles in his arms at his every movement. During the last month she had studied every part of him so completely that she could create him in her imagination whenever she chose, and lately she chose often. She had to fight not to laugh when they gave him the worst meat and he had to spit into his hand and act as though it were delicious. She watched the way his fingers held the plate, the way he sat so compact and attentive. She waited for the sound of his soft voice and wondered what he would say when he could speak in private. She made a game of observing his eyes until just the second before they turned to her, and believed she had been discovered only once.

13

Bernard ate almost all of his meals at Blanche's house now, and gradually became more relaxed. For one thing, his distribution increased in both quality and quantity, and he could now expect a reasonable piece of meat or salmon. For another, Blanche's and Bonnie's husbands had begun to join him on his hunts, to show him places to fish that only members of this household knew. He found he liked these men and began to call them "uncle."

Blanche herself still frightened him, but not all the time. There were moments when he found approval in her gaze, times when some word of hers sounded almost like a joke. Bonnie was warmer, more solicitous of his needs, more delighted at the food he brought, and Bernard regarded her as an ally.

As far as Marie was concerned, he still had no clue to her feelings. Even Pete and Theodore observed that this game was lasting longer than the usual and debated whether something might be wrong. They were full of advice for Bernard, full of ideas of how to please Marie, full of reminders that it was her agreement, more than anyone's, that was necessary. But no matter what Bernard did, Marie would not look at him or give him any sign of encouragement. He grew despondent, lost his appetite, found himself thinking once again of Doris and the ease of their association. Marie seemed totally beyond his reach, the focus of mystery and impossible desire. And so he was unprepared on the night, just before the first frost of winter, when, with shaking hands, Marie herself passed him a plate of food.

"This is for you," she said so softly he could barely hear, and she sat beside him while, slowly and with great emotion, he ate.

14

A year later, while waiting for the birth of Marie's first child, Blanche and Martha passed the time by nibbling strips of dried eel. Martha, who had no love for the oily skin, threw hers into the fire, where it sizzled briefly.

"The midwife predicts a girl," Blanche said. "When she spun the charm above Marie's stomach, it revolved to the left."

"A girl is most rewarding," Martha nodded. "But there is a special satisfaction in raising boys. So often I think of times when Bernard was young, so often I miss him around the house."

Blanche reached for another stick of *baleek* and did not answer. Her silence was immediately noticed, as she knew it would be.

"How is he doing?" Martha asked at last.

"He will learn," Blanche said. "He has potential. It is clear he cares greatly for Marie, and she is patient."

"That is one word for it." Martha tossed a handful of scraps into the flame and watched the light flare and dance. "Of course, Bernard was used to . . ." She shifted her weight, cleared her throat. "He had such a *happy* home that I'm sure it has taken some adjusting on his part in new surroundings."

"Yes, he *was* somewhat spoiled. But I think he has a good heart."

"As well he must, to remain loyal to such a chinless girl."

"One only hopes their child will inherit the mother's disposition and not be sulky and resentful of every request."

"One can but pray it will have the father's looks and personality."

A single rope of eel remained on the plate. Both women extended a hand toward it, hesitated, and withdrew. It rested between them as they cleaned their teeth with fine bone picks, carefully wiped their fingers, and when, at the sound of Marie's first muffled protest, they rose together and rushed to her side, it remained behind.

PART 5

PHYSICAL DEVELOPMENT, HEALTH AND AGING

PHYSICAL DEVELOPMENT, HEALTH AND AGING

A multlicultural perspective on physical development, health and aging includes a consideration of the intersection between normative physical changes that all adults experience, stage of life, and life style factors that are often related to ethnicity, class, gender, able-bodiedness, sexual orientation, and so on. And an adult's subjective assessment of his or her own physical condition is as important, if not more so, than one's actual condition. This subjective framing of one's physical appearance or state of health colors the view of the self and impacts behavior.

Unlike childhood wherein a timetable of physical changes can be charted, from learning to walk and talk to becoming a sexually mature man or woman, the adult's biological clock is unrelated to any age or stage-specific behavior. The only universal change, in fact, is the climacteric, or the cessation of reproductive ability. However, this is a very gradual change for men, and occurs over a period of several years for middle-aged women. And while popular culture might suggest that there may be a "male menopause" or that menopausal women experience increased anxiety or depression, there is little empirical research to substantiate these "myths" (Bee, 1996).

Although the climacteric is the only *universal* physical change in adulthood that everyone is sure to experience at some point, there are also a number of physical and health-related changes that are increasingly likely to occur as one ages. For example, there is a slowing down as we age, especially in terms of reaction time. Older adults simply do not react as quickly as younger adults; the rate of change in the central nervous system varies widely among individuals, however. In addition, a person's previous life experiences and the nature of the task may make a difference in reaction time. This slowing

227

down is seen most acutely in timed learning tasks, a factor adult educators need to consider when planning learning experiences.

Another common physical change in adulthood is a decline in the acuity of all five senses—touch, taste, sight, hearing, and smell. As with reaction time, the rate of change varies widely from person to person. Some older adults hear very well, while other younger adults may experience a hearing loss. Vision is the other sense that can have an effect on learning as one ages, but as with hearing, corrective measures can compensate. Interestingly, environmental factors may impact the changes in senses. Bee (1996) notes that there is evidence to suggest that hearing loss may relate to the noise level in the person's environment: "Within U.S. samples, men with greater noise exposure have far more hearing loss than do those with less exposure. Women . . . show still less, while samples from other cultures in which noise levels are very low show still less" (p. 110). The relationship between sun exposure and skin changes and stress and changes in the immune system are other environmental threats where sex, ethnicity, and socioeconomic class make a difference (Bee, 1996). These variables—sex, race/ethnicity, and class—determine to some extent, the amount of protection one has from environmental factors. For example, working-class adults are more likely to work outside and in noisy, polluted environments, while professional and managerial positions are associated with high levels of stress.

The incidence of chronic health problems also increases with age, with the most common being cardiovascular disease, cancer, and arthritis. Again, heredity and lifestyle play a role in the severity and instance of these diseases. It is common knowledge that exercise, healthy eating habits, cessation of smoking, and reduction of excessive drinking can decrease the chances of succumbing to some of these diseases.

In addition to environment and heredity, physical development and health are related to gender, social class, and race, and ethnicity. In the Western Hemisphere, women outlive men, but have higher rates of nonfatal chronic diseases, and greater instances of emotional problems, with depression being twice as common among women as men (Strickland, 1992). Although it is not clear why women live longer but have more health problems than men, a number of explanations have been advanced. Women's hormonal make-up is different from men's, with the greater ratio of estrogen "protecting" women from fatal diseases. Women typically seek medical attention earlier in the disease process, perhaps take better care of themselves in terms of health practices, and have, at least until recently, not experienced as much environmental work-related stress.

As with other aspects of development, socioeconomic class plays a role in physical aging and health care. Poor and working class men and women are more likely to have jobs that demand physical activity, are located in hazardous environments, provide less than satisfactory healthcare benefits, and so on. When class is combined with race and ethnicity, higher income adults within African American, Hispanic, or Asian American communities experience less illness and greater longevity than lower income adults of the same group (Guralnik, Land, Blazer, Fillenbaum & Branch, 1993). Level of education, which is highly correlated with socioeconomic class, may explain some of the these differences. Adults with more education know better how to take care of themselves as well as have the income to obtain medical care before it's too late.

With regard to ethnic differences in the United States, Bee (1996) presents the following pattern of health and longevity: "Native Americans have the poorest health, Asian Americans, the best. African Americans have a shorter life expectancy than whites; Hispanics have significantly lower rates of heart disease but suffer from other diseases at higher rates. Some of these differences appear to be linked to variations in health habits and social class; some appear to be genetic" (p. 148).

The four selections in this section underscore the importance of the relationship between the physical and the mental; that is, one's sense of self is related to appearance, actual physical condition, and age or life stage.

Two very different stories, *What I Know from Noses,* and *Finch the Spastic Speaks,* deal with physical conditions and how those conditions influence development. The Jewish protagonist of *What I Know from Noses* has her nose fixed as an adolescent allowing her to stop "seeing noses everywhere I turned," and to concentrate on "my whole self" and the "people around me." Now, fourteen years later, she is ambivalent about the decision and wonders whether she lost more of herself than just her nose. Through a feminist lens, she now sees that she succumbed to external definitions of beauty—"it is the rules, not our bodies, that need repair."

Finch, in *Finch the Spastic Speaks,* is trapped in a body over which he has little control, "locked forever in his prison of chaotic muscles." His mind is simultaneously free and indeed, he revels in challenging "graduate students ten years his senior," or "the holder of the endowed chair in history!" His story of struggling to do even the simplest physical tasks takes second stage to his emotional growing pains. Like other young adults, he wants to be accepted and he wants to have relationships with the opposite sex. In a poignant episode, a date ends in acute embarrassment, with Finch asking, "Should not Finch, like you, feel?" As a young adult college student, Finch is trying to define who he is, both apart from and in relation to his physical condition. At this point in his life, he says he "cannot know what is, or is not, Finch."

Two other selections have to do with physical and psychological well-being and stage of life. "*Combustion*" by Susan Hauser, is a about a menopausal woman who interprets her hot flashes as a cleansing, an "organic sauna" that others might envy. This positive rendering of midlife physical changes, leads to a positive sense of self. The protagonist of the final selection, *The Hector Quasadilla Story,* wants to play baseball for just one more season. Through "the game that never ends," where "the grass is always green, the lights always shining," Hector can forget, indeed deny, that he is getting old. It matters little that he hasn't played regularly or that he "can barely trot to first." In a game that stretches into thirty-two innings, Hector alternates between old memories and fantasies of his macho, younger years, and the brutal reality of his aging body. This game becomes his last chance to be the hero of his youth.

As these stories illustrate, there is a strong interaction between appearance, physical condition, stage of life, and developmental issues. In particular, the definition of self cannot be severed from the physical, and physical condition is often related to class, gender, and other sociocultural variables.

What I Know from Noses

Anndee Hochman

From the time I was eight years old, I understood that noses, even if they were not broken, could be mended.

My aunt had had a nose job, and she wasn't shy about it. I sat next to her on the couch while we paged through old photo albums. "There I am with my old nose," she sometimes said, as if the old nose were a childhood friend who had moved away.

I never asked my aunt why she had her nose fixed. The question seemed too obvious. The old one was too big and too bumpy. Who would pick a bumpy nose, a Jewish nose, if she had the choice? My aunt's new nose looked normal—not too wide or too thin, not too flared at the nostrils or uneven at the bridge. Not a nose anyone would look at twice in a crowded elevator. Which was, I guessed, the idea.

My aunt seemed happy with her new nose. When she smiled, her whole face thrilled—her teeth gleamed and her cheekbones nudged upward, and her nose did not do anything at all. Everyone in the family said she was very photogenic. I thought she was beautiful.

I am in high school, sitting in music class. The wooden chair prods hard against my back; tears burn my eyes. I am fifteen. At just under five feet, I've grown as tall as I'm going to get, and my body has changed. In the sixth grade, my straight dark hair crinkled first into waves, then wiry, unruly links. I'm no longer underweight. And my nose, true to family form, has developed a bump.

I look at photographs from before I grew, before my face turned traitor, and I want to cry. I rub my finger down the length of my nose. It feels huge where the bone rises. I think it is growing. At home, with the bathroom door locked, I turn sideways in front of the mirror and hold one hand over my nose, imagining how much better I'd look if it fell straight and smooth from bridge to tip.

On buses, in department stores, at the movies, I see noses attached to people. I judge the noses—too big, too snubbed, better than mine, worse than mine. I hardly see any that are worse then mine.

I am determined not to cry in music class. But Bob Fitzsimmons has just called me "suicide slope." Not for the first time. Across the room, he is snickering about my nose, his shoulders twitching as he whispers to the boy sitting next to him. Bob Fitzsimmons has too many freckles, he wears ugly clothes, and I hate him. I hate my nose.

After dinner that night, I sob to my mother. Everyone thinks I'm ugly, I tell her. I want a new nose. I want this one fixed. She hugs me tightly. OK, she says, OK. We'll go see some doctors.

I started my junior year in high school with crisp looseleaf binders, several medium-point black Bic pens, and a new nose. The operation wasn't so bad. At one point I started to surface out of the anesthesia and felt someone tapping in the middle of my face. It didn't hurt; it just felt annoying, like a headache you wish would go away.

For a week, I wore a bandage and didn't leave the house; for the rest of the summer, I had to be careful not to let my nose get sunburned. In August my father took a picture of me standing on our front walk. I had let my hair grow long since school let out; I wore a wide-brimmed straw hat and a white sundress. I angled my head at the camera, letting my nose show, and smiled widely. It was the first photograph of myself I remember liking.

Back at school, my life was much the same as the year before. I got A's in my classes, wrote for the newspaper, woke up at 6:15 every morning so I could spend forty-five minutes blow-drying the curls out of my hair. But inside myself, I felt changed.

My boyfriend told me, in cramped printing on a sheepishly sweet card, that he thought I was pretty. I believed him. When I acted in school plays, I didn't hesitate to turn my profile to the audience. And on buses, eventually, I stopped noticing the noses first.

More than a decade later, I'm still just barely five feet tall and weigh the same as I did at fifteen. In college, I quit wrestling my hair straight; now I wash it and let it dry in random curls. I rarely use makeup. In the summer, I shave my legs from the knees down. "My concession to polite society," I tell my mother.

Sometimes I stand in line at Safeway, turning the glossy pages of women's magazines. Hair dyes, depilatories, plastic surgeries, polymer fingernails, page after page of creams and blushes and eyeliners and lip glosses, page after page of implicit promises: Use this and you'll be beautiful, slender, deliriously happy. These women don't look like me; they don't look like anyone I've ever met. I stuff the magazines back in their racks and pay for my tofu, my spinach, my mineral water. I feel pleased that I'm not buying nail polish.

As a matter of principle, I declare I will never dye grey out of my hair, wear blue contact lenses on my brown eyes, or buy clothes that feel terrible just because they're in style. I tell myself that wearing one's natural face out in the world is not only an honest act, but a political one.

And for all these fourteen years I have carried a secret glitch in my principles, a bump as big as an old nose.

Unlike my aunt, I never talked about my nose job once I left high school. Not even my lovers knew. If friends came to visit at my parents' house, I made sure they saw only baby pictures with my cute snub of a nose, not the telltale "before" photos of adolescence.

It wasn't the nose itself that bothered me so much as the raw spot in my consciousness. I didn't want to remember a time of cringing at nose jokes and hiding my profile from my father's camera. I didn't want to recall how I stung with embarrassment and shame and the desperate hunger to look "right."

As I grew older, questions and arguments haunted my decision. Who says a bumpy nose is bad? Who cares what people think? Why is it mostly Jewish girls who get their noses fixed, Jewish noses that poke across the boundaries of what is considered beautiful? If you change a part of your physical self permanently, what happens to the intangible parts; does your psyche also shift to fit the new shape?

Sometimes, in the bathroom with the door locked, I looked in the mirror and cupped my hand against my nose, making a space where the bump used to be. I wondered then what I had lost when I asked the surgeon to scrape my bone down to smooth—and how I could get it back.

In the last few years, I have begun to tell friends about my nose. The whole story comes back to me vividly: the burn I felt at fifteen, wanting so badly to be pretty. The relief afterward, then all the years of embarrassed, guilty silence. And this realization: that when I stopped seeing noses everywhere I turned, my vision gained room for other things—my whole self, people around me, the desires that webbed us together.

Maybe I would have shed that self-consciousness anyway, slipped gradually out of it and into adulthood. Maybe if I hadn't had a nose job, I would be the same person I am now, just with a rougher profile. I don't believe that chromosomes drive destiny. But I do know that removing the bump on my nose somehow helped me to see past it.

If I ever have a daughter, and her nose takes after mine, and it makes her miserable, I'm not sure what I will tell her. Maybe I'll discuss sexist codes of attractiveness and tell her she's gorgeous just as she is. Maybe I'll hold her tightly and say, OK, let's go talk to some doctors.

I would want my daughter to know this: On the subject of women and beauty, it is the rules, not our bodies, that need repair. But even as I talk, I will remember myself at fifteen—how much, how fervently I wanted and deserved to feel fixed.

Finch the Spastic Speaks

Gordon Weaver

The doctor's achievements with problems like mine are famous; his connection with the university—research and occasional lectures—accounts for my choice of this state, city, school. I had, of course, my pick of institutions. He is, I think, basically kind, but too great a scientist to obscure his ministrations with mercy or pity, and for this I am grateful. Though we have met each month for the past five years, we have no . . . what you would call *rapport*.

Answer a leading question: what is Finch? Is he the body, the badly made bundle of nerve ends and motor responses? Or is he the mind, the intelligence, the scholarships and fellowships, the heap of plaques, medallions, scrolls, given in testimony to his brilliance? Or is he something even more than these, a total greater than the sum of his parts? I ask you, does not Finch . . . feel?

Ah, you mock! Finch, you say, Finch of all people! Finch? Poor, pathetic Finch, with his tested and recorded intelligence quotient of two hundred and thirty-three, locked forever in his prison of chaotic muscles. Poor Finch, who falls as easily over a curbstone as an infant toddler over a toy. Unfortunate Finch, whose large, staring eyes often roll wildly behind his thick glasses. Tragic Finch, who must choke and strain like some strangling madman if he is to ask for so much as a drink of water.

You underestimate me.

Stripped to shorts and undershirt, I sit on the edge of the doctor's examination table, legs dangling. With an ordinary tape measure, he checks my calves, thighs, forearms, biceps, to see if any disparity has developed. Kneeling, he exerts pressure on each foot as I pull up against him, testing for any distinction in muscular strength. "Okey doke," he says, pausing to jot conclusions in the thick folder bearing my name that will doubtless one day yield monographs, to his ever-spreading renown. "Ready?" he says, handing pen and folder to the attentive nurse. I do not speak needlessly.

He stands near me, raises his hands, spreads his fingers like a wrestler coming to close with an opponent in the center of the ring. And I see it just that way, a contest, for my amusement. I am very strong.

Relaxation is the secret. I half-close my eyes to concentrate, bombarding my shoulders, arms, hands, fingers, with commands: relax! Gradually, the fingers twitch, release the edge of the table, and slowly my arms rise, fingers open to meet his. He meets me halfway, interlocks his fingers with mine, and we push, face to face. I watch his skin flush, eyes protrude ever so slightly, teeth clench. We push, as earnest as two fraternity boys arm wrestling for a pitcher of beer. I am very strong.

He grunts without meaning to, catches himself, pushes again, then gives up, exhales loudly. "Okay," he says. I smell the aroma of some candied lozenge on his breath. Is there a trace of sweat on his tanned brow? "Okay," he says, "okay now." To save time, the nurse helps him unlace our fingers.

There was an impressive formal reception when I came to the university, five years ago. Not for me alone, of course. Invited were perhaps a hundred new students with some claim to distinction: merit scholars, recipients of industrial science fellowships, national prize-winning essayists, valedictorians in great number. But, except for a small covey of timid and meticulous Negro boys and girls, to whom all the dignitaries paid solemn if perfunctory court, I was easily the center of attention.

Imagine Finch, the spastic, dressed for the occasion. (The habitual fraternity jacket was not to come until my sophomore year, when Delta Sigma Kappa, campus jocks, coming to know me from my work at the gymnasium, adopted me something of a mascot, perhaps their social service project for the year—the jacket was free, as are the passes to football and basketball games. I could, if I cared to, sit on the players' bench.) I wear a dark suit with vest, and the dormitory housemother has tied a neat, hard little knot in my tie for me. I stand near the refreshment table, as erect as my balance will permit. My left arm is locked into place, palm up, whereon I place a napkin, a saucer, and a clear glass cup of red punch which I have no interest in tasting. With utmost care, I have tenderly grasped the cup's handle between thumb and forefinger, and there I stand, listening, questioning, answering, discussing (I speak extraordinarily well this day!) with a crowd of deans, departmental chairmen, senior professors, polite faculty wives, the president of the student body, and a handful of upper-class and graduate honor students. From time to time a few wander away to make a ritual obeisance to the Negroes, but they return.

Finch, Finch is the main attraction! Finch, with his certified intelligence quotient of two hundred and thirty-three, Finch who probes and reveals yawning gaps in the reading of graduate students ten years his senior, Finch who speaks with authority of science, literature, and contemporary politics, Finch who dares to contradict the holder of the endowed chair in history! Oh, there is glory in this! Finch, who cannot tie a shoelace, cannot safely strike a match, has trouble inserting dimes in vending machine slots—Finch is master here!

The other new students stand on the fringe of my audience, bewildered, or stroll off to stare dumbly at the obligatory portraits of past university presidents and trustees that dot the walls. I grow weary, but the tremor of my head can pass for judicious nodding, the tick of my cheek for chewing gum. The punch in my cup rocks a little. Who is the free man here?

Is it the scholar-professor who must think hard to recall specific points in his dissertation if he is to answer me? Is it the hatchet-faced, balding Dean of Letters and Science who carefully defends the university against its out-of-state rival, which also sought Finch? Is it the beautiful girl who won a regional science fair, but stands here, open-mouthed and silent as Finch explicates the relationship between set theory and symbolic logic? Is it the faculty wife with bleached hair, calculating her sitter's wages, who dares not depart for fear of offending Finch? Or is it Finch, whose brain roars with commands of discipline to his muscles, achieved only with the excruciating tenuous force of his will?

What you might think a disaster was actually the climax of my triumph. I had almost no warning. I felt the spasm that plunged my chin down against my chest, felt a stiffening come over my arms and hands, but no more. As nicely as if I wished it, I tossed my cup of punch up and back over my shoulder, while the saucer snapped in two in my left hand, giving me a rather nasty cut across the palm. There was a fine spray of punch in the air, the cup shattering harmlessly against the wainscotted wall behind me. Only the beautiful winner of the regional science fair forgot herself so far as to shriek as if she had been goosed.

I allowed no time for tension or embarrassment. I spoke quickly, clear as a bell, "Please excuse me," and reached up with the napkin to wipe punch from my forehead and hair. I asked for a chair, was seated, and the conversation continued as before while my hand was bandaged.

Which of you, I ask, would dare such a thing outside your dreams? When I smiled they laughed. And the winner of the science fair blushed, mortified by her outburst, as I related other such experiences in my past for their entertainment.

Above all, do not underestimate me.

The doctor breathes heavily. At my sides, my hands still hold their clawlike, grappling shape. A small victory, I am stronger than he; something to savor for a short time each month. He writes again, says, "I trust you're keeping up with the schedule." I nod, or what passes for a nod. The nurse helps me into my shirt and trousers.

"I can't emphasize that enough, James," the doctor said. He has called me by my first name since I met him; I was, after all, only seventeen when my parents arranged the first consultation.

"I don't want to alarm you," he said, "but there is evidence of unilateral deterioration—" I know the jargon as well as he—"your right side's progressing fairly rapidly. I want you to stay with the schedule, and don't miss the medication. I'm going to write your folks . . ."

I have always kept the schedule. Ever since I can remember, there has been a schedule, exercises, work with weights, isometrics, special breathing and relaxation drills. At home, in my dormitory room, in classes, on regular visits to the gymnasium, I have faithfully kept the schedule. And medication. Pills, occasional injections as new serums and theories prevail. My wristwatch is equipped with a small but persistent buzzer to keep me precisely on the schedule.

"Your know the literature on progression yourself . . ." he is saying. The nurse is fastening the buckles on my shoes; I once counted it a great breakthrough to go from snaps to buckles. I looked forward to laces, but no longer care about such matters. The nurse brings my fraternity jacket.

"You do understand the import of what I'm saying, James?" the doctor said. I realized he wanted more than a nod or flutter of eyelids. I must speak.

I did not forget the beautiful winner of the regional science fair. I saw her now and again during my first quarter at the university. We passed in corridors, joined the same lines in the cafeteria and bookstore, and once, sat in the same aisle in the auditorium to watch a foreign film. Whether she seemed to notice me or not (how, I ask, does one *not notice* Finch?), I never forgot her face as I saw it when my hand was being bandaged at the reception, flushed with distress for her unmannerly and callous shriek at my misfortune with the punch cup. I understood she was emotionally in my debt until I should release her.

As these weeks passed, I began to pay attention, to sometimes go out of my way to meet her as she left a class or walked one of the narrow paths crossing the wide, green campus on her way to or from her dormitory. I found stations, fixed and concealed points, from which to observe her at length. It was not until the first long vacation, however, that I recognized how affected I was by her beauty. Her name was Ellen.

Picture Finch: his father or mother drives him to the public library for a day's work, and he burrows into his books and three-by-five notecards with a determination the envy of any serious scholar. A librarian helps him carry books to a far, quiet corner near a window, where the sun's warm rays belie the frozen, cold stillness of the snow-covered streets and buildings outside. He begins, reads, writes, outlines, and times passes without his knowing it, or caring. But a dingy cloud throws him into shade, or the day has already faded to that dark, chill cast that is a deep winter afternoon. He lifts his trembling head, closes his eyes, sore with strain, and suddenly sees nothing, thinks of nothing, but the beautiful Ellen. History of political science or biology evaporate, and his reality consists only of her pale blond hair, the hazel tint of her bright, large eyes, the unbelievably fresh smoothness of her skin, the light downy hair on her arm, the sparkle of her white, even teeth; to the exclusion of even his lifelong awareness of his insane, spastic body, Finch knows only this beautiful Ellen!

I see, I *feel* the beauty of her movement: her hand glides to gesture, her fingers curl around a pencil, artless as the flow of water, no more self-conscious than the law of gravity; her head tilts, or she throws it to cast her hair back out of her eyes; she sits, crosses one long, sleek leg over the other, and it bobs in time to the animation of her conversation; she arches her back, thrusts out her breasts, and lets her coat slide down her stiffened arms as if they were greased rails; she climbs the steps to her dormitory, her knees churning like pistons, and pauses before the door to stomp snow from her high, black boots; alone on a path (but Finch, hidden, watches!) she holds her books against her stomach, runs, slides like a tightwire walker on a streak of silvery ice.

Ah, thinks Finch, oblivious to his books and the dry, clean smell of the library, *beauty*! She walks and runs, this beautiful Ellen, sits, jumps, with the floating, liquid perfection of some gaudy reptile.

It was Christmas, and I was home with my family, and I had reading and research papers to do, but I—why should I not say it—was in love. Finch was eighteen, and in love for the first time in his life. Yes, *Finch loves*! Or, thought he did. Loved, once.

"Jim?" says a voice outside this absorbing, warming reality—it is his father, or his mother, come at the agreed hour. "Jim, it's time to go, we'll be late for supper." Finch opens his eyes, and it is winter again, cars make slushy noises outside the window, and he must re-order his mind, recall where he left off his research, stack his cards and papers, answer questions, think of real things, when and where and what he is.

It is Christmas Eve night, and my family gathers at the huge tree the dominates our living room. There are special things to eat, and I am allowed a little whiskey for the occasion. My mother is happy in her Christmas way, tears in her eyes as she hands me many expen-sive gifts, elaborately wrapped—a new fountain pen, made in Ger-many, with a thick barrel, so much easier for the fingers to circle; a cowhide briefcase with a manacle fitted to the handle so I can lock it to my wrist (this will require new feats of balance, but, to please her, I say nothing of it); an astrakhan hat, in vogue among students this year—she will not have me lack what others have!

I appear to enjoy this annual ceremony as much as they. I give, and get, an enthusiastic hug and kiss as I open each gift, being care-ful not to too badly smash or tear the fluffy bows and ribbons and bright paper as I unwrap each package, labeled, as always, *To Jim from Santa*. I faithfully follow my father's direction as he films all this, stooped behind his camera and tripod, his words just a bit thick with too much whiskey. I pose, seated on the floor between my younger brother and sister (they are both perfectly ordinary), put my arms around their necks, do my best to smile so that I will not look drunk or half-witted in the movie.

But I got to bed early, pleading fatigue, the ritual splash of whiskey, the research to be done even on Christmas day. I leave them, to seek Ellen, to be alone in my bed and nourish this thrilling, weakening sensation of love that for the first time in my left lets me, makes me, forget myself. My taut body relaxes in stages, by degrees, while my brain whirls gently with real and imaginary visions of this exquisite Ellen. I still hear music, the rattle of happy, sentimental talk as my parents sit up late, drinking and watching old Christmas films—and for the first time in my life, I am not ashamed of the erec-tion that keeps me from sleep.

The good doctor has just informed me that my future is limited. The paralysis, unknown to me as I labor faithfully at my schedules, as I dose myself to the point of nausea, has been progressing. Subtle as a tiny worm, my malady has eaten away at this comic body, devouring days of my life. The figures noted in my folder already record the shrinkage from atrophy. The ultimate and sure end, if progression is not arrested, will be a spasm of sufficient duration, somewhere vital, the throat, the diaphragm, and I will suffocate in a final paroxysm, no different than if I had swallowed a fishbone. Yet he asks me to speak now, reassure him that I understand and face his diagnosis calmly.

He waits, brows lifted, expectant, needing; the nurse returns my file to the cabinet drawer. I speak, for us both, a lie.

"I'm . . . not . . . alarmed," I say, almost effortlessly. True, my mouth twists in shapes wholly unrelated to the words. My tongue emerges as I finish, and I am in danger of drooling idiotically, but the words, slow-paced, are only a little distorted, like the stridency in the voices of the deaf when they sing.

True, no one could take me for normal, but that I speak at all is a minor wonder.

"Good," the doctor said, "good," washing his hands. The nurse has left the room.

I have said, does not Finch feel? But feeling brings on paralysis, interrupts the constant stream of impulses from brain to muscle—feeling means stasis, immobility. I must be alone if I am to allow myself grief or wonder. Solitude waits only on my tortured passage through the waiting room, a perilous descent of the stairs, a short ride on my bicycle to the dormitory.

Back at the university, I determined to call her. Though I might have known she would not refuse me, I shook as if I suffered Saint Vitus' dance, telephone receiver in hand, until she said yes, she would accompanying me to a movie. "Will we be walking, Jimmy?" she asked. I faltered, choked, not having thought to the point of specific arrangements. Finch, pride of the history department, flustered like any juvenile! *No*, I managed to stammer: even the closest theater was a trek across the campus, far enough to be humiliating. I cringed, imagining us, arm in arm perhaps, floundering and swaying on the icy paths. "Oh," Ellen said, and waited for me to speak. I rocked fitfully on the small seat in the booth in the empty dormitory corridor. It might have sounded, in her ear, like the wild and frantic banging of someone prematurely buried.

I nearly mentioned my bicycle, but this was unsafe in winter for me alone—with her, perched on the handlebars, it would have been macabre. "I have a car, Jimmy," she said sweetly. And so we went in her car.

I do not remember what film we saw, for through most of the feature I sat rigid, inching my hand closer and closer to hers. Something happened in the film, something loud, action with bombastic musical accompaniment, and damning myself eternally a coward if I failed to act, at last, with a short, convulsive, clutching thrust, I slipped my hand over hers. She was kind enough to turn her head to me, and smile. We sat that way until the house lights came up, my sweaty palm covering the back of her smooth, cool hand. Surreptitiously, I breathed her delicious perfume, and from the corner of my eye, exulted in the delicate turn of her ear, her nostril, the way her blond hair swept upward on the back of her neck, the soft line of her throat, the faint heaving of her bosom.

We parked at the dormitory complex. It was very cold, and the other cars raised thick, steady clouds of exhaust. Their occupants, clasped in long, intense embraces, moved as shadows behind the frosted windows, all about us. Every few minutes, an engine died, a door opened, and a couple emerged to walk to one or another of the buildings. In the doorway lights we saw clearly their final kissing and fondling.

Ellen left the motor running, and we sat, silent. She wore a heavy coat, open, with a hood, a ring of snowy rabbit fur framing her face. We sat, quiet, while my brain raced, wondering what I should, or would, or could do. I did not want, at first, to touch her, but felt I must. I could feel the tick in my cheek grow worse, knew my limbs were frozen, hands balled in fists in my lap.

"Do you want me to walk with you to your dorm, Jimmy?" she said, and quickly, she leaned toward me, perhaps to open the door for me, I do not know. Somehow it terrified me, and I lurched, as if I had been given an electric shock, and I spoke.

"No!" I said. I did not mean to touch her, not at first.

My left arm came up, swiftly enough to have given her a jarring slap, but stopped short, and I caressed her cheek and chin. She seemed to lean further toward me. I willed my right hand to take her shoulder and turn her fully toward me. I think she wanted me to kiss her, or thought I wanted to—I looked into her face, and she was, again, smiling, as she had in the theater. Her mouth was open slightly, her eyelids fluttering.

It was then I decided to kiss her, and let myself feel fully the love I had not permitted myself before, ever. I think I may have begun to cry.

I was not in love, I understand now, not in love with this beautiful Ellen, this precocious student of science, with her skin like milk, her grace of movement so inherent and unconscious as to put a dancer or an animal to shame. I did not love her, I say. I felt, then, as I moved my head closer to hers, the welling up of my response to all the love showered on me before, by my family, doctors, nurses, therapists, teachers.

Should not Finch, like you, feel?

I was, surely, crying, making a grotesque sound like the growling of a beast. I was moved by the collective force of all that love—my weepy mother, standing at the end of the parallel handrails, holding back her tears, whispering, *step Jimmy, step, one more step to mother, Jimmy*; my father, carrying me high on his shoulders in the teeth of a biting wind at a football game, cheering, *look at him go, Jimmy!,*

suddenly letting me drop into his arms, hugging me to his chest, saying, *it's okay, Jim, it's okay,* because he thought I felt hurt, unable
ever to run like that anonymous halfback; my teachers, *see, James
knows, you're all so smart aleck, but James always has the right answer;* my sister, *Jimmy, are you the smartest person in the world?;* an
auditorium filled with parents, the state superintendent of education saying, *I cannot say enough in praise of James Finch,* rolls of applause as I move, like some crippled insect, to the podium, everyone's
eyes wet . . . I draw Ellen's face close to mine, my hand tightening on
her shoulder. Stupidly, I try to speak.

Kiss me, I want to say, with all the force muted by all the tenderness of my need. And I am betrayed once more by my odious body.
Ellen's mouth is closed to meet mine, and I gargle some ugly distor-
tion of my intention: *Kwaryoup,* I say, and her eyes pop open in hor-
ror. I hold her tightly, feel her resistance, try again—*Keeeebryumbee!*
erupts from my throat. She tries to release herself. *Sochavadeebow,*
I am saying, trying to reassure her.

"Jimmy!" she says, and pulls at my wrists. "Let go, Jimmy!" I want
to comply, but my left hand, nerves along my arm seeming to explode
like a string of firecrackers, raises, comes down on her breast.
"Jimmy!" she shrieks, and is crying now. "Get away from me, Jimmy,
let go of me! Get your hands off me, you're hurting me, Jimmy!"

And it is over, mercifully. The door is open, I crawl or fall out, scram-
ble through the snow on my hands and knees, slobbering, falling,
thrashing. Behind me, I hear Ellen's nearly hysterical sobbing.

Ah, Finch, to think you might love! I no longer need to remember
this, but when I do, am amused, recalling fairy tales of frogs and
princesses, recited, sometimes hour after hour, in an effort to relax
me for sleep, by my patient mother. A student of history, I remind myself, should have known better.

No matter. Before the following year was out, I had ceased avoiding her. When we meet now, we can even smile, though we do not
speak.

As I leave, other patients in the waiting room pretend not to see
me. An old woman with a cane and a platform shoe covers her eyes
with a magazine. A palsied man, no more than forty, looks down at
his shuddering hands. Another woman, younger, with a perfectly
healthy looking child on her lap, suddenly becomes interested in her
son's hair, like a grooming, lice- and salt-seeking primate. Yet another woman, her face set in a lopsided grimace, one shoulder permanently higher than the other, merely yawns, closes her eyes,
pinches the bridge of her nose between two fingers until I am beyond
her, as if she cannot bear her affliction so long as I am before her to
remind her of it.

I walk to the door. I stagger like an old wino, head whipping from side to side with the thrust of each leg, as if I keep time to some raucous, private music. My arms are cocked, ready to catch me if I slip. My feet point inward, and my torso tips forward to provide the continuity of momentum, my broad shoulders thrown back to maintain a risky balance.

It is a gait to embarrass, to make children laugh, a clumsy cantering locomotion that results from only the most exacting and determined attention to control. Inside my rolling head, behind my shocked, magnified eyeballs, my brain orders, with utmost precision, each awkward jerk of thigh, leg, foot. Just as I reach the door to the stairs, a voice greets me cheerfully.

"Hello, Jimmy," sings out in a lilting feminine rush of genuine delight. I bang loudly against the door as I stop, gripping the knob with both hands for support. My head nearly hits the panel of thick, opaque glass. I turn with difficulty. "Hello, Jimmy," she says again.

I know her, but not well. She is a disgusting thing to see, a fellow-student. Fat of face and body, her legs are little more than pale pink, waxy skin stretched over bone, her feet strapped to the steel platform of her wheelchair. One arm is horribly withered, the thin, useless fingers held curled in her broad lap. The other is braced for strength to allow her to work the levers that steer her chair. Beneath her seat squats a large, black battery, her source of power. Her neck angles slightly to one side. Someone has recently given her jet black hair a hideous pixie cut.

I know her. She is one of the small, cohesive platoon of handicapped, crippled, maimed university students. They have an association of sorts, advised by a conscientious faculty member who lost an eye in Korea. The university provides a specially equipped Volkswagen van to take them about campus. They have keys to operate freight elevators, and the buildings have ramps to accommodate them. When I came to the university I was invited, by the one-eyed professor, to join their ranks. I even attended one meeting—mostly polio victims and amputees. The agenda was devoted to a discussion of whether or not to extend membership to an albino girl whose eyesight was so bad she could not read mimeographed class handouts. I declined to join, of course, but still receive their randomly published newsletter. We have nothing in common.

She smiles now, lipstick and powder, rouge and eyebrow pencil making a theater mask of her face. "I've never seen you up here before, Jimmy, have you just started coming?" I am struck, suddenly with the awareness that she has an . . . an *interest* in me! I grope frantically to open the door.

I must, and do, speak, but badly, without thinking, so shaken am

I with my understanding. *Haroyoup* comes groaning from my lips, like the creaking of a heavy casket lid. Startled and embarrassed, she smiles all the harder, and I push open the door to begin the slow descent of the steep stairs leading to the street where my bicycle waits. Mad Finch, who dared to think he might feel!

At the top of the stairs I turn around, for I must descend backwards. I take the rail with both hands, regulate my breathing, concentrate, then step back, into the air, with one foot . . . I have a special sense of freedom, for I can never know if the foot will find the stair just below, or if I will step backward into space, find nothing, and fall. I am, for an instant, like a blindfolded highdiver who steps off the springboard, uncertain if there is water below.

I am able, momentarily at least, to forget my self-pity in this kind of freedom only I know.

I must not despair! Though Finch wields the chalk no better than a child does a crayon, he cuts surely as a surgeon to the heart of the problem on the blackboard. Though his pronunciation is atrocious, his syntax is exact, his structure flawless, vocabulary well beyond his years. Though his eyes, enlarged behind thick lenses, stare, sometimes roll up in his head, no one reads more or faster, and for amusement he will commit a paragraph or a page to memory in record time.

It is Finch who is free to traverse the lines of caste and class in our community. Finch is the locker room pet of brainless athletes. They challenge him to feats of strength, and lose goodnaturedly. From the heights of their chickenwire and toilet paper float thrones, Junoesque sorority queens wave to Finch in the crowd, call him by name. Filthy and morose, the bearded politicals and bohemians, who lurk in the basement of the student union, will take time to read Finch their latest throwaway or poem. Serious students, praying for futures in government or academia, consult Finch before submitting seminar reports.

Oh, I am not lonely!

So, with an effort of will, informed by the discipline of my regimen in physical therapy, weightlifting, my schedules, I heave, lifting my center of balance upward with an exaggerated shrug of my broad, strong shoulders; then, at the exact moment, a second divided into several parts for precision, I lean to the right, forcing all my weight onto my right leg, onto the raised pedal of my bicycle. There is no continuity, no fluid evolving process of motion, but my timing is correct—my mind has once more concentrated this fool's body into a preconceived pattern—the pedal depresses, the bike rolls forward.

There is an instant when disaster is possible—I am thrown forward with the bike, but my locked left hand grips the handlebar, stops me short of an ignominious and bruising tumble to the pave-

ment. I remember to pull with my right arm, to isolate the individual muscles that will steer out, away from the curb, past the hulk of
a parked florist's truck.

I move. Out now, near the center line, I assert the series of stiff,
dramatic thrusts of hip and leg that pump me along, past the campus shops, the bus stop.

Students throng the sidewalk, and they call to me. The frat boys,
the unmercifully attractive girls, golden and creamy in their expensive clothes, jocks in their letter sweaters and windbreakers, mal-
contents in old military jackets. They call: "Ho Finch!" "Jimbo!" "Hi
Jimmy!" They grin, wave. "Baby Jim boy!" "Hi Jim," they call.

With careful, paced breathing, I multiply the complexity of my ordeal. Almost one by one, I unlock my fingers from the handlebar.
With the strained deliberation of a weight-lifter, I raise it above my
head, steering and balance both entrusted to my left arm. Aloft, the
tingling spasms are sufficient to produce a casual wave. Like a swimmer shaking water from his inner ear, I rock my head, once, twice,
three times, until I face them. Opening my jaw is enough to pull my
lips back over my teeth: a smile.

In this instant I am helpless. Were a car to swerve into my path,
a pedestrian dart in front of me, all would end in an absurd, theatri-
cal collision—perhaps serious injury. But I prevail.

Now, the breeze in my ears, my glasses vibrating on the bridge of
my nose, threatening to fall across my mouth, I speak. My tongue
bucks and floats, the stiff planes of my throat shiver, and I respond.

"Jimmy!" they cry. "How you doing, Jimbo!"

Hyaroul explodes my voice, and I can almost see their delight, the
fullness of quick and easy tears of sentimental pity form in their
eyes. *Hyarouffa!* I say, already plotting how I will lower my right
hand, face the road again. *Haluff!* I make of unexpelled breath, not
knowing if it is my cry of joy at being alive, known, loved, or a curse
far more terrible than any profane cliché they will ever know—because . . . I suspect . . . simply because I cannot answer my own questions, cannot know what is, or is not, Finch.

Combustion

Susan Carol Hauser

I took a sauna once, long ago, in a shed on the shore of a northern lake. I leaned back, closed my eyes, and let the heat come over me. My heart rate picked up. My shoulders slumped. I might as well have been standing in rain, my body awash in water. I was the chicken sort and did not finally dive into the lake, but I did stand out in the night and let the air nibble me dry.

I felt good afterward, lighter and emptied, relieved of the weight of all that sweat that had been lurking inside me. I sat for a long time content to just sit, and then had a good sleep, the kind that comes when you've left one day behind and the next is still in shadow.

That was about twenty-five years ago. I've had a lot of good sleeps since then, but forgot about the beauty of a gratuitous sweat. Forgot about it until a few years ago when my personal female sauna kicked in. Hot flashes. Hormone storms. The fireworks that signal the end of fecundity. A prolonged celebration of the rite of passage that is menopause.

Back on that night of the induced sweat, my younger son Aaron declined to join us. One ladle of water on those benign looking rocks sent him and his five-year-old body fleeing into the safety of the night. He couldn't quite leave us though. He pressed his face against the rough wall and peered at us through a large crack. We could see his one eye, opened wide like a mouth.

When I have a hot flash, part of me feels like Aaron. I watch, astounded, as an invisible hand tosses water on the stones of my body, and I ignite. How can flesh not melt? Then, of necessity, I give up the watch and close my eyes and float on the water, and then the fire expends itself, and I pick up my little fan and create a breeze something like the ones that frequent northern lakes at night. Then I just sit in the quiet puddle of my flesh. If it is the middle of the night I sleep the good sleep of a person cleansed.

Of course, not all of the storms come in the privacy of my home. They come during meetings, during lunch downtown, at the grocery store, on the street corner while I am in conversation with a passerby friend. Awe strikes the company I keep, their eyes widening as a child's at the scene: my face turning red, water erupting on my brow, my glasses steamed, my arms windmills as I cast off as many layers of clothing as decorum allows while searching for a tissue to sop the water out of my eye wells.

Yes, I'm all right, I tell them. Not having a heart attack, just a hot flash, news from the body front: this woman is shedding the garment of the lunar clock. Marvel at it with her, at her luck in carrying within herself an organic sauna. Any time, any place, she may slip away for a few minutes into a wash of free-flowing sweat.

Envy her. It is making her strong, is tempering her with the fire and water contained whole within her human body.

The Hector Quesadilla Story

T. Coraghessan Boyle

He was no Joltin' Joe, no Sultan of Swat, no Iron Man. For one thing, his feet hurt. And God knows no legendary immortal ever suffered so prosaic a complaint. He had shin splints too, and corns and ingrown toenails and hemorrhoids. Demons drove burning spikes into his tailbone each time he bent to loosen his shoelaces, his limbs were skewed so awkwardly that his elbows and knees might have been transposed and the once-proud knot of his *frijole*-fed belly had fallen like an avalanche. Worse: he was old. Old, old, old, the graybeard hobbling down the rough-hewn steps of the senate building, the ancient mariner chewing on his whiskers and stumbling in his socks. Though they listed his birthdate as 1942 in the program, there were those who knew better: it was way back in '54, during his rookie year for San Buitre, that he had taken Asunción to the altar, and even in those distant days, even in Mexico, twelve-year-olds didn't marry.

When he was younger—really young, nineteen, twenty, tearing up the Mexican League like a saint of the stick—his ears were so sensitive he could hear the soft rasping friction of the pitcher's fingers as he massaged the ball and dug in for a slider, fastball, or change-up. Now he could barely hear the umpire bawling the count in his ear. And his legs. How they ached, how they groaned and creaked and chattered, how they'd gone to fat! He ate too much, that was the problem. Ate prodigiously, ate mightily, ate as if there was a hidden thing inside him, a creature of all jaws with an infinite trailing ribbon of gut. *Huevos con chorizo* with beans, *tortillas, camarones* in red sauce, and a twelve-ounce steak for breakfast, the chicken in *mole* to steady him before afternoon games, a sea of beer to wash away the tension of the game and prepare his digestive machinery for the flaming *machaca*-and pepper salad Asunción prepared for him in the blessed evenings of the home stand.

Five foot seven, one hundred eighty-nine and three-quarters pounds. Hector Hernán Jesús y María Quesadilla. Little Cheese, they called him. Cheese, Cheese, Cheesus, went up the cry as he stepped in to pinch-hit in some late-inning crisis, Cheese, Cheese, Cheesus, building to a roar until Chavez Ravine resounded as if with the holy name of the Saviour Himself when he stroked one of the clean line-drive singles that were his signature or laid down a bunt that stuck like a finger in jelly. When he fanned, when the bat went loose in the fat brown hands and he went down on one knee for support, they hissed and called him *Viejo*.

One more season, he tells himself, though he hasn't played regularly for nearly ten years and can barely trot to first after drawing a walk. One more. He tells Asunción too—One more, one more—as they sit in the gleaming kitchen of their house in Boyle Heights, he with his Carta Blanca, she with her mortar and pestle for grinding the golden, petrified kernels of maize into flour for the tortillas he eats like peanuts. *Una más*, she mocks. What do you want, the Hall of Fame? Hang up your spikes, Hector.

He stares off into space, his mother's Indian features flattening his own as if the legend were true, as if she really had taken a spatula to him in the cradle, and then, dropping his thick lids as he takes a long slow swallow from the neck of the bottle, he says: Just the other day, driving home from the park, I saw a car on the freeway, a Mercedes with only two seats, a girl in it, her hair out back like a cloud, and you know what the license plate said? His eyes are open now, black as pitted olives. Do you? She doesn't. Cheese, he says. It said Cheese.

Then she reminds him that Hector Jr. will be twenty-nine next month and that Reina has four children of her own and another on the way. You're a grandfather, Hector—almost a great-grandfather, if your son ever settled down. A moment slides by, filled with the light of the sad, waning sun and the harsh Yucatano dialect of the radio announcer. *Hombres* on first and third, one down. *Abuelo*, she hisses, grinding stone against stone until it makes his teeth ache. Hang up your spokes, *abuelo*.

But he doesn't. He can't. He won't. He's no grandpa with hair the color of cigarette stains and a blanket over his knees, he's no toothless old gasser sunning himself in the park—he's a big-leaguer, proud wearer of the Dodger blue, wielder of stick and glove. How can he get old? The grass is always green, the lights always shining, no clocks or periods or halves or quarters, no punch-in and punch-out: this is the game that never ends. When the heavy hitters have fanned and the pitchers' arms gone sore, when there's no joy in Mudville, taxes are killing everybody, and the Russians are raising hell in Guatemala, when the manager paces the dugout like an attack dog, mind racing, searching high and low for the canny veteran to go in and do single combat, there he'll be—always, always, eternal as a monument—Hector Quesadilla, utility infielder, with the .296 lifetime batting average and service with the Reds, Phils, Cubs, Royals, and L.A. Dodgers.

So he waits. Hangs on. Trots his aching legs round the outfield grass before the game, touches his toes ten agonizing times each morning, takes extra batting practice with the rookies and slumping millionaires. Sits. Watches. Massages his feet. Waits through the scourging road trips in the Midwest and along the East Coast, down to muggy Atlanta, across to stormy Wrigley, and up to frigid Candlestick, his gut clenched around an indigestible cud of meatloaf and instant potatoes and wax beans, through the terrible night games with the alien lights in his eyes, waits at the end of the bench for a word from the manager, for a pat on the ass, a roar, a hiss, a chorus of cheers and catcalls, the marimba pulse of bat striking ball, and the sweet looping arc of the clean base hit.

And then comes a day, late in the season, the homeboys battling for the pennant with the big-stick Braves and the sneaking Jints, when he wakes from honeyed dreams in his own bed that's like an old friend with the sheets that smell of starch and soap and flowers, and feels the pain stripped from his body as if at the touch of a healer's fingertips. Usually he dreams nothing, the night a blank, an erasure, and opens his eyes on the agonies of the martyr strapped to a bed of nails. Then he limps to the toilet, makes a poor discolored water, rinses the dead taste from his mouth, and staggers to the kitchen table, where food, only food, can revive in him the interest in drawing another breath. He butters tortillas and folds them into his mouth, spoons up egg and melted jack cheese and *frijoles refritos* with the green *salsa*, lashes into his steak as if it were cut from the thigh of Kerensky, the Atlanta relief ace who'd twice that season caught him looking at a full-count fastball with men in scoring position. But not today. Today is different, a sainted day, a day on which sunshine sits in the windows like a gift of the Magi and the chatter of the starlings in the crapped-over palms across the street is a thing that approaches the divine music of the spheres. What can it be?

In the kitchen it hits him: *pozole* in a pot on the stove, *carnitas* in the saucepan, the table spread with sweetcakes, *buñuelos*, and the little marzipan *dulces* he could kill for. *Feliz cumpleaños*, Asunción

pipes as he steps through the doorway. Her face is lit with the smile
of her mother, her mother's mother, the line of gift givers descendant
to the happy conquistadors and joyous Aztecs. A kiss, a *dulce*, and
then a knock at the door and Reina, fat with life, throwing her arms
around him while her children gobble up the table, the room, their
grandfather, with eyes that swallow their faces. Happy birthday,
Daddy, Reina says, and Franklin, her youngest, is handing him the
gift.

And Hector Jr.?

But he doesn't have to fret about Hector Jr., his firstborn, the boy
with these same great sad eyes who'd sat in the dugout in his Reds
uniform when they lived in Cincy and worshiped the pudgy icon of
his father until the parish priest had to straighten him out on his ha-
giography; Hector Jr., who studies English at USC and day and night
writes his thesis on a poet his father has never heard of, because here
he is, walking in the front door with his mother's smile and a store-
wrapped gift—a book, of course. Then Reina's children line up to kiss
the *abuelo*—they'll be sitting in the box seats this afternoon—and
suddenly he knows so much: he will play today, he will hit, oh yes,
can there be a doubt? He sees it already. Kerensky, the son of a
whore. Extra innings. Koerner or Manfredonia or Brooksie on third.
The ball like an orange, a mango, a muskmelon, the clean swipe of
the bat, the delirium of the crowd, and the gimpy *abuelo*, a big-
leaguer still, doffing his cap and taking a tour of the bases in a stately
trot, Sultan for a day.

Could things ever be so simple?

In the bottom of the ninth, with the score tied at 5 and Reina's kids
full of Coke, hotdogs, peanuts, and ice cream and getting restless,
with Asunción clutching her rosary as if she were drowning and Hector Jr.'s nose stuck in some book, Dupuy taps him to hit for the
pitcher with two down and Fast Freddie Phelan on second. The
eighth man in the lineup, Spider Martinez from Muchas Vacas, D.R.,
has just whiffed on three straight pitches, and Corcoran, the Braves'
left-handed relief man, is all of a sudden pouring it on. Throughout
the stadium a hush has fallen over the crowd, the torpor of supper-
time, the game poised at apogee. Shadows are lengthening in the
outfield, swallows flitting across the face of the scoreboard, here a fan
drops into his beer, there a big mama gathers up her purse, her knit-
ting, her shopping bags and parasol, and thinks of dinner. Hector
sees it all. This is the moment of catharsis, the moment to take it out.

As Martinez slumps toward the dugout, Dupuy, a laconic, embit-
tered man who keeps his suffering inside and drinks Gelusil like water, takes hold of Hector's arm. His eyes are red-rimmed and paunchy,

doleful as a basset hound's. Bring the runner in, champ, he rasps.
First pitch fake a bunt, then hit away. Watch Booger at third. Uh-
huh, Hector mumbles, snapping his gum. Then he slides his bat from
the rack—white ash, tape-wrapped grip, personally blessed by the
archbishop of Guadalajara and his twenty-seven acolytes—and
starts for the dugout steps, knowing the course of the next three minutes as surely as his blood knows the course of his veins. The familiar cry will go up—Cheese, Cheese, Cheesus—and he'll amble up to
the batter's box, knocking imaginary dirt from his spikes, adjusting
the straps of his golf gloves, tugging at his underwear, and fiddling
with his batting helmet. His face will be impenetrable. Corcoran will
work the ball in his glove, maybe tip back his cap for a little hair
grease, and then give him a look of psychopathic hatred. Hector has
seen it before. Me against you. My record, my career, my house, my
family, my life, my mutual funds and beer distributorship against
yours. He's been hit in the elbow, the knee, the groin, the head. Nothing fazes him. Nothing. Murmuring a prayer to Santa Griselda, pa-
troness of the sun-blasted Sonoran village where he was born like a
heat blister on his mother's womb, Hector Hernán Jesús y María
Quesadilla will step into the batter's box, ready for anything.

But it's a game of infinite surprises.

Before Hector can set foot on the playing field, Corcoran suddenly
doubles up in pain, Phelan goes slack at second, and the catcher and
shortstop are hustling out to the mound, tailed an instant later by
trainer and pitching coach. First thing Hector thinks is groin pull,
then appendicitis, and finally, as Corcoran goes down on one knee,
poison. He'd once seen a man shot in the gut at Obregón City, but the
report had been loud as a thunderclap, and he hears nothing now but
the enveloping hum of the crowd. Corcoran is rising shakily, the
trainer and pitching coach supporting him while the catcher kicks
meditatively in the dirt, and now Mueller, the Atlanta *cabeza*, is
striding big-bellied out of the dugout, head down as if to be sure his
feet are following orders. Halfway to the mound, Mueller flicks his
right hand across his ear quick as a horse flicking its tail, and it's all
she wrote for Corcoran.

Poised on the dugout steps like a bird dog, Hector waits, his eyes
riveted on the bullpen. Please, he whispers, praying for the inter-
cession of the Niño and pledging a hundred votary candles—at least,
at least. Can it be?—yes, milk of my mother, yes—Kerensky himself
strutting out onto the field like a fighting cock. Kerensky!

Come to the birthday boy, Kerensky, he murmurs, so certain he's
going to put it in the stands he could point like the immeasurable
Bambino. His tired old legs shuffle with impatience as Kerensky
stalks across the field, and then he's turning to pick Asunción out of

the crowd. She's on her feet now, Reina too, the kids come alive beside her. And Hector Jr., the book forgotten, his face transfigured with the look of rapture he used to get when he was a boy sitting on the steps of the dugout. Hector can't help himself: he grins and gives them the thumbs-up sign.

Then, as Kerensky fires his warm-up smoke, the loudspeaker crackles and Hector emerges from the shadow of the dugout into the tapering golden shafts of the late-afternoon sun. That pitch, I want that one, he mutters, carrying his bat like a javelin and shooting a glare at Kerensky, but something's wrong here, the announcer's got it screwed up: BATTING FOR RARITAN, NUMBER 39, DAVE TOOL. What the—? And now somebody's tugging at his sleeve and he's turning to gape with incomprehension at the freckle-faced batboy, Dave Tool striding out of the dugout with his big forty-two-ounce stick. Dupuy's face locked up like a vault, and the crowd, on its feet, chanting Tool, Tool, Tool! For a moment he just stands there, frozen with disbelief. That Tool is brushing by him and the idiot of a batboy is leading him toward the dugout as if he were an old blind fisherman poised on the edge of the dock.

He feels as if his legs have been cut out from under him. Tool! Dupuy is yanking him for Tool? For what? So he can play the lefty-righty percentages like some chess head or something? Tool, of all people. Tool, with his thirty-five home runs a season and lifetime BA of .234; Tool, who's worn so many uniforms they had to expand the league to make room for him—what's he going to do? Raging, Hector flings down his bat and comes at Dupuy like a cat tossed in a bag. You crazy, you jerk, he sputters. I woulda hit him, I woulda won the game. I dreamed it. And then, his voice breaking: It's my birthday, for Christ's sake!

But Dupuy can't answer him, because on the first pitch Tool slams a real worm burner to short and the game is going into extra innings.

By seven o'clock, half the fans have given up and gone home. In the top of the fourteenth, when the visitors came up with a pair of runs on a two-out pinch-hit home run, there was a real exodus, but then the Dodgers struck back for two to knot it up again. Then it was three up and three down, regular as clockwork. Now, at the end of the nineteenth, with the score deadlocked at 7 all and the players dragging themselves around the field like gut-shot horses, Hector is beginning to think he may get a second chance after all. Especially the way Dupuy's been using up players like some crazy general on the Western Front, yanking pitchers, juggling his defense, throwing in pinch runners and pinch hitters until he's just about gone through the entire roster. Asunción is still there among the faithful, the foolish, and the self-deluded, fumbling with her rosary and mouthing prayers for Jesus Christ Our Lord, the Madonna, Hector, the home team, and her departed mother, in that order. Reina too, looking like the survivor of some disaster, Franklin and Alfredo asleep in their seats, the *niñitas* gone off somewhere—for Coke and dogs, maybe. And Hector Jr. looks like he's going to stick it out too, though he should be back in his closet writing about the mystical so-and-so and the way he illustrates his poems with gods and men and serpents. Watching him, Hector can feel his heart turn over.

In the bottom of the twentieth, with one down and Gilley on first— he's a starting pitcher but Dupuy sent him in to run for Manfredonia after Manfredonia jammed his ankle like a turkey and had to be helped off the field—Hector pushes himself up from the bench and ambles down to where Dupuy sits in the corner, contemplatively spit- ting a gout of tobacco juice and saliva into the drain at his feet. Let me hit, Bernard, come on, Hector says, easing down beside him.

Can't, comes the reply, and Dupuy never even raises his head. Can't risk it, champ. Look around you—and here the manager's voice quavers with uncertainty, with fear and despair and the dull edge of hopelessness—I got nobody left. I hit you, I got to play you.

No, no, you don't understand—I'm going to win it, I swear.

And then the two of them, like old bankrupts on a bench in Miami Beach, look up to watch Phelan hit into a double play.

A buzz runs through the crowd when the Dodgers take the field for the top of the twenty-second. Though Phelan is limping, Thorkelsson's asleep on his feet, and Dorfman, fresh on the mound, is the only pitcher left on the roster, the moment is electric. One more inning and they tie the record set by the Mets and Giants back in '64, and then they're making history. Drunk, sober, and then drunk again, saturated with fats and nitrates and sugar, the crowd begins to come to life. Go, Dodgers! Eat shit! Yo Mama! Phelan's a bum!

Hector can feel it too. The rage and frustration that had consumed him back in the ninth are gone, replaced by a dawning sense of won- der—he could have won it then, yes, and against his nemesis Keren- sky too—but the Niño and Santa Griselda have been saving him for something greater. He sees it now, knows it in his bones: he's going to be the hero of the longest game in history.

As if to bear him out, Dorfman, the kid from Albuquerque, puts in a good inning, cutting the bushed Braves down in order. In the dugout, Doc Pusser, the team physician, is handing out the little green pills that keep your eyes open and Dupuy is blowing into a cup of coffee and staring morosely out at the playing field. Hector watches as Tool, who'd stayed in the game at first base, fans on three straight pitches, then he shoves in beside Dorfman and tells the kid he's looking good out there. With his big cornhusker's ears and nose like a tweezer, Dorfman could be a caricature of the green rookie. He says nothing. Hey, don't let it get to you, kid—I'm going to win this one for you. Next inning or maybe the inning after. Then he tells him how he saw it in a vision and how it's his birthday and the kid's going to get the victory, one of the biggest of all time. Twenty-four, twenty-five innings maybe.

Hector had heard of a game once in the Mexican League that took three days to play and went seventy-three innings, did Dorfman know that? It was down in Culiacán. Chito Marití, the converted bullfighter, had finally ended it by dropping down dead of exhaustion in center field, allowing Sexto Silvestro, who'd broken his leg rounding third, to crawl home with the winning run. But Hector doesn't think this game will go that long. Dorfman sighs and extracts a bit of wax from his ear as Pantaleo, the third-string catcher, hits back to the pitcher to end the inning. I hope not, he says, uncoiling himself from the bench; my arm'd fall off.

Ten o'clock comes and goes. Dorfman's still in there, throwing breaking stuff and a little smoke at the Braves, who look as if they just stepped out of *The Night of the Living Dead*. The home team isn't doing much better. Dupuy's run through the whole team but for Hector, and three or four of the guys have been in there since two in the afternoon; the rest are a bunch of ginks and gimps who can barely stand up. Out in the stands, the fans look grim. The vendors ran out of beer an hour back,and they haven't had dogs or kraut or Coke or anything since eight-thirty.

In the bottom of the twenty-seventh Phelan goes berserk in the dugout and Dupuy has to pin him to the floor while Doc Pusser shoves something up his nose to calm him. Next inning the balls-and-strikes ump passes out cold, and Dorfman, who's beginning to look a little fagged, walks the first two batters but manages to weasel his way out of the inning without giving up the go-ahead run. Meanwhile, Thorkelsson has been dropping ice cubes down his trousers to keep awake, Martinez is smoking something suspicious in the can, and Ferenc Fortnoi, the third baseman, has begun talking to himself in a tortured Slovene dialect. For his part, Hector feels stronger and more alert as the game goes on. Though he hasn't had a bite since breakfast he feels impervious to the pangs of hunger, as if he were preparing himself, mortifying his flesh like a saint in the desert.

And then, in the top of the thirty-first, with half the fans asleep and the other half staring into nothingness like the inmates of the asylum of Our Lady of Guadalupe, where Hector had once visited his half-wit uncle when he was a boy, Pluto Morales cracks one down the

first-base line and Tool flubs it. Right away it looks like trouble, because Chester Bubo is running around right field looking up at the
sky like a birdwatcher while the ball snakes through the grass, car-
oms off his left foot, and coasts like silk to the edge of the warning
track. Morales meanwhile is round second and coming on for third,
running in slow motion, flat-footed and hump-backed, his face
drained of color, arms flapping like the undersized wings of some big
flightless bird. It's not even close. By the time Bubo can locate the
ball, Morales is ten feet from the plate, pitching into a face-first slide
that's at least three parts collapse, and that's it, the Braves are up
by one. It looks black for the hometeam. But Dorfman, though his
arm has begun to swell like a sausage, shows some grit, bears down,
and retires the side to end the historic top of the unprecedented
thirty-first inning.

Now, at long last, the hour has come. It'll be Bubo, Dorfman, and
Tool for the Dodgers in their half of the inning, which means that
Hector will hit for Dorfman. I been saving you, champ, Dupuy rasps,
the empty Gelusil bottle clenched in his fist like a hand grenade. Go
on in there, he murmurs, and his voice fades away to nothing as Bubo
pops the first pitch up in back of the plate. Go on in there and do your
stuff.

Sucking in his gut, Hector strides out onto the brightly lit field like
a nineteen-year-old, the familiar cry in his ears, the haggard fans on
their feet, a sickle moon sketched in overhead as if in some cartoon
strip featuring drunken husbands and the milkman. Asunción looks
as if she's been nailed to the cross, Reina wakes with a start and
shakes the little ones into consciousness, and Hector Jr. staggers to
his feet like a battered middleweight coming out for the fifteenth
round. They're all watching him. The fans whose lives are like empty
sacks, the wife who wants him home in front of the TV, his divorced
daughter with the four kids and another on the way, his son, pride of
his life, who reads for the doctor of philosophy while his crazy
padrecito puts on a pair of long stockings and chases around after a
little white ball like a case of arrested development. He'll show them.
He'll show them some *cojones*, some true grit and desire: the game's
not over yet.

On the mound for the Braves is Bo Brannerman, a big musta-
chioed machine of a man, normally a starter but pressed into desperate relief service tonight. A fine pitcher—Hector would be the first
to admit it—but he just pitched two nights ago and he's worn thin as
wire. Hector steps up to the plate, feeling legendary. He glances over
at Tool in the on-deck circle, and then down at Booger, the third-base
coach. All systems go. He cuts at the air twice and then watches
Brannerman rear back and release the ball: strike one. Hector

smiles. Why rush things? Give them a thrill. He watches a low outside slider that just about bounces to even the count, and then stands
like a statue as Brannerman slices the corner of the plate for strike
two. From the stands, a chant of *Viejo, Viejo*, and Asunción's piercing
soprano, Hit him, Hector!

Hector has no worries, the moment eternal, replayed through
games uncountable, with pitchers who were over the hill when he
was a rookie with San Buitre, with pups like Brannerman, with big-
leaguers and Hall of Famers. Here it comes, Hector, 92 MPH, the big
gringo trying to throw it by you, the matchless wrists, the flawless
swing, one terrific moment of suspended animation—and all of a
sudden you're starring in your own movie.

How does it go? The ball cutting through the night sky like a
comet, arching high over the center fielder's hapless scrambling form
to slam off the wall while your legs churn up the base paths, you
round first in a gallop, taking second, and heading for third . . . but
wait, you spill hot coffee on your hand and you can't feel it, the
demons apply the live wire to your tailbone, the legs give out and
they cut you down at third while the stadium erupts in howls of ex-
ecration and abuse and the *niñitos* break down, faces flooded with
tears of humiliation, Hector Jr. turning his back in disgust and Asunción raging like a harpie, *Abuelo! Abuelo! Abuelo!*

Stunned, shrunken, humiliated, you stagger back to the dugout in
a maelstrom of abuse, paper cups, flying spittle, your life a waste, the
game a cheat, and then, crowning irony, that bum Tool, worthless all
the way back to his washerwoman grandmother and the drunken
muttering whey-faced tribe that gave him suck, stands tall like a giant and sends the first pitch out of the park to tie it. Oh, the pain.
Flat feet, fire in your legs, your poor tired old heart skipping a beat
in mortification. And now Dupuy, red in the face, shouting: The game
could be over but for you, you crazy gimpy old beaner washout! You
want to hide in your locker, bury yourself under the shower-room
floor, but you have to watch as the next two men reach base and you
pray with fervor that they'll score and put an end to your debase-
ment. But no, Thorkelsson whiffs and the new inning dawns as inevitably as the new minute, the new hour, the new day, endless, im-
placable, world without end.

But wait, wait: who's going to pitch? Dorfman's out, there's nobody
left, the astonishing thirty-second inning is marching across the
scoreboard like an invading army, and suddenly Dupuy is standing
over you—no, no, he's down on one knee, begging. Hector, he's saying, didn't you use to pitch down in Mexico when you were a kid,
didn't I hear that someplace? Yes, you're saying, yes, but that was—

And then you're out on the mound, in command once again, elevated like some half-mad old king in a play, and throwing smoke. The first two batters go down on strikes and the fans are rabid with excitement, Asunción will raise a shrine, Hector Jr. worships you more than all the poets that ever lived, but can it be? You walk the next three and then give up the grand slam to little Tommy Oshimisi! Mother of God, will it never cease? But wait, wait, wait: here comes the bottom of the thirty-second and Brannerman's wild. He walks a couple, gets a couple out, somebody reaches on an infield single and the bases are loaded for you, Hector Quesadilla, stepping up to the plate now like the Iron Man himself. The wind-up, the delivery, the ball hanging there like a *piñata*, like a birthday gift, and then the stick flashes in your hands like an archangel's sword, and the game goes on forever.

PART 6
LEARNING IN ADULTHOOD

LEARNING IN ADULTHOOD

As everyone knows, learning is part of being alive. Yet most adults when asked if they've learned something recently, think only in terms of formal, classroom activities and many respond, "No, I haven't had the time," or "No, I haven't taken any classes for awhile." Learning is so intertwined with living that we hardly notice when it's taking place, or how it's taking place. Yet, as many as 90% of adults are engaged in at least one learning project annually, and most average five such projects at 100 hours each over the course of a year (Tough, 1979). These projects can range from learning to cook ethnic food, to how to deal with adolescent children, to how to add on a deck. Some adults even devise their own "study" program to, for example, use a computer, appreciate opera, or explore Civil War history.

Much of adult learning is utilitarian in nature in that we *add* to our stock of knowledge and skills. Other learning can be developmental; that is, learning, particularly that derived from life experiences, can lead to some aspect of self-change. Subtle changes may occur when we encounter people from other cultures and find they don't fit our preconceived stereotypes, or when we really listen to another's view and recognize that he or she has made some credible points. When our *entire* worldview changes including the underlying values and assumptions, we experience what is called transformational learning. This kind of learning is usually precipitated by a dramatic life event—a loved one dies, we are diagnosed with a terminal disease, we experience a natural disaster such as an earthquake or a flood. We find our old coping strategies inadequate which leads us to question our values, assumptions, and priorities. We look for new ways to deal with the situation, one of which is to change our perceptions. This kind of learning shapes who we are—we are different afterwards in ways that others can see (Clark, 1993).

To a large extent, the historical and social context in which we live determines the nature of our learning. Today it is imperative that we learn to keep up with the changes going on around us. "The norm of a successful life [today]" observes Bateson (1994)

> more often involves repeated new beginnings and new learning. All those who become immigrants and refugees, displaced housewives and foreclosed farmers, workers whose skills are obsolete and entrepreneurs whose businesses are destroyed will have to learn new skills. Increasingly, returning to the classroom and sometimes totally shifting gears from one identity to another will be fundamental to adult development. . . . Beyond a certain level of economic and technological development, any society must become a learning society. (p. 82)

As with other facets of development, learning is also very much a function of the personal and social factors that structure our lives. Learning rarely occurs "in splendid isolation from the world in which the learner lives; . . . it is intimately related to that world and affected by it" (Jarvis, 1987, p. 11). Jarvis (1992) also writes that "the process of learning is located at the interface of people's biography and the sociocultural milieu in which they live, for it is at this intersection that experiences occur" (p. 17). Where we happen to live, the color of our skin, whether we are male or female, young or old, rich or poor, converge to shape the kinds of life experiences that we have, which in turn leads to what and how we learn. An older adult of Scandinavian heritage living in a rural midwestern town is likely to have different life experiences than the young African American professional living in New York City and thus learn different things. While social class, race, gender, and so on often determine the nature of our learning, they can also be obstacles. Bateson (1994) underscores this point with the observation that "wealth and power are obstacles to learning. People who don't wear shoes learn the languages of people who do, not vice versa" (p. 69).

Our sociocultural milieu not only influences *what* we learn, but *how* we learn. In other words, culture affects our learning style. Anderson (1988) writes, "Because the social, cultural and environmental milieus of ethnic and racial groups differ, one should expect these differences to be reflected in their respective cultural cognitive styles" (p. 4). The culture of American learning institutions is primarily Eurocentric and values independence, analytic thinking, objectivity and accuracy" (Guild, 1994, p. 16). In contrast, non-Western cultures promote a relational approach which is more field-dependent, holistic and affective (Anderson, 1988).

Of course, individual learning styles can vary from the qualities associated with the group learning style. However, different cultures tend to promote different values. Mexican Americans, among others, are said to value personal relationships and cognitive generalities (Cox & Ramirez, 1981; Vasquez, 1992), while African Americans emphasize oral expression and are more attuned to non-verbal cues and affect (Shade, 1989). Native Americans are thought to perceive globally and value time to reflect (More, 1990). Group cooperation and achievement are emphasized above individual achievement for those from many non-Western cultures including Chinese Americans, Vietnamese Americans and Puerto Rican Americans (Anderson, 1988).

How we are socialized as males and females also affects what we learn. Girls and young women in patriarchal cultures are often steered toward such school subjects as art, music and the language arts. Boys and young men are encouraged to pursue math and science and are expected to do better at math (Lummis & Stevenson, 1990). Girls are rewarded for being neat, quiet and considerate in learning situations, while boys' assertive behavior is valued in the classroom.

Finally, social class can also impact learning. Since learning institutions promote middle-class activities and middle-class values, those from working class backgrounds are disadvantaged. Allison Davis, an early African American multicultural education scholar, discussed the influence of class on learning. He stated that a person's "goals . . . symbolic world, and its evaluation were largely selected from the narrow culture of that class" (Davis, 1948, p. 11).

The readings about learning in adulthood illustrate different kinds of learning (additive and transformative) and represent different sociocultural factors that shape the learning. In *La Tortillera,* for example, the Hispanic protagonist is being instructed by her mother on how to make homemade tortillas. What is being passed down from one generation to the next, is not only a skill, but an ethnic heritage. As the mother says about the importance of knowing how to make tortillas: "Do you want your niños to grow up without culture and underprivileged? How can you expect them to know the meaning of life?"

Cultural and developmental factors converge in Watanabe's *Talking to the Dead.* Set in Hawaii, Yuri, the Japanese-Hawaiian protagonist becomes an apprentice to the village mortician, Aunty Talking to the Dead. When there is a death in the village, Aunty is sent for first—"for it was she who understood the wholeness of things—the significance of directions and colors." Yuri learns ancient ways of preparing bodies for cremation, but remains uneasy and afraid of doing such tasks on her own. When faced with Aunty's death, Yuri must carry out Aunty's wishes to be cremated in the traditional ways of her Hawaiian ancestors. Yuri finally takes control of the situation—

"Then I knew. In that instant, I stopped trembling. This was *it:* My moment had arrived." She has not only learned a vocation, she has grown in her sense of authority and control. Yuri exemplifies the notion that the self *itself* is learned: "The self fluctuates through a lifetime and even through the day, altered from without by changing relationships and from within by spiritual and even biochemical changes, such as those of adolescence and menopause and old age" (Bateson, 1994, p. 66).

Similarly, in *Mountain Biking and the Pleasures of Balance* a woman not only learns a skill, but also becomes empowered as she is freed from depending on male mentors. She bemoans the dearth of female mentors throughout her life, and says that she has had to "repeat the ritual of turning to men for knowledge about cycling . . . before owning balance completely for [herself] in [her] mid-30s." Gender initially defines this experience as it does later on during her "metamorphosis into a mountain biker" when she discovers other women racers from whom she feels support even in competition.

In summary, learning in adulthood is a complex phenomenon intricately related to the setting in which it takes place, and the personal and psychosocial characteristics of the learner. Adult learning is also intertwined with growth and change. On the one hand, life events and experiences evoke learning, and on the other hand, what one learns often impacts the self and the situation in such a way that one is changed in the process.

La Tortillera

The Tortilla Maker

Patricia Preciado Martin

Casa donde no hay harina, todo se hace remolina.[1]

There are a few things I must explain about my mother. She has
an inborn and natural elegance and grace, a genetic exquisiteness.
People turn their heads and stare in admiration when she walks by.
I have spent most of my life following a few paces behind her,
pretending to carry the train of an imagined magnificent gossamer
cape.

She is regal. And there is no place where she reigns more absolutely than in the Kingdom of the Kitchen. There she has decreed
irrevocable laws with monarchical absoluteness. There she is the
queen and I, alas, the court jester.

These are the Laws of the Kitchen:

Law Number 1: Tamales are not made; they are sculpted.
Law Number 2: Sopa is not soup; it is "the lovely broth."
Law Number 3: One must always wear an apron when em-
    barking on a kitchen mission. The apron must be handmade
    and embroidered with the days of the week (preferably in
    cross-stitch), and the correct one must be worn each day.

---

[1]In the house where there is no flour, everything will turn to shambles.
(Where there is no discipline, all will be lost.)

Law Number 4: A dining table must always have a starched and
ironed cloth—never, never placemats.

Law Number 5: Tortillas are the essence of life, the symbol of
eternity, the circle that is unbroken, the shortest distance between two points.

Law Number 6: Law Number 5 takes precedence over laws
number one through four and the Six Precepts of the Roman
Catholic Church.

Law Number 7: The unfortunates who buy their tortillas from
the supermarket, wrapped in plastic, might as well move to
Los Angeles, for they have already lost their souls.

A day in the kitchen with my mother is an oft-repeated disaster
echoing past scenarios:

"Patricia, es lástima that you don't make homemade tortillas more
often. Pobres de tus criaturas.[2] Do you want your niños to grow up
without culture and underprivileged? How can you expect them to
know the meaning of life?"

"You are right, Mamá. I just don't ever seem to have the time. And
anyway, they never seem to come out right. One time I forgot to put
in the baking powder, and they were as hard as soda crackers. The
next time I put in too much baking powder, and they puffed up like
balloons. They're either too salty or too bland. Sometimes I add too
much water, and they have the consistency of glue, or not enough,
and they are like rubber. And when I try to roll them out, they're
shaped funny."

"That's all right, mihijta. You are here today, and you have the
time, so let's make them together. I'll go through it with you [for the
hundredth time] step by step." (An audible sigh.)

"Well, Mamacita, it would be most helpful if you would give me
some measuring spoons and cups. We could measure the ingredients,
and then I could write down all the amounts, and then perhaps when
I made them at home [wishful thinking] they would turn out better."

"Measure? Who needs to measure? You can feel it in your alma if
the amounts are right. Your heart will tell you. See? I cup my hand
like this, and I know it's enough baking powder. The flour—just
make a lovely snowy mound of it in the middle of the bowl. And add
the salt in the form of La Santa Cruz to bless the bread. Don't worry.
La Virgen de Guadalupe will guide you."

I have already broken one of her favorite china cups during our
morning coffee session. There is a stain of my scrambled egg glowing

---

[2]Your poor children.

fluorescently on her white linen tablecloth with the crocheted hem. She has told me three times to lower my voice and put on an apron— the one that says "martes." She always has a candle burning for me on her bedroom altar with its army of saints, virgins, Santos Niños, and Almighty Poderosos. Her intentions are unspecified, but I think it has something to do with the fact that I cook with frozen food and use paper napkins.

She pours, spoons, sifts, stirs, mixes, and kneads with grace and deliberation. I watch with feigned interest and intensity. I am thinking about the tortillas at the supermarket in the plastic wrappers. The candle on the little altar flares and dies out.

The dough is ready. Now we must make little bolitas of perfectly uniform masa that must "rest" for half an hour under a cross-stitched embroidered cloth that says "Tortillas."

It is now time to roll the tortillas out. We take the cloth off ceremoniously. Mamá's bolitas of masa have expanded into symmetrical mounds of dough. Mine, however, are lumpy and misshapen.

Mamá: Now we will roll them out. I will let you use the palote[3] that my father made for me when I was but a little girl of six. Have I ever told you the story of how I began making tortillas for our family of eight when I was so small that I used to have to stand on a wooden box to reach the counter?

"Yes, Mamá." This story has been so often recited that it has become part of my family folklore with mythic importance equal to Popocatépetl and Ixtacihuatl.

"You roll them out gently. Now watch," Mamá demonstrates. "Put your right foot forward so that your body will be balanced in its weight as you lean forward to roll out the dough. That will ensure that the tortilla will be uniform." [And, incidentally, my life.]

The sweat is forming on my upper lip. I take the palote in my right hand, arrange my feet as directed, and try to roll out the dough into the shape of a circle. The masa had a mind of its own. It resists, gathers strength, overpowers and subdues me.

Mamá comments with a patient sigh, "That doesn't look too bad, mihijta. It is not quite round, it's true, but let's cook it and see how it comes out."

She places my Rorschach tortilla on the comal. It energizes with the heat. It browns, it puffs, it grows appendages, it hardens. The morning's lesson progresses. My stack of tortillas grows at a precarious tilt, a leaning tower. I am dusted with white flour from head to foot. My fingernails are luminous with dough. I am exhausted.

---

[3]rolling pin

Mamá announces with pious finality, "There. Now we're done. That was not so hard, now was it? Children! Come and see the tortillas your mother has made!"

From the mouths of little children: "Your tortillas look funny, Mom! How come they don't look like Nani's? That one looks like a rabbit. That one looks like a mushroom. That one looks like Florida! And that one looks like Texas!"

It wouldn't be so bad, I suppose, if one of them had been shaped like the state of Chihuahua. But Texas is unacceptable.

Mamacita relights the candle to St. Jude, the patron of hopeless cases.

A la mejor cocinera se le ahuma la olla.[4]

---

[4]Even the best cook can burn the pot. (No one is perfect.)

Talking to the Dead

Sylvia A. Watanabe

We spoke of her in whispers as Aunty Talking to the Dead, the half-Hawaiian kahuna lady. But whenever there was a death in the village, she was the first to be sent for—the priest came second. For it was she who understood the wholeness of things—the significance of directions and colors. Prayers to appease the hungry ghosts. Elixirs for grief. Most times, she'd be out on her front porch, already waiting—her boy, Clinton, standing behind with her basket of spells—when the messenger arrived. People said she could smell a death from clear on the other side of the island, even as the dying person breathed his last. And if she fixed her eyes on you and named a day, you were already as good as six feet under.

I went to work as her apprentice when I was eighteen. That was in '48—the year Clinton graduated from mortician school on the G.I. Bill. It was the talk for weeks—how he returned to open the Paradise Mortuary in the very heart of the village and brought the scientific spirit of free enterprise to the doorstep of the hereafter. I remember the advertisements for the Grand Opening—promising to modernize the funeral trade with Lifelike Artistic Techniques and Stringent Standards for Sanitation. The old woman, who had waited out the war for her son's return, stoically took his defection in stride and began looking for someone else to help out with her business.

At the time, I didn't have many prospects—more schooling didn't interest me, and my mother's attempts at marrying me off inevitably failed when I stood to shake hands with a prospective bridegroom and ended up towering a foot above him. "It's bad enough she has the face of a horse," I heard one of them complain.

My mother dressed me in navy blue, on the theory that dark colors make everything look smaller; "Yuri, sit down," she'd hiss, tugging at my skirt as the decisive moment approached. I'd nod, sip my tea, smile through the introductions and boring small talk, till the time came for sealing the bargain with handshakes all around. Then nothing on earth could keep me from getting to my feet. The go-between finally suggested that I consider taking up a trade. "After all, marriage isn't for everyone," she said. My mother said that that was a fact which remained to be proved, but meanwhile, it wouldn't hurt if I took in sewing or learned to cut hair. I made up my mind to apprentice myself to Aunty Talking to the Dead.

The old woman's house was on the hill behind the village, in some woods, just off the road to Chicken Fight Camp. She lived in an old plantation worker's bungalow with peeling green and white paint and a large, well-tended garden out front—mostly of flowering bushes and strong-smelling herbs I didn't know the names of.

"Aren't you a big one," a gravelly voice behind me rasped.

I started, then turned. It was the first time I had ever seen the old woman up close.

"Hello . . . uh . . . Mrs. . . . Mrs. . . . Dead," I stammered.

She was little—way under five feet—and wrinkled, and everything about her seemed the same color—her skin, her lips, her dress—everything just a slightly different shade of the same brown-grey, except her hair, which was absolutely white, and her tiny eyes, which glinted like metal. For a minute, those eyes looked me up and down.

"Here," she said finally, thrusting an empty rice sack in my hands, "For collecting salt." And she started down the road to the beach.

In the next few months, we walked every inch of the hills and beaches around the village, and then some.

"This is *a'ali'i* to bring sleep—it must be dried in the shade on a hot day." Aunty was always three steps ahead, chanting, while I struggled behind, laden with strips of bark and leafy twigs, my head buzzing with names.

"This is *awa* for every kind of grief, and *uhaloa* with the deep roots—if you are like that, death cannot easily take you." Her voice came from the stones, the trees, and the earth.

"This is where you gather salt to preserve a corpse," I hear her still. "This is where you cut to insert the salt," her words have marked the places on my body, one by one.

That whole first year, not a single day passed when I didn't think of quitting. I tried to figure out a way of moving back home without making it seem like I was admitting anything.

"You know what people are saying, don't you?" my mother said, lifting the lid of the bamboo steamer and setting a tray of freshly-steamed meat buns on the already-crowded table before me. It was one of the few visits home since my apprenticeship—though I'd never been more than a couple of miles away—and she had stayed up the whole night before, cooking. The kitchen table was near-overflowing—she'd prepared a canned ham with yellow sweet potatoes, wing beans with pork, sweet and sour mustard cabbage, fresh raw yellow-fin, pickled egg plant, and rice with red beans. I had not seen so much food since the night she tried to persuade her younger brother, my Uncle Mongoose, not to volunteer for the army. He went anyway, and on the last day of training, just before he was shipped to Italy, he shot himself in the head when he was cleaning his gun. "I always knew that boy would come to no good," was all Mama said when she heard the news.

"What do you mean you can't eat another bite," she fussed now. "Look at you, nothing but a bag of bones."

I allowed myself to be persuaded to another helping, though I'd lost my appetite.

The truth was, there didn't seem to be much of a future in my apprenticeship. In eleven and a half months, I had memorized most of the minor rituals of mourning and learned to identify a couple of dozen herbs and all their medicinal uses, but I had not seen—much less gotten to practice on—a single honest-to-goodness corpse.

"People live longer these days," Aunty claimed.

But I knew it was because everyone—even from villages across the bay—had begun taking their business to the Paradise Mortuary. The single event which established Clinton's monopoly once and for all was the untimely death of old Mrs. Pomadour, the plantation owner's mother-in-law, who choked on a fishbone during a fundraising luncheon of the Famine Relief Society. Clinton was chosen to be in charge of the funeral. He took to wearing three-piece suits—even during the humid Kona season—as a symbol of his new respectability, and was nominated as a Republican candidate to run for the village council.

"So, what are people saying, Mama," I said, finally pushing my plate away.

This was the cue she had been waiting for. "They're saying that That Woman has gotten herself a new donkey . . ." She paused dramatically, holding my look with her eyes. The implication was clear.

I began remembering things about being in my mother's house. The navy blue dresses. The humiliating weekly tea ceremony lessons at the Buddhist Temple.

"Give up this foolishness," she wheedled. "Mrs. Koyama tells me the Barber Shop Lady is looking for help . . ."

"I'll think I'll stay right where I am," I said.

My mother drew herself up. "Here, have another meat bun," she said, jabbing one through the center with her serving fork and lifting it onto my plate.

A few weeks later, Aunty and I were called just outside the village to perform a laying-out. It was early afternoon when Sheriff Kanoi came by to tell us that the body of Mustard Hayashi, the eldest of the Hayashi boys, had just been pulled from an irrigation ditch by a team of field workers. He had apparently fallen in the night before, stone drunk, on his way home from Hula Rose's Dance Emporium.

I began hurrying around, assembling Aunty's tools and bottles of potions, and checking that everything was in working order, but the old woman didn't turn a hair; she just sat calmly rocking back and forth and puffing on her skinny, long-stemmed pipe.

"Yuri, you stop that rattling around back there!" she snapped, then turned to the Sheriff. "My son Clinton could probably handle this. Why don't you ask him?"

"No, Aunty," Sheriff Kanoi replied. "This looks like a tough case that's going to need some real expertise."

"Mmmm . . ." The old woman stopped rocking. "It's true, it was a bad death," she mused.

"Very bad," the Sheriff agreed.

"The spirit is going to require some talking to. . . ."

"Besides, the family asked special for you," he said.

No doubt because they didn't have any other choice, I thought. That morning, I'd run into Chinky Malloy, the assistant mortician at the Paradise, so I happened to know that Clinton was at a mortician's conference in the city and wouldn't be back for several days. But I didn't say a word.

Mustard's remains had been laid out on a green formica table in the kitchen. It was the only room in the house with a door that faced north. Aunty claimed that you should always choose a north-facing room for a laying-out so the spirit could find its way home to the land of the dead without getting lost.

Mustard's mother was leaning over his corpse, wailing, and her husband stood behind her, looking white-faced, and absently patting her on the back. The tiny kitchen was jammed with sobbing, nose-blowing relatives and neighbors. The air was thick with the smells of grief—perspiration, ladies' cologne, last night's cooking, and the faintest whiff of putrefying flesh. Aunty gripped me by the wrist and pushed her way to the front. The air pressed closer and closer—like someone's hot, wet breath on my face. My head reeled, and the room broke apart into dancing dots of color. From far away I heard somebody say, "It's Aunty Talking to the Dead."

"Make room, make room," another voice called.

I looked down at Mustard, lying on the table in front of me—his eyes half-open in that swollen, purple face. The smell was much stronger close up, and there were flies everywhere.

"We're going to have to get rid of some of this bloat," Aunty said, thrusting a metal object into my hand.

People were leaving the room.

She went around to the other side of the table. "I'll start here," she said. "You work over there. Do just like I told you."

I nodded. This was the long-awaited moment. My moment. But it was already the beginning of the end. My knees buckled and everything went dark.

Aunty performed the laying-out alone and never mentioned the episode again. But it was the talk of the village for weeks—how Yuri Shimabukuro, assistant to Aunty Talking to the Dead, passed out under the Hayashi's kitchen table and had to be tended to by the grief-stricken mother of the dead boy.

My mother took to catching the bus to the plantation store three villages away whenever she needed to stock up on necessaries. "You're my daughter—how could I *not* be on your side?" was the way she put it, but the air buzzed with her unspoken recriminations. And whenever I went into the village, I was aware of the sly laughter behind my back, and Chinky Malloy smirking at me from behind the shutters of the Paradise Mortuary.

"She's giving the business a bad name," Clinton said, carefully removing his jacket and draping it across the back of the rickety wooden chair. He dusted the seat, looked at his hand with distaste before wiping it off on his handkerchief, then drew up the legs of his trousers, and sat.

Aunty picked up her pipe from the smoking tray next to her rocker and filled the tiny brass bowl from a pouch of Bull Durham. "I'm glad you found time to drop by," she said. "You still going out with that skinny white girl?"

"You mean Marsha?" Clinton sounded defensive. "Sure, I see her sometimes. But I didn't come here to talk about that." He glanced over at where I was sitting on the sofa. "You think we could have some privacy?"

Aunty lit her pipe and puffed. "There's nobody here but us. . . . Oh, you mean Yuri. She's my right hand. Couldn't do without her."

"The Hayashis probably have their own opinion about that."

Aunty waved her hand in dismissal. "There's no pleasing some people. Yuri's just young; she'll learn." She reached over and patted me on the knee, then looked him straight in the face. "Like we all did."

Clinton turned red. "Damn it, Mama!" he sputtered. "You're making yourself a laughing stock!" His voice became soft, persuasive. "Look, you've worked hard all your life, but now, I've got my business—it'll be a while before I'm really on my feet—but you don't have to do this. . . ." He gestured around the room. "I'll help you out. You'll see. I'm only thinking about you. . . ."

"About the election to village council, you mean!" I burst out.

Aunty was unperturbed. "You thinking about going into politics, son?"

"Mama, wake up!" Clinton hollered, like he'd wanted to all along. "The old spirits have had it. We're part of progress now, and the world is going to roll right over us and keep on rolling, unless we get out there and grab our share."

His words rained down like stones, shattering the air around us.

For a long time after he left, Aunty sat in her rocking chair next to the window, rocking and smoking, without saying a word, just rocking and smoking, as the afternoon shadows flickered beneath the trees and turned to night.

Then, she began to sing—quietly, at first, but very sure. She sang the naming chants and the healing chants. She sang the stones, and trees, and stars back into their rightful places. Louder and louder she sang—making whole what had been broken.

Everything changed for me after Clinton's visit. I stopped going into the village and began spending all my time with Aunty Talking to the Dead. I followed her everywhere, carried her loads without complaints, memorized remedies and mixed potions till my head spun and I went near blind. I wanted to know what *she* knew; I wanted to make what had happened at the Hayashis' go away. Not just in other people's minds. Not just because I'd become a laughing stock, like Clinton said. But because I knew that I *had* to redeem myself for that one thing, or my moment—the single instant of glory for which I had lived my entire life—would be snatched beyond my reach forever.

Meanwhile, there were other layings-out. The kitemaker who hung himself. The crippled boy from Chicken Fight Camp. The Vagrant. The Blindman. The Blindman's dog.

"Do like I told you," Aunty would say before each one. Then, "Just give it time," when it was done.

But it was like having the same nightmare over and over—just one look at a body and I was done for. For twenty-five years, people in the village joked about my "indisposition." Last year, when my mother died, her funeral was held at the Paradise Mortuary. I stood outside on the cement walk for a long time, but never made it through the door. Little by little, I had given up hope that my moment would ever arrive.

Then, one week ago, Aunty caught a chill after spending all morning out in the rain, gathering *awa* from the garden. The chill developed into a fever, and for the first time since I'd known her, she took to her bed. I nursed her with the remedies she'd taught me—sweat baths; eucalyptus steam; tea made from *ko'oko'olau*—but the fever worsened. Her breathing became labored, and she grew weaker. My few hours of sleep were filled with bad dreams. She kept slipping and slipping away from me. In desperation, aware of my betrayal, I finally walked to a house up the road and telephoned for an ambulance.

"I'm sorry, Aunty," I kept saying, as the flashing red light swept across the porch. The attendants had her on a stretcher and were carrying her out the front door.

She reached up and grasped my arm, her grip still strong. "You'll do okay, Yuri," the old woman whispered hoarsely, and squeezed. "Clinton used to get so scared, he messed his pants." She chuckled, then began to cough. One of the attendants put an oxygen mask over her face. "Hush," he said. "There'll be plenty of time for talking later."

The day of Aunty's wake, workmen were repaving the front walk and had blocked off the main entrance to the Paradise Mortuary. They had dug up the old concrete tiles and carted them away. They'd left a mound of gravel on the grass, stacked some bags of concrete next to it, and covered them with black tarps. There was an empty wheelbarrow parked on the other side of the gravel mound. The entire front lawn was roped off and a sign put up which said, "Please use the back entrance. We are making improvements in Paradise. The Management."

My stomach was beginning to play tricks, and I was feeling a little dizzy. The old panic was mingled with an uneasiness which had not left me ever since I had decided to call the ambulance. I kept thinking maybe I shouldn't have called it since she had gone and died anyway. Or maybe I should have called it sooner. I almost turned back, but I thought of what Aunty had told me about Clinton and pressed on. Numbly, I followed the two women in front of me through the garden along the side of the building, around to the back.

"So, old Aunty Talking to the Dead has finally passed on," one of them, whom I recognized as the Dancing School Teacher, said. She was with Pearlie Mukai, an old classmate of mine from high school. Pearlie had gone years ago to live in the city, but still returned to the village to visit her mother.

I was having difficulty seeing—it was getting dark, and my head was spinning so.

"How old do you suppose she was?" Pearlie asked.

"Gosh, even when we were kids it seemed like she was at least a hundred."

"'The Undead,' my brother used to call her."

"When we misbehaved, my mother used to threaten to send us to Aunty Talking to the Dead. She'd be giving us the licking of our lives and hollering, 'This is gonna seem like nothing, then!'"

Aunty had been laid out in one of the rooms along the side of the house. The heavy wine-colored drapes had been drawn across the windows, and all the wall lamps turned very low, so it was darker in the room than it had been outside.

Pearlie and the Dancing School Teacher moved off into the front row. I headed for the back.

There were about thirty of us at the wake, mostly from the old days—those who had grown up on stories about Aunty, or who remembered her from before the Paradise Mortuary.

People were getting up and filing past the casket. For a moment, I felt faint again, but I remembered about Clinton (how self-assured and prosperous he looked standing at the door, accepting condolences!), and I got into line. The Dancing School Teacher and Pearlie slipped in front of me.

I drew nearer and nearer to the casket. I hugged my sweater close. The room was air conditioned and smelled of floor-disinfectant and roses. Soft music came from speakers mounted on the walls.

Now there were just four people ahead. Now three. I looked down on the floor, as the blackness welled up inside me.

Then Pearlie Mukai shrieked, "Her eyes!"

People behind me began to murmur.

"What . . . whose eyes?" The Dancing School Teacher demanded.

Pearlie pointed to the body in the casket.

The Dancing School Teacher peered down and cried, "My God, they're open!"

My heart turned to ice.

"What?" voices behind me were asking. "What about her eyes?"

"She said they're open," someone said.

"Aunty Talking to the Dead's Eyes Are Open," someone else said.

Now Clinton was hurrying over.

"That's because she's Not Dead," still another voice put in.

Clinton looked into the coffin, and his face turned white. He turned quickly around again, and waved to his assistants across the room.

"I've heard about cases like this," someone was saying. "It's because she's looking for someone."

"I've heard that too! The old woman is trying to tell us something."

I was the only one there who knew. Aunty was talking to *me*. I clasped my hands together, hard, but they wouldn't stop shaking.

People began leaving the line. Others pressed in, trying to get a better look at the body, but a couple of Clinton's assistants had stationed themselves in front of the coffin, preventing anyone from getting too close. They had shut the lid, and Chinky Malloy was directing people out of the room.

"I'd like to take this opportunity to thank you all for coming here this evening," Clinton was saying. "I hope you will join us at the reception down the hall. . . ."

While everyone was eating, I stole back into the parlor and quietly—ever so quietly—went up the casket, lifted the lid, and looked in.

At first, I thought they had switched bodies on me and exchanged Aunty for some powdered and painted old grandmother, all pink and white, in a pink dress, and clutching a white rose to her chest. But the pennies had fallen from her eyes—and there they were. Open. Aunty's eyes staring at me.

Then I knew. In that instant, I stopped trembling. This was *it*: *My* moment had arrived. Aunty Talking to the Dead had come awake to bear me witness.

I walked through the deserted front rooms of the mortuary and out the front door. It was night. I got the wheelbarrow, loaded it with one of the tarps covering the bags of cement, and wheeled it back to the room where Aunty was. It squeaked terribly, and I stopped often to make sure no one had heard me. From the back of the building came the clink of glassware and the buzz of voices. I had to work quickly—people would be leaving soon.

But this was the hardest part. Small as she was, it was very hard to lift her out of the coffin. She was horribly heavy, and unyielding as a bag of cement. It seemed like hours, but I finally got her out and wrapped her in the tarp. I loaded her in the tray of the wheelbarrow—most of her, anyway; there was nothing I could do about her feet sticking out the front end. Then, I wheeled her through the silent rooms of the mortuary, down the front lawn, across the village square, and up the road, home.

Now, in the dark, the old woman is singing.

I have washed her with my own hands and worked the salt into the hollows of her body. I have dressed her in white and laid her in flowers.

Aunty, here are the beads you like to wear. Your favorite cakes. A quilt to keep away the chill. Here is *noni* for the heart and *awa* for every kind of grief.

Down the road a dog howls, and the sound of hammering echoes through the still air. "Looks like a burying tomorrow," the sleepers murmur, turning in their warm beds.

I bind the sandals on her feet and put the torch to the pyre.

The sky turns to light. The smoke climbs. Her ashes scatter, filling the wind.

And she sings, she sings, she sings.

Mountain Biking and the Pleasures of Balance

Marti Stephen

Looking back over my metamorphosis into a mountain biker, I realize that sometimes, in order to achieve balance, you have to go to extremes. In my case, it took a love for the extreme, the passionate and even the epic, to sign up to race twenty miles of fire roads and single-track (narrow, one-bike trails) in drizzling rain and through snowbanks at the summit of a mountain. But I didn't see it as extreme then, I saw it as initiation, and I had a powerful, though vague, longing to be on the other side of an experience I'd never had before.

My memories of my life-long cycling odyssey begin at age seven or eight and center around two things: a bike borrowed from the boys across the street, and the infallible sense that I could learn this new physical skill. Now I know that some girls were lucky enough to learn from other girls, but in my neighborhood there were no girls riding bikes, and I had to approach the very font of physical prowess—a boy.

I repeated the ritual of turning to men for knowledge about cycling at least two more times before owning balance completely for myself in my mid-30s. But after those first years on the bike—when I felt I could learn anything—I lost my childlike trust in my body, my sense of balance, and my place in the sporting world. The rediscovery of that trust, which I made on a touring bike in my mid-20s, is now made substantial every time I line up for a mountain bike race.

After the boy next door, my second tutor in the world of the wheel was a bike racer—an architecture student who was my boyfriend and who had a passion for the history, the cliquishness, the working-class values and the outlandishness of road racing in these United

States (as opposed to Europe, where it is as well understood as football is here). I was in my 20s then, and he reintroduced me to the bike. At the time, mountain biking was in its infancy, and while I was vaguely aware of it, I was busy worshipping male role models and discovering that the brutal physical requirements of road racing were far beyond my fitness level. As a little girl, I'd had a nonathletic childhood and had been brought up, as many girls were, to avoid risk. I'd also developed a case of self-loathing during numerous failures in coed kickball games, recess hours and p.e. classes. In road riding terms, I felt permanently o.t.b. (off-the-back, a term used to describe the rider who can't keep up with the pack). At the time, I adored the idea of road racing so much that I couldn't even speak about my own racing aspirations above a whisper. So my dreams, born somewhere deep within me and diametrically opposed to anything I had dared in a long, long time, took control of my soul.

As I moved beyond the transitional boyfriend and into my own halting self-discovery as a racer, I discovered other women racers (what a blessing) and, on a particularly memorable century ride in the Santa Ynez Valley of California, another boyfriend. He became another guide on my bicycle quest, and probably the last male tutor I would ever need. He lived at the base of Mt. Tamalpais in Marin County, California, a mountain named after a woman and a location famous as the birthplace of mountain biking. He took my road bike elitism (carefully copied from the old boy school) and rubbed it in the dirt. It was the beginning of the lesson that would eventually set me free.

Oh, he made me suffer. Four-hour-long, bone-jarring rides that were approximately half uphill and half downhill, each presenting a completely different set of obstacles. My only real taskmaster was the incline of the earth, and she was the only real audience, too. Bless her, she was impartial, and her challenges made me fitter than I had ever been. We made an unspoken bargain: as long as I would honor the suffering, she would make me fit.

This bargain with the dirt was a cold one. I honored it sometimes while shrinking from the effort required, sometimes in the exhilaration of strength. I kept my side of it in violent gusts of wind that blew me off my bike on the tops of ridges and I broke it on fine, sunny days when the challenge—particularly the challenge of balance—made me wither in self-disgust and stay close to the hearth instead of close to the heart. But I would keep it again on mild rides and wild ones. I remember one in particular where hip-deep water at a stream crossing nearly washed away my bike. But as long as I came back, Nature extended the terms, and I grew fitter. Fit enough, in fact, to race mountain bikes.

I agreed to the challenge with my eyes shut and with the hope that the experience would be alchemical—that the base metal of a rider would finally, gloriously, be turned into the gold of a racer. Since I held such a simple, grandiose view of racing, no such thing would happen, but there were transformative moments, nonetheless.

I arrived at the race with the man who had conducted my studies in mountain biking so far, and he was about to relinquish his mentorship as I discovered the wealth of support I felt from other women—my competitors. I remember how I expected him to be all-knowing in regards to pre-race jitters, and how I followed his example of reading a book before the warm-up of my race, and how I nearly missed the start of my own race because I was slavishly not looking out for myself. (Obvious enough, but I was expecting absolute knowledge from this man).

My race rode off without me—it seems hilarious in the retelling—and I was forced to chase the field. But I caught them and even passed a number of riders—solidly—while climbing. I was instantly in an elated, anaerobic state (which anyone will tell you is not always elated) and flew up the mountain for the first several miles. Both the will and the ability to go on at this level seemed to be on a slow-drip transfusion into my veins. I'd never felt more at home or more centered. Neither, in my perception, has the presence of trees and clouds and dirt seemed more immediate to me—or closer to my marrow.

I met several memorable women along the way. When I was forced in the second mile to stop at a bottleneck clogged with racers and wipe my wet, mud-spattered glasses, the first one stepped off the sidelines. She said, "Here, let me wipe them for you. I have watched this race for years, and I've never had the guts to do what you're doing."

During the first half of the race, I had kept company with another woman rider. In the years since then I've forgotten her name, but I remember how we paced one another; how we passed men together (who unkindly joked that they were useless if women were passing them); how we looked out for each other as we tipped over in the snowbanks, waiting for each other—the competitor—to get back on her bike. As the climb changed to a descent halfway through the race, and the drizzle to a steady rain, I could no longer see the track or stay upright. She could do both, and I had to relinquish her company.

Left on my own and growing increasingly colder in what were really hypothermic conditions, my friend Mother Nature and I did a dance down the mountainside.

On the way down, my long-sought-after ideal of racing revealed that sport isn't always about competition—sometimes it's about compassion. As I descended, about three quarters of the way through the race, I found a racer from the longer elite event sitting near the stone stairstep section, holding his face in his hands. His group was crashing and hopping down the steps while he was immobilized by the mud in his eyes. The technical demands of riding in this section were so consuming that no one noticed him—but I was walking. I gave him a water bottle to wash out his eyes, and he called me an angel. Given the contrast between my solo act of kindness and the obliviousness of others to his plight, I half believed that my intervention was heavenly.

I threaded past the sections of the descent that were too technical for me, and as the rain stopped, I was on my bike again for the final quarter of the race. At a broad stream crossing, I picked up another woman competitor, who came charging from behind. My numbness gave way to that elevated, anaerobic dance again, and spectators began to reappear and shout that the finish was only two miles away, and then one, and then around the next bend. When the finish banner appeared, it was suspended over the end of a quagmire filled with peanut-butter mud. I moved into place beside my latest traveling companion, and 250 meters away from the conclusion of my first epic, I heard my name being shouted by the woman I'd climbed the first half of the course with. "Go Marti, go!" It was like the trumpet blast of real angels, and I got out of my saddle and sprinted to the finish line, determined to expend any energy I hadn't already squandered on this spending spree of exertion. My latest partner responded, and then faltered—either giving up or just plain losing—but it didn't matter what she did, because for me the last four hours of experience were being distilled into one final outburst of love for being in a human body, trying to find its limits.

And then it was over, and it was so remarkably concluded that real time seemed to come back with a thwack, and I couldn't imagine riding my bike out of the muck in the staging area that I had just sprinted through. Someone handed me an electrolyte drink, and its chemicals tasted dry. I made my way back to my boyfriend's car, unlocked the door and promptly sat down on his fastidiously kept upholstery in all my muddy glory. I was no longer captive to a male sport, I had found my own kingdom of balance—with a little nudge from the wild side. In it reigned the feminine aspects of both mountain biking and competition.

I found the feminine in mountain biking because I realized that the ability to balance requires the quality of yielding and of working with something rather than against it—if you fight gravity, it will conquer you; if you work with it, it will grant you balance. The struggle to find this quality often means leaning to extremes. In my case, it meant the extremes of worshipping the concept of racing and then psyching myself out of ever attaining it. In my first mountain bike race, I also discovered the feminine quality of competition when I realized that for me, competing meant striving *with* people to surpass myself, rather than striving *against* them—the idea of competitors as community.

Since that race, I would like to say that I have kept both that balance and that spirit alive in a little shrine in my heart—but I haven't. I've lost the path and rediscovered it. Led others to it, and then failed to follow myself. Owned it and then completely squandered it. But it has always called to me, and in my own way, I have always kept its value in mind. Finally, I think I have surrendered to it, and it's no longer a matter of will for me to train and ride—it's a simple matter of breathing the air I was meant to breathe.

References

Anderson, J. R., "Cognitive styles and multicultural populations. *Journal of Teacher Education,* 1988, *39*, (1), 2–9.

Bateson, M. C. (1994). *Peripheral visions: Learning along the way.* New York: HarperCollins.

Blank, J. W. (1998). *The death of an adult child: A book for bereaved parents.* In J. D. Morgan (Ed.), *Death, value and meaning series.* Amityville, New York: Baywood.

Bee, H. L. (1996). *The journey of adulthood.* Upper Saddle River, New Jersey: Prentice Hall.

Blood, R. O., Jr. (1967). *Love match and arranged marriage: A Tokyo-Detroit comparison.* New York: Free Press.

Clark, M. C. (1993). Transformational learning. In S. B. Merriam (Ed.). *An update on adult learning theory* (pp. 47–56). New Directions for Adult and Continuing Education, No. 57. San Francisco: Jossey-Bass.

Costa, P. T., & McCrae, R. R. (1984). Personality as a lifelong determinant of well-being. In C. Z. Malatesta & C. E. Izard (Eds.), *Emotion in adult development* (pp. 141–158). Beverly Hills, CA: Sage.

Cox, B., & Ramirez, M., III. (1981). Cognitive styles: Implications for multiethnic education. In J. Banks, & B.J. Shin (Eds.), *Education in the '80's* (pp. 61–71). Washington, D.C.: National Education Association.

Davis, A. (1948). *Social class influences upon learning.* Cambridge, MA: Harvard University Press.

Delany, S., & Delany, A. E. (1993). *Having our say: The Delany sisters' first 100 years.* New York: Kodansha International.

Erikson, E. H. (1963). *Childhood and society.* (2nd ed.). New York: Norton.

Erikson, E. H. (1968). *Identity, youth and crisis.* New York: Norton.

Erikson, E. H. (1980). *Identity and the life cycle.* New York: Norton.

Gilligan, C. (1982). *In a different voice: Psychological theory and women's development.* Cambridge, MA: Harvard University Press.

Guild, P. (1994). The culture/learning style connection. *Educational Leadership, 51,* (8), 16–21.

Guralnik, J. M., Land, K. C., Blazer, D., Fillenbaum, G. G., & Branch, L. G. (1993). Educational status and active life expectancy among older blacks and whites. *New England Journal of Medicine, 329,* 110–116.

287

288 References

Hocker, W. V. (1988). Parental loss of an adult child. In O. S. Margolis, A. H. Kutscher, E. R. Marcus, H. C. Raether, V. R. Pine, I. B. Seeland, & D. J. Cherico (Eds.), *Grief and loss of an adult child* (pp. 37–49). New York: Praeger.

Holland, J. L. (1992). *Making vocational choices: A theory of vocational personalities and work environments.* (2nd ed.). Odessa, FL: Psychological Assessment Resources.

Jarvis, P. (1987). *Adult learning in the social context.* London: Croom Helm.

Jarvis, P. (1992). *Paradoxes of learning.* San Francisco: Jossey-Bass.

Johnson, C. L. (1995). Cultural diversity in the late-life family. In R. Blieszner & V. H. Bedford (Eds.). *Handbook of aging and the family* (pp. 307–331). Westport, CT: Greenwood Press.

Levinson, D. J. (1978). *The seasons of a man's life.* New York: Ballantine Books.

Lewis, C. S. (1960). *The four loves.* New York: Harcourt Brace.

Lorde, A. (1984/1995). Age, race, class and sex: Women redefining difference. In B. Guy-Sheftall (Ed.). *Words of fire: An anthology of African-American feminist thought* (pp. 283–291). New York: New Press.

Lummis, M., & Stevenson, H. W. (1990). Gender differences in beliefs and achievement: A cross-cultural study. *Developmental Psychology, 26,* 254–263.

Maslow, A. H. (1968). *Toward a psychology of being* (2nd ed.). New York: Van Nostrand-Reinhold.

McAdams, D. P. (1989). *Intimacy: The need to be close.* New York: Doubleday.

More, A. J. (1990). Learning styles of Native Americans and Asians. Paper presented at the Annual Meeting of the American Psychological Association, Boston. (ERIC Document Reproduction Service No. ED 330 535)

Nahas, R., & Turley, M. (1979). *The new couple: Women and gay men.* New York: Seaview Books.

Neugarten, B. (1976). Adaptation and the life cycle. *Counseling Psychologist, 6,* 16–20.

Phinney, J. S. (1993). Multiple group identities: Differentiation, conflict and integration. In J. Kroeger (Ed.), *Discussions in ego identity* (pp. 47–74). Hillsdale, NJ: Erlbaum.

Rohrlich, J. B. (1980). Work and love: The crucial balance. New York: Summit.

Shade, B. J. (1989). The influence of perceptual development on cognitive style: Cross ethnic comparisons. *Early Child Development and Care, 51,* 137–155.

Shorter-Gooden, K., & Washington, C. N. (1996). Young, black, and female: The challenge of weaving an identity. *Journal of Adolescence, 19,* 465–475.

Sternberg, R. J. (1987). Liking versus loving: A comparative evaluation of theories. *Psychological Bulletin, 102,* 331–345.

Stiver, I. P. (1991). Work inhibitors in women. In J. V. Jordan, A. G. Kaplan, J. B. Miller, I. P. Stiver, & J. L. Surrey, (Eds.) *Women's growth in connection: Writings from the stone center* (pp. 223–236). New York: Guilford Press.

Strickland, B. R. (1992). Women and depression. *Current Directions in Psychological Science, 1,* 132–135.

Super, D. E. (1986). Life career roles: Self-realization in work and leisure. In D. T. Hall and Associates (Eds.), *Career development in organizations* (pp. 95–119). San Francisco: Jossey-Bass.

Tennant, M. C., & Pogson, P. (1995). *Learning and change in the adult years: A developmental perspective.* San Francisco: Jossey-Bass.

Thorton, M. C. (1996). Hidden agendas, identity theories and multiracial people. In M. P. Root (Ed.), *The multiracial experience: Racial borders as the new frontier* (pp. 101–120). Thousand Oaks, CA: Sage.

Tough, A. (1979). *The adult's learning projects: A fresh approach to theory and practice in adult learning* (2nd ed.). Austin, TX: Learning Concepts. (Original work published in 1971).

Vasquez, J. A. (1992). Cognitive style and academic attainment. In J. Lynch, C. Modgil, & S. Modgil (Eds.), *Cultural diversity and the schools: Equity and excellence: Education and cultural reproduction.* London: Falmer Press.

Whitbourne, S. K., & Weinstock, C. S. (1986). *Adult development.* (2nd ed.). New York: Praeger.

Willis, P. E. (1977). *Learning to labour: How working class kids get working class jobs.* Farnborough, England: Saxon House.

Wilson, A. (1996). How we find ourselves: Identity development and the two-spirit people. *Harvard Educational Review, 66 (2),* 303–317.

Acknowledgment for Permissions

The following authors and publishers have generously given permission to use extended quotations from previously published material.

Jaimi Carter. "Are You Writing a Book?" in *Miscegenation Blues: Voices of Mixed Race Women,* ed. Carol Camper, pp. 243–46 (Sister Vision Press, 1994). Copyright © 1994 by Jaimi Carter. "Flip Flops." From Baby *Doctor* by Perri Klass, M.D. Copyright © 1992 by Perri Klass, M.D. Reprinted by permission of Random House, Inc. and the author. All rights reserved. "You're Short, Besides!" by Sucheng Chan. Copyright © 1989. Reprinted by permission of the author. From *Making Waves* by Asian Women United of California © by Asian Women United of California. "Three Steps a Minute by Ruth Shigezawa. Reprinted by permission of the author. Greenfield Review Press, New York, 1996. "How I Got to Be Jewish" appeared as chapter 4 in *Fear of Fifty* by Erica Jong, published by HarperCollins, 1994. Reprinted by permission of the author. "A Dictionary of Japanese Terms." Copyright © 1996 by R. A. Sasaki. Reprinted with permission of the author. First appeared in *Into the Fire: Asian American Prose*, Greenfield Review Press, New York, 1996. "Dear Aunt Nanadine" by Alexis De Veaux, previously published in *Essence Magazine* in 1982. "Learning to Work: A Story by a Learning Disabled Person" by Dale Brown was published in *American Rehabilitation* January-February-March edition, volume 9, number 1, (1983). "Sweetheart" by Molly Martin, Copyright © 1990, first published in *Tradeswomen Magazine.* "Piecework" from *Piecework* by Mona Elaine Adilman, pp. 27–29, Borealis Press Limited, 1980. Permission granted by S. Soloman, executor of Elaine Adilman's estate. All pages from "The Linden Tree" from *Last Courtesies and Other Stores* by Ella Leffland. Copyright © 1972 by Ella Leffland. Reprinted by permission of Harper Collins Publishers, Inc. "The Linden Tree" by Ella Leffland. Copyright © 1980 by Ella Leffland. From *Last Courtesies and Other Stories* (Harper & Row, 1980). Used by permission of the Wallace Literary, Inc. "Is This a Reward of a Catholic Girlhood?" by Margaret Cruikshank. Copyright © 1980. Reprinted by permission of the author. Published by Persephone Press. "Between" by Elizabeth Graver originally published in *Story* magazine. Autumn 1994. Copyright © by Elizabeth Graver 1994. Reprinted by permission of the Richard Parks Agency. "First Love" copyright © 1991 by R. A. Sasaki. Reprinted from *The Loom and Other Stories* with permission of Graywolf Press, Saint Paul, Minnesota. "The Management of Grief" from *The Middleman and Other Stories* by Bharati Mukherjee. Copyright © 1988 by Bharati Mukherjee. Used by permission of Penguin Books Canada Limited and Penguin Books of the United States. "The Management of Grief" from *The Middleman and Other Stories* by Bharati Mukherjee. Published by Virago Press, London. "This Place" by Beth Brant from *Food and Spirits* by Beth Brant. Published by Firebrand Books, Ithaca, New York. Copyright © 1991 by Beth Brant. "1895 Honeymoon Hotel" by Marie M. Hara. Published by Bamboo Ridge Press in 1994. "Groom Service" from *Working Men* by Michael Dorris. Copyright © 1993 by Michael Dorris. Reprinted by permission of Henry Holt and Company, Inc. "What I Know from Noses" by Anndee Hochman. Copyright © 1994. Reprinted with permission of the author. "Finch the Spastic Speaks" by Gordon Weaver. Reprinted by permission of Louisiana State University Press from *The Entombed Man of Thule* by Gordon Weaver. Copyright © 1972 by Louisiana State University. "Combustion" by Susan Carol Hauser is reprinted by permission from *I am Becoming a Woman I've Wanted* (1994), edited by Sandra H. Martz, and *Full Moon: Reflections on Turning Fifty* (1996) by Susan Carol Hauser, both published by Papier-Mache Press. "The Hector Quesadilla Story," from *Greasy Lake and Other Stories* by T. Coraghessan Boyle. Copyright © 1979, 1981, 1982, 1983, 1984, 1985 by T. Coraghessan Boyle. Used by permission of Viking Penguin Press, a division of Penguin Putnam, Inc. "La Tortillera," From *El Milagro and Other Stories*. Copyright © 1996 by Patricia Preciado Martin. Reprinted by permission of the University of Arizona Press. "Excerpts" from *Talking to the Dead* by Sylvia Watanabe. Copyright © 1992 by Sylvia Watanabe. Used by permission of Doubleday, a division of Bantam Doubleday Dell Publishing Group, Inc. "Mountain Biking and Pleasures of Balance" was reprinted from *Another Wilderness: Notes from the New Outdoors-woman* edited by Susan Fox Rogers and published by Seal Press. Copyright © 1994 by Marti Stephen. The following authors could not be located: "A Sistah Outsider" by Shamara Shantu Riley, published by W. W. Norton, 1994. "Church" by G. Winston James. Published by Avon, 1996. "The Storyteller" by Jason Laus Baluyut. Published by Greenfield Review Press in 1996.